# LEADER RESILIENCE

## The NEW Frontier
## of Leadership

*A practical guide to building your resilience and
transforming your ability to Lead*

# Dr Lynda Folan

Copyright © 2021 Lynda Folan

ISBN: 978-1-922565-73-0
Published by Vivid Publishing
A division of Fontaine Publishing Group
P.O. Box 948, Fremantle
Western Australia 6959
www.vividpublishing.com.au

NATIONAL LIBRARY OF AUSTRALIA    A catalogue record for this book is available from the National Library of Australia

# CONTENTS

# TABLE OF FIGURES

# ACKNOWLEDGEMENTS

Unlike most academics and writers, I never set out to complete a doctorate or write a book. Neither of these were in my life plan; in fact, after completing my master's degree in 1998, I was very clear that I would never study again. Surprisingly, I now find myself writing acknowledgements for my book which is based on the findings from my doctorate that I recently completed. Completing both of these has taken a significant effort on my part, as I am not a natural academic, nor has writing been a part of my career aspirations. In school, I was definitely not a 'swot', and I achieved average results both in school and at university. Just before entering university, I recall my father telling me I was going to have to work hard, as 'I was not really university material'. He was absolutely right; academia is not my natural place—I have to work hard to achieve results.

So how did it come about that I spent eight years completing a research doctorate and another eighteen months converting this research into a book? The answer is very simple: I have a passion for developing and supporting leaders, their teams, and their organisations to achieve excellence.

This book, and the research that forms the foundation of the book, would not have been possible without the support of family, friends, work colleagues and my university supervisors. Managing the challenges of running my own business, completing a doctorate and writing a book has placed pressure on family and friends alike. I am eternally grateful to all those who have supported me in small and big ways throughout these very time-consuming activities.

In particular, I want to acknowledge my son, Matthew, who is and always will be the most precious person in the world to me. Matt, your absolute belief in yourself and your personal resilience in the face of challenges, both big and small, are such a delight to behold. You are a force to reckoned with, and it is my hope that you find a direction for your incredible drive and unlimited potential. Thank you for the lessons you have taught me and for your unconditional love. I hope that, in years to come, I will have the pleasure of seeing you find your place in the world and that your choices will bring you joy, fulfilment and a life that is even more amazing and satisfying than mine has been.

I also want to acknowledge my Mum and Dad. Dad, I owe my personal drive to you, not because you ever asked me to work hard or to continue to study, but because you challenged me to be all that I could be. Mum, I owe my love of education to you; you just assumed I would get an education and there was no question that I could achieve anything I set out to do. I am very sure that no one, not you or my teachers, would have anticipated me becoming a Doctor of Psychology, but you never set limits on my potential.

Finally, I want to acknowledge my academic supervisors and my amazing clients who supported me in the completion of my doctorate. Thank you for your assistance and the invaluable contribution you made to achieving a great outcome. I could not have done it without you.

# DEDICATION

I dedicate this book to all those leaders who tirelessly and selflessly dedicate themselves to growing and developing their skills, daily delivering transformational leadership to the people who work for and with them.

My career has been dedicated to working with leaders, their teams and their organisations to achieve excellence. I feel hugely privileged to do the work that I do, and it is out of this work that the vision for my research and this book evolved. From my years of working with leaders across the globe, I have come to understand that leadership is both a choice and an honour. The choice to lead is not an easy one, as it requires consistent work and ongoing personal development. However, those that make the decision reap the benefits, for they make a significant difference for the people they lead and the organisations they run.

Leadership does not happen as a result of being appointed to a position of power; it is a choice. When we hold a position of power, we have a choice: to lead or not to lead. There is no middle road on this. We can find many examples of individuals in positions of power who have demonstrated a total lack of leadership. Identifying these people is fairly easy, as they demonstrate a total lack of regard for their responsibilities as leaders and often demonstrate egotistical, self-promoting behaviours. This lack of leadership results in people being damaged and teams becoming dysfunctional. Over time, this creates a toxic culture that undermines the organisation's ability to deliver results. These people are not leaders; they are individuals who hold positions of power and choose to do so for their own ends or for some other self-directed motive that does not support organisational success. Those that lead using this egotistical style are now described in research as corporate sociopaths or narcissists. If you have ever worked with one of these types, you know exactly the type of person that is being referred to here. If you have been subjected to the impact of these egotistical individuals in positions of power, you understand very clearly the importance of leadership and why it is such a key part of organisational effectiveness.

The time has come for true leaders to rise up and show the world what leadership really is. For individuals in positions of power to act as role models and deliver transformational leadership that makes a positive contribution to their organisation and the people that work for them. What we need in today's world is leaders who focus on building the capacity and capability of their people, uniting teams, enhancing collaboration and building an organisational culture that is focused on achieving success for everyone. This type of leadership stands in stark contrast to some of the examples of people who use their positions of power for self-interest. Individuals exhibiting divisive, unethical, immoral and narcissistic behaviour are not leaders. Rather, they are corporate sociopaths who happen to be in a position of power and are therefore able to manipulate and damage others to achieve their own ends.

This book evolved from observing the impact of leaders who choose daily to deliver a transformational leadership style and who tirelessly work to enhance their leadership and personal impact. I have therefore dedicated the findings of my research and this book to those people in positions of power, who:

- Choose to lead and not just to manage,

- Continually strive to be their best,

- Are brave enough to acknowledge their mistakes and find a better way,

- Face difficulties and see them as challenges,

- Daily pick themselves up after being knocked down,

- Are passionate about doing better for themselves, their teams and their organisations,

- Do the right thing even when no one is looking,

- Truly value diversity and inclusion,

- Remain humble, no matter how powerful their positions,

- Demonstrate authenticity and empathy,

- Work tirelessly to make their organisations better places to work, and

- Choose to continually grow and develop to become the best version of themselves.

These are the true heroes in organisations; they are the transformational leaders that will find success for themselves, their teams and their organisations, no matter how tough the challenges.

It is my sincere hope that, as we start to hand over positions of power to the next generation, they will choose to take the route of leadership. And that they will discontinue the power-hungry, narcissistic behaviours that are being demonstrated in organisations and the political arena across the globe. True transformational leadership requires, first and foremost, learning how to lead yourself and manage your own internal reactions and emotions. Then, from a healthy sense of self, to make the choice to develop the skills and ability to lead others, help them to reach their potential and build organisations with a positive culture.

In dedicating this book to leaders across the globe, my sincere hope is that the contents of this book will inspire people in positions of power to step up and make the decision to lead and do the work required to be truly transformational leaders.

"Every success story is a tale of constant adaptation, revision and change"

Richard Branson

# CHAPTER 1

# INTRODUCTION AND OVERVIEW

Having spent over three decades working with leaders across the globe to enhance their leadership and build sustainable organisational outcomes, I want you to know that if you take up the challenge to build your leadership, you will see a significant shift. This book will provide you with insights and strategies to build your resilience, empower you to deliver transformational leadership and exponentially shift the outcomes you achieve. After attending the leadership resilience workshops that we run people have repeatedly commented, that the program has transformed their life both personally and professionally. I hope that, in reading this book, you too will have the opportunity to transform your thinking and your life. Everything you will discover in the pages that follow started with observing leaders in action and working with them and supporting them to be their best. While you will be provided with all research evidence for these observations, please understand that everything you read has been put into practice, tried and tested in organisations and with leaders. As a dedicated practitioner in the leadership and organisational development arena, I am not excited by the academics and the statistics but by the practical application of sound research principles. The research aspects will be presented to provide clarity on the importance of the link between resilience and leadership. However, my hope is that you will not only read the research evidence, but that you will take this opportunity to apply the learning in a very practical way to transform your leadership. Chapters 9, 10 and 11 will provide a pragmatic set of strategies to enhance your resilience and build your leadership capacity.

But let's start by looking at the foundational concepts that will be tackled in the book and begin the journey to understanding the New Frontier of Leadership.

**Resilience.** Noun. 'The capacity to recover quickly from difficulties. Toughness'.

Main domain of research: clinical psychology.

**Leadership.** Noun. 'The action of leading a group of people or an organisation.'

Main domain of research: organisational psychology.

These two seemingly unconnected nouns and previously unrelated areas of research, now more than ever before, have a remarkably important relationship to one another. During the last ten years, we have seen the emergence of research identifying the importance of the relationship between resilience and leadership (Folan, 2019; Garbowski, 2010; Offutt, 2011; Sylvester, 2009; Wasden, 2014). Clear evidence now indicates that they go hand-in-hand and that being a successful leader is almost impossible without first being resilient and capable of bouncing back from the challenges and adversity. The greatest leaders of our time—the ones that will go down in the history books as positive role models and icons of leadership—build their own resilience, support the people around them to enhance their teams' resilience and grow their organisations' capacities to succeed and bounce back from challenge and adversity.

A synergistic relationship exists between resilience and transformational leadership. Our ability to deliver a transformational leadership style that engages and motivates others relies on our commitment to the development of our resilience. Leaders and practitioners who work with leaders have intuitively known for a long time that resilience and leadership are intricately linked, and research is now supporting this understanding. This understanding requires a new focus in leadership and leadership development. Organisations need to realign their development strategies towards enhancing resilience in order to build leadership capacity. A leader without resilience is like a car without gas—it just won't get you very far. No matter how many skills the leader has developed or how competent they are, like the car without gas, the leader is going nowhere. The importance of resilience in leadership cannot be overstated: it is the fuel that enables effectiveness.

This book summarises eight years of research investigating the relationship between resilience and leadership.

The title of the research: *Defining a Research Model of Leader Resilience and Evaluating the Dispositional Effect of Resilience on Transformational Leadership* (Folan, 2019).

The thesis included a multidisciplinary review of the existing research to understand the relationship between resilience and leadership and to define a model of resilience in an organisational context. The research provided confirmation of the model of leader resilience and established the strength of the relationship between resilience and transformational leadership. It also showed the positive impact of developing resilience on leadership capability.

The model of leader resilience defines three dimensions required to build resilience:

1. Locus of control;

2. Self-concept well-being; and

3. Constructive thinking.

Figure 1: Model of resilience (Folan, 2019)

Each of these dimensions has been shown in previous research to enhance a leader's ability to bounce back and remain optimistic, ensuring that the individual can consistently deliver a transformational leadership style (Campbell, 1990; Epstein, 2014, Rotter, 1990). This organisational model of leader resilience informed the design of the two field-based studies conducted as part of the research.

**Study 1** was designed to investigate the relationship between resilience and the transformational leadership style and to validate the model of leader resilience. The participants were leaders from a range of private and public-sector organisations across Australia. The analysis of this study employed structural equation modelling (a sophisticated form of statistical analysis) to provide statistical support for the three dimensions of leader resilience and the strength of the relationship between resilience and leadership.

**Study 2** first examined whether resilience could be enhanced as a result of attending a three-day workshop designed to build resilience. It also investigated whether improving resilience had a positive impact on an individual's leadership style. Workshop participation resulted in a significant positive shift in the scores of resilience and the dimensions of resilience. The analysis also confirmed that the delegates and their bosses assessed that the participants' levels of transformational leadership underwent a significant positive shift.

The results of both these studies confirmed the relationships between resilience and leadership and showed that an increase in resilience caused an improvement in measures of transformational leadership. Academics aside, what does this mean for you as a leader or a developer of leaders? Well, the conclusions of these studies confirm that:

- To be a great leader, you first need to be resilient,

- Resilience is an essential prerequisite for transformational leadership,

- Resilience can be developed and enhanced through workshops,

- The more resilient the leader, the more transformational the leadership and therefore the more positive the culture, and

- If you are not resilient, you need to get to work building this capacity if you want to be an effective leader.

As you read this book, my hope is that you find a path by which you, your team and your organisation can not only recognise the value of resilience but can also diligently and thoughtfully work to develop resilience. This will prepare you for challenges and allow you to respond quickly to your changing business environment, while personally flourishing. As you do so, you will find that you and your team are in a better position to build a positive culture where everyone is developing and growing in competence and exceeding expectations.

The book will guide you to an understanding of the evolution of leadership research, as well as outline the importance of building resilience in the present business context, while offering you suggestions on how to enhance your resilience and leadership.

In terms of the content of the book, Chapter 2 provides an overview of leadership in our changing world, where leaders must navigate a new and unique set of challenges. It defines a new era of leadership, emphasising the importance of shifting our focus to a more contemporary view of leadership.

Chapter 3 provides insights into the research around leadership development practices and some of the limitations of existing models of development. It also includes a discussion of the importance of first building personal attributes prior to teaching leadership skills and style.

Chapter 4 elaborates on what transformational leadership is and includes an overview of the research findings that support this model of leadership. This is one of the most researched and well-validated models of leadership, and these discussions provide clarity on why you would want to be seen as a transformational leader.

Chapter 5 reviews the resilience research and discusses the evolution of this construct across a multidisciplinary research base. This chapter outlines the research basis for why your resilience determines your ability to lead others effectively, and it wraps up by presenting the model of leader resilience that was developed.

Chapter 6 focuses on presenting the research basis for the link between resilience and transformational leadership and articulates the importance of building the attribute of resilience.

Chapter 7 takes the leadership discussion to the next level and discusses the seven habits of resilient organisations. This is an introduction to the organisational level of leadership and provides the broader focus of creating organisations that support the growth of resilient leaders.

Chapter 8 tackles the issue of measurement, and you will have the opportunity to reflect on your own resilience and the resilience of your team. The Folan Resilience scale will allow you to measure your present level of resilience and to self-evaluate and determine what aspects of your resilience you need to enhance. The Team Resilience Scale will give you an opportunity to reflect on your team's resilience and what aspects you may want to develop.

Chapter 9 opens a discussion on stress and pressure and looks at the importance of managing this in the world we live in. We look at stress and warning signs of stress because, if our resilience is low, we are more likely to become stressed in the constantly changing world of work.

Chapters 10, 11 and 12 provide strategies for enhancing your resilience by building each of the dimensions of resilience, self-concept well-being, locus of control and constructive thinking. An overview of each construct is also provided, as well as their importance in an organisational setting.

Read on, as your path to becoming a more resilient leader lies ahead.

"Leadership is not about a title or a designation. It's about impact influence and inspiration"

Robin Sharman

# CHAPTER 2

# A NEW ERA, A NEW FRONTIER OF LEADERSHIP

Leadership has been a major topic of discussion in business over the past hundred years, and in the present economic, social and business context, it is now the key topic on people's agendas. Bennis and Nanus (1985) commenced describing our world as a VUCA (Volatile, Uncertain, Complex and Ambiguous) world in 1985. Never before has this concept been as relevant as it is now, in the context of COVID-19 and the plethora of global phenomena that are impacting our world (Black Lives Matter, the US election challenges, global climate change protests, and demonstrations across the globe on a variety of issues). We are living in truly exceptional times and facing challenges that can't be overcome with the leadership styles of the past. These exceptional times are calling for exceptional leaders to step up and be counted.

Researchers have been telling us for a long time that a major shift needs to take place in how we define, identify, promote and develop leaders to ensure that they are capable of being successful in today's VUCA world. We can no longer allow managers to get away with being 'old school' and choosing not to lead their people, teams and organisations effectively. A new focus is needed on developing leadership, and particularly on developing the leader's internal capacity to cope in these challenging times.

For years, we have educated people on the leadership behaviours that they need to deliver to enhance outcomes, and yet we can still look around and see people who do not deliver these behaviours. Regardless of whether this is by choice or due to inability, the time has arrived for businesses to make some tough decisions. Organisations need to stop appointing people who are not prepared, are uninterested or don't have the ability to lead people. The focus into the future needs to be on appointing people who want to lead and who are actively developing their capacity for leadership. Discussions have to shift from the focus of the last two decades, which was on developing leadership skills and teaching leadership behaviours. We need to alter the focus to develop the person's internal capacity and changing their attitude, which will then result in a shift in behaviour.

In many ways, leadership of the past was quite linear: a boss or manager would outline a strategy or game plan, provide guidance on what needed to be achieved and then expect each team member to simply execute their part of the roadmap. There weren't nearly as many internal and external factors impacting the ability to deliver. Times have changed, however, and the focus of leaders now needs to change. In today's VUCA world, setting a plan, giving direction and assuming your team will deliver the plan are no longer sufficient strategies. The VUCA world requires a new focus for leaders and a new direction for researchers and practitioners in this arena.

The business imperative for quality leadership and quality leadership research has consistently been articulated within the field of organisational psychology (Landy & Conte, 2016). Researchers and practitioners of leadership have known for many years that effective leadership is an essential component of organisational success and that different ways of leading produce dramatically different results (Bass, 1985; Avolio, Bass & Jung, 1999). Much of the early work and more recent research indicate disagreement on how and why leaders produce different organisational results (Hollander & Julian, 1969; Saunders & Barker, 2001; Stogdill, 1948; Yukl, 1998). The key to meeting the demands of the VUCA world is to lucidly define why leaders produce different results so that we can be clear on what is required to enhance leadership.

Today, more than ever before, we see leadership as a challenging and complex set of capabilities and personal characteristics that few have truly mastered. The backdrop of leadership is constantly evolving. The last ten years have seen a global transformation of information and data exchange, with online communication and connections occurring at the speed of light. Added to this is a global uprising against discrimination in all its forms, with movements like the #MeToo movement and Black Lives Matter. Needless to say, the effects of these changes and the first global pandemic in 2020 have precipitated a new age of leadership focus with more demands than ever before. This transformation requires a change in leadership. If we are going to develop great leaders in today's VUCA world, we will have to usher in a new era of leadership.

## 2.1 Leadership Today and into the Future

Having supported leaders across the globe for the last thirty-five years, I have lots of stories to tell of great successes and even greater failures. One thing is clear: in today's world, the need for leadership has never been greater. Leadership is a crucial component of organisational success. Without effective leadership, organisations will fail to achieve their potential, and in some cases, poor leadership will be the demise of an organisation. Over time, a lack of effective leadership will result in negative repercussions for all involved. Yet, if we look across a range of organisations, we find as many varieties of leadership as there are flavours of ice cream. This variety, while interesting, does not support consistent outcomes for organisations. The business imperative for quality leadership is clear. Equally imperative is that research provides clarity on what effective leadership is, as well as defining how to effectively build leadership capacity. For a long time, research has told us that certain styles of leadership are more effective. Now is the time to define how to effectively build these styles.

Debate and discussion are ongoing regarding some key questions related to leadership:

- How is it that one leader can create amazing engagement, while other leaders who have had the same development and training can't seem to connect with their teams and instead actively disengage them?

- Why do leaders who were once incredibly successful suddenly fail?

- And... how come an untrained leader might succeed, whereas a well-trained leader just can't seem to get the job done?

In short, the answers to these questions lie in the most recent leadership research into attributes (Folan, 2019; Garbowski, 2010; Offutt, 2011). The abilities of leaders to consistently deliver high-quality results rely on the focus they put into developing their internal leadership capacities, rather than on their external leadership styles. Leaders in today's world need to first develop their internal attributes of leadership to enable them to deliver consistent and effective leadership styles (Folan, 2019). Research tells us that the starting point of effective leadership is the individual's ability to develop and maintain the internal attribute of resilience. Developing resilience enables a leader to thrive in the context of the VUCA world, while also maintaining well-being to effectively deliver a constructive leadership style.

Unfortunately, traditional leadership training has been designed to build skills, style and capability. It has not been designed to develop the person's internal leadership attributes. For years, developers and researchers in the leadership space have been aware of the lack of evidence in relation to traditional leadership development strategies (Day & Sin, 2009; Howard & Wellins, 2009). Practitioners have also known intuitively that an individual who is lacking in resilience and a strong internal leadership capacity will struggle to be effective in leading others. Research is now catching up with what has been known intuitively by those responsible for developing leaders, making a clear point that leadership starts at the intra-personal level. We know that an individual can attend all the leadership training on offer and have the best coaches and mentors, but without a high level of resilience, that person will not be a consistently effective leader.

The role of leadership and the competencies required by leaders to deliver organisational results has shifted dramatically in the past decade, and research has battled to keep pace with these changes (Landy & Conte, 2016). In the present business context, with its volatile economic and social environments and constantly changing sector requirements, the ability to manage and lead as we did in the past is no longer sufficient. Leadership 2021 and beyond requires that we learn to adapt to the VUCA world; at the same time, leaders need to be able to maintain and enhance organisational performance and ensure alignment with the broader business context (Judge, Naoumova & Douglas, 2009). The maintenance of business outcomes in today's world requires leaders to stay ahead of the changing business requirements and to deliver competitive advantages for their organisations by continuing to achieve in the face of constant change (Draghici & Draghici, 2007).

This might all sound overwhelming and challenging. If so, that's because it can be, but achieving it is far from impossible. In fact, the feeling can be quite empowering when you know that you, and only you, can craft your leadership and that if you first build your resilience, you can and will achieve far greater success than you ever imagined. In the work that I do with leaders, I have seen individuals make dramatic changes and turn their leadership around by focusing on building their resilience. If you want to achieve dramatic changes and enhance your leadership outcomes, you will first need to do the internal work to build your resilience.

The fact that leadership comes from within doesn't mean leadership cannot be taught, developed or improved. It can be. Not only do we have lots of examples of people who have improved their leadership, we also have research evidence that shows that leadership can be developed and enhanced by developing leaders' resilience (Folan, 2019). Research shows that adaptive and flexible leadership competencies are critical in delivering the achievements mentioned above and ensuring that organisations remain competitive in today's world (Bass & Avolio, 1990; Mann, 1959). Therefore, you cannot and should not be so set in your ways that you refuse to consider how shifts and adjustments in your personal attributes can lead to greater results for you, your team and your organisation. Leadership is not a one-size-fits-all, and we are not trying to create cookie cutter versions of what a leader should look like. However, there are key attributes that you must develop to enable your ability to lead others.

For companies to meet the challenge of working in a VUCA world, their leaders must develop new attributes, skills and ways of working that result in sustainable outcomes for themselves and their businesses (Landy & Conte, 2016; Schein, 2009; Taffinder, 1995). In fact, this is the reason why large companies shift, change, exit and replace leaders. Businesses that are leading the way are searching for something new, for a change in outcomes and results. In so doing, they frequently make a change in their leaders. Unfortunately, these changes don't always bring about the required shift. For organisations to grow and flourish, they need to reassess the requirements of leadership and address the issues of resilience, either with the existing leaders or with a new set of leaders. Research must provide meaningful guidance to businesses in their pursuit of leadership excellence. Clearly, the solution to a leadership shift does not lie in simply changing the people. Research tells us it lies in building the resilience of the leaders.

The ability to ensure effective leadership is one of the essential components in the delivery of an organisation's competitive advantage and allows it to operate successfully in a dynamic marketplace (Smith & Kelly, 1997). Just look at the most successful companies in the world. Many of them share a commonality—strong leadership that delivers an organisational culture that enhances dialogue, empowerment and engagement of everyone. They aren't standing still, or resting on their laurels, or hanging out waiting for the tides to turn. Rather, they are innovating, reinventing and working their tails off to improve their businesses, no matter what the context. Doing this requires strong internal leadership and the capacity to flourish in the context of challenges.

Given the importance of leadership in the organisational context, an interesting point to note is that repeated references have been made to the lack of adequate leadership and leadership development in organisations (Howard & Wellins, 2009). Ashford and DeRue (2010) noted that nearly sixty percent of companies are facing leadership shortages and that thirty-one percent expect a lack of leadership capability to negatively impact organisational outcomes. To make matters worse, these failures are estimated to cost businesses billions of dollars. Therefore, further research on this critical business issue remains a priority. What is needed is research that informs and guides organisations on how to achieve effective leadership, thereby enhancing organisational outcomes (Avolio, Sosik & Berson, 2013). As the business community navigates the present complex environmental factors, it requires practical research-based guidance on new ways of understanding leadership and leader development. Should we choose to ignore the trends and changing tides, then leaders, their teams and their businesses will ultimately fail to achieve their full potential.

Frankly, leadership in the VUCA world is falling even further behind than previously. The most recent research is showing, yet again, that the requirements for leadership have dramatically changed and that we require a new set of competencies to lead in this new world, with agility, flexibility and the ability to manage well-being high on the agenda (Johnson, Dey, Nguyen, Groth, Joyce, Tan, Glozier & Harvey, 2020). The findings of the most recent research on how we can enhance leadership capability note the importance of building resilience in leaders to manage these new frontiers of business (Folan, 2019).

## 2.2 Overview of 100 Years of Leadership Research

The empirical study of leadership has evolved over more than 100 years (Lippit, 1939). Numerous theoretical conceptualisations of leadership have been put forward and many have attempted to define how leadership differs from management (Fiedler, 1967). A substantial body of research now exists, with a broad focus on two areas:

1. Leadership characteristics, and

2. Leadership effectiveness.

The area of **leadership characteristics** dates back to the earliest research, commencing with the 'Great Man' theories (Stogdill, 1948). This body of research sought to understand the characteristics of leaders and the impact of these characteristics on organisational outcomes and success (Hollander & Julian, 1969; Stogdill, 1948). Results were inconsistent and did not offer clarity on the link between leadership and traits or characteristics (Hollander & Julian, 1969). We are also now very clear that both women and men have the capacity to lead.

The second broad area of research attempted to define models of leadership with a particular focus on **leadership** behaviours associated with **effectiveness** (Hogan et al., 1994; Landy & Conte, 2016). The main model that emerged from this research was the transformational leadership model (Bass, 1985). This model evolved into Bass's (1985) full-range leadership model, which remains the dominant model of leadership effectiveness (Howell & Avolio, 1993; Lowe et al., 1996; Waldman, Ramirez, House & Puraman, 2001). The development of what Bass and Avolio (1997) termed a full-range model of transformational leadership was a significant development in the broad leadership debate. The articulation of this model has offered opportunities for the revision and extension of research on leadership and leadership development.

Besides these broad areas of research, more specific research topics have dominated the research arena over the years.

**Trait Theories:** The very early trait theories of leadership commenced with the 'Great Man' theories (Stogdill, 1948). While we now know that leadership is not gender specific, men in positions of power were the focus of those early theories. This research sought to understand the specific traits of leaders and their impact on effectiveness. The view at this time was that you either had the qualities to lead or you didn't. Ongoing debates also questioned whether some people were simply born to lead while others were simply born to be followers. Trait research has not delivered consistent results, and over time, we have moved away from a trait-based focus in research. If these theories were accurate, someone with the effective traits should be a great leader all the time. However, we see leaders who are highly effective for a period of time and then fail. We would also expect to see a specific set of personality traits that ensured you would be a great leader. Again, this is not borne out in reality; if we look around, we can see effective leaders with very different personalities.

These theories do, however, provide insights into the connection between some specific traits, such as extroversion and leadership. However, personality and traits do not fully explain the differences in leadership. You will have worked with or seen leaders who are introverts who are exceptional leaders and leaders who are extroverts who are exceptional leaders. So, what is really at play here? If both an introvert and an extrovert can be exceptional leaders, their traits are not what are defining their effectiveness. Something way more important than personality and traits is in play that requires research and investigation.

**Behavioural Theories:** The next dominant research area commenced in the early 1950s, focusing on behavioural theories of leadership. This research evolved in response to some of the inconsistencies found in trait theories. The University of Michigan and Ohio State University simultaneously began studying leadership behaviours. Fleishman and Harris (1962), from Ohio State University, defined two basic dimensions of leadership behaviours that produced enhanced outcomes: consideration (concern for the welfare of subordinates) and initiating structure (structuring subordinates' activities and tasks and group activities). The University of Michigan researcher Likert (1967) identified three key behavioural dimensions that differentiated great leaders: being task-orientated or relation-orientated and indulging in participative behaviour. Yukl (1998) noted, however, that the results in this area were inconsistent and that the predominance of the use of questionnaires in the studies led to measurement errors and bias. A fairly substantial body of research, however, shows the impact of certain behaviours on leadership outcomes and the impact of changing behaviours on subordinates (Landy & Conte, 2016).

**Power Theories:** The next area of research was power-based theories of leadership, which developed in the 1950s as an attempt to better understand leadership from the perspective of the distribution of power. The theory of power relations in leadership was initiated by French and Raven (1959), who defined five power bases that influence leadership outcomes: legitimate, expert, referent, reward and coercive power. The concept that power plays a part in leadership outcomes was reviewed further by several researchers, such as Salancik and Pfeffer (1977). While the research in this area has shown some positive results (Salancik & Pfeffer, 1977), these power-based theories are not grounded in a fully defined model of leadership; they focus on this very limited aspect of power. Yukl (1998) raised questions about the theories and their validity, showing that they are limited in their ability to explain the breadth and depth of leadership. Everyone has observed individuals who, without any form of power, demonstrate highly effective leadership, while other people in positions of power definitely don't demonstrate leadership.

**Contingency Theories:** One aspect that became apparent was that the use and effectiveness of both power and behaviour theories were contingent on other factors not accounted for by these theories (Fiedler, 1967). Out of this, a new area of research evolved that focused on the contingent factors relevant to leadership. These contingency theories include theories such as Fiedler's (1967) contingency model and Hersey and Blanchard's (1972) situational theory.

Contingency theories presumed that the leadership approach utilised should be determined by the characteristics of the subordinates and the contextual setting. These theories have some validity, in that we do see some leaders thriving in one context and then not in another context. However, they don't fully explain the leader who is able to engage and motivate a team in multiple contexts and with a range of subordinates.

**Participative Theories:** These theories of leadership evolved in the 1970s from the earlier behavioural research, with some of the initial investigation being undertaken by Ohio State University. This area of research developed as an attempt to define the characteristics and advantages of a participative style of leadership (Vroom & Yetton, 1973). Landy and Conte (2016) described these theories of participative leadership as one of the stronger contributions to the leadership debate. Elements of participative leadership are incorporated in the transformational leadership model.

**Leader–Member Exchange Theories:** A further approach to leadership that evolved in the 1970/80s looked at the relationship between the leader and the subordinate, i.e. the leader–member exchange theory (Dansereau et al., 1975). This theory evolved from the contingency and participative leadership theories and postulated that leaders adopt different behaviours with different individuals who report to them. Over time, these behaviours form a consistent pattern and influence the experience of the subordinate and the group. Positive leader–member exchange relationships lead to increased subordinate satisfaction, better job performance, enhanced creativity and reduced intention to quit (Gerstner & Day, 1997; Tierney, Farmer & Graen, 1999). Gerstner and Day (1997) argued that, although this theory offers a compelling proposition for understanding leadership, it requires further research and definition to substantiate its position in the leadership debate.

**Charismatic and Visionary Theories:** The study of leadership styles further evolved in the 1980s and 1990s, incorporating elements of participative leadership and behavioural leadership research (Bass, 1985). The focus for this research was on defining a leadership style that delivers positive impact and enhanced outcomes (Bass & Riggio, 2006). Research looking at the impact of charismatic and visionary leadership styles demonstrated that these styles have a positive impact on organisational outcomes (Conger, 1989; Sashkin, 1988; Tichy & Devanna, 1986). Again, however, they did not provide a comprehensive model of leadership.

**Transformational Theories:** Alongside visionary and charismatic research was a new development: investigating the relationship between transformational and transactional leadership styles. This research demonstrated that transformational leadership produces enhanced business outcomes (Bass, 1998). Out of these early conceptualisations of transformational leadership evolved one of the most extensively researched models of leadership: the transformational leadership model (Bass, 1998; Bass & Avolio, 1990). This research culminated in the development of the first full-range model of leadership (Avolio et al., 1999; Bass et al., 2003; Bass & Riggio, 2006).

So, where do we stand today?

In the ever-changing environment of leadership, the transformational model has withstood the test of time as a model of leadership effectiveness. It offers us the most strategic and relevant prediction and explanation of how to build leadership capability. While this brief history lesson might feel overly academic, it is crucial for understanding how we got to this point in our discussion of leadership. To be able to take the leadership debate forward, experts on leadership need to pull away from the past, look into the future and then shape the focus for today. We would be naive to ignore the evolution of leadership research or to abandon what we have learned so far. Rather, we should be building on what has gone before to better understand leadership today.

Diverse perspectives exist on the achievements of leadership studies to date. Hogan and Ghufran (2011) argued that the empirical study of leadership has failed, and they noted the lack of substance provided by popularist business books within the leadership field. Conversely, Avolio et al. (2013) argued that substantial achievements have been made in the understanding of leadership, particularly over the past decade.

A relatively sizeable shift in thinking has occurred around leadership in recent times. For example, Lowe and Gardner's (2000) review of published articles noted some important developments, one of which is the focus on transformational leadership developed by Bass (1998). The development of Bass and Avolio's (1997) full-range model of leadership was a significant development in the broad leadership debate (Gardner, 1993; Weiner et al., 2012). This model of leadership has been repeatedly revised and extended to provide greater levels of clarity (Antonakis, Avolio & Sivasubramaniam, 2003; Avolio, Sosik & Berson, 2013; Bass, 1998). We know from the comprehensive research in this area that transformational leadership is a driver of excellence in the workplace. It builds individual capacity and enhances engagement, and the visionary aspect is extremely important in adapting to surrounding environments. Transformational leadership adjusts to challenges and obstacles as they arise and ensures that people are taken on the journey. Should you want to be a better leader or to develop into your leadership role, then you should not only understand how leadership has evolved over time, but you should also know how transformational leadership will shape the future of business effectiveness.

Until very recently, research on leadership has only told one part of the story. We also need to look at the practice of leadership in organisations. Leadership has evolved over time, leading us to where we stand today, with a much clearer understanding of what is and isn't effective in leadership. However, we also know that a lot of managers in our organisations who have been trained in best practice leadership still don't deliver effective leadership to their teams and their organisations. We really need to look below the surface of leadership in order to answer the question: Why do we still have people in positions of power who don't lead their people effectively, even when they have had all the training necessary to deliver a transformational leadership style?

The answer to this question is not something that is blatantly evident and certainly not something that has been identified in earlier leadership research. Indications of what might be an answer to this very important question are apparent in some recent research showing that if you want to be a transformational leader, you need to first build your internal leadership capacity, which is defined as your dispositional attributes (Garbowski, 2010). A need is apparent not only to develop the transformational capability of a leader, but also to build dispositional leadership attributes in order to deliver a transformational style. Developing the dispositional attributes of a leader will allow consistent delivery of an effective leadership style. Without this, the individual will be driven by unconscious actions and reactions that manifest in inconsistency and ineffective leadership.

For many years, the age-old question, 'Are leaders born or made?' has misled us. Leaders are neither born nor made; leadership is a choice. Developing as a leader requires that the person develops their dispositional attributes that will enable them to leverage an effective style of leadership. Some individuals have a more natural ability to lead than others, but we also know that these people can fail hopelessly at times. Once we understand that the internal leadership attributes are what require development, we will unlock the key to a transformational leadership style. This change in focus from external leadership style to internal leadership attributes is essential if we are to deliver real and lasting change in the leadership space.

"One of the important techniques of becoming a better leader is self-reflection. Once you get into the habit you begin to see common themes"

David Gevorkyan

# CHAPTER 3

# THE REQUIREMENTS FOR A NEW WAY OF ASSESSING AND DEVELOPING LEADERSHIP

Now, more than ever, transformational leadership is essential for progressive, innovative businesses to flourish and succeed. Truly successful organisations need to look beyond profit or the bottom line and focus on creating an environment that allows the organisation, the people that work in it and the customers to flourish and succeed. Does this mean that all organisations that succeed in some aspect of business are run by transformational leaders? Definitely not. Numerous organisations are still found worldwide that have a dearth of leadership but are successfully delivering financial returns. However, if those businesses were able to transform their leadership and culture, they would deliver a far higher return, the people in the organisation would flourish and the organisation would build true sustainability.

We can all point out businesses, boards, councils, governments and government departments that publicise success but are being managed by individuals who are not demonstrating transformational leadership in their positions of power. Very often, these people who choose not to demonstrate true leadership are either displaying a laissez-faire attitude or narcissistic behaviour in the pursuit of their own self-interest. Both of these are delivered at the expense of those around them and hinder the organisation's success. These individuals are not leaders; they are simply individuals who happen to be in positions of power, driving their own personal agenda, either consciously or unconsciously. In their book, *The narcissistic epidemic— Living in the age of entitlement*, Twenge and Campbell (2009) discuss the rise of narcissistic tendencies in our world today. This behaviour is prevalent in organisations across all sectors and is particularly evident at the moment in the political arena. Unfortunately, where narcissists are in positions of power, success will be achieved at the expense of people, culture and a sustainable business environment. The price paid by these organisations is evident in the revolving door of senior people exiting the organisation, the stress levels of people in the organisation and the lack of ethical and moral behaviour that becomes a standard part of these businesses or entities.

In 2001, we all watched the demise of Enron, an organisation that publicised its success as a very profitable and outwardly successful company, as evidenced by its trading value on the stock market. The collapse of this organisation was the result of narcissistic individuals in positions of power pursuing their own ends, openly stealing and lying for personal gain. These individuals also convinced their accounting firm to cover up the systemic corruption that was happening in the organisation. This resulted in the downfall of both Enron and Arthur Anderson, one of the big five accounting firms of that time. It also damaged the stock market and put hundreds of hard-working people out of work. As a result, a lot of effort has been made globally to attempt to stop this kind of self-interested and unethical behaviour from happening in organisations. However, as we all know, it still happens; narcissistic people still end up in very powerful positions, demonstrating a lack of ethics coupled with open self-interest. I can't say strongly enough that these people are not leaders; they are simply individuals in powerful positions.

Leadership is a choice, and that choice is to effectively lead others, build sustainable success and create added value for the organisation, the team and the customers. In fact, if you were to drill a hole from the outer layer to the innermost core of any highly successful business, you would discover leaders who are focused on transforming themselves, their teams and their organisations. You would find a company culture that supports people to be their best, and business practices that are ethical and sustainable. This is achieved through the way in which those in power choose to lead, the manner in which they empower employees and the environment they create for everyone to flourish.

At its core, transformational leadership is a people-centred style that inspires individuals and teams to take action to enhance the organisational outcomes and deliver improved customer satisfaction. The ability to lead in this way requires that we take a step back and look at the underlying attributes that support transformational leadership. An unbelievably powerful secret to truly successful leadership lives in the pages ahead. It is one that, if you are prepared to take up the challenge, will reinvent your leadership and energise you, your team and your organisation. You will be given the blueprint for building your capacity to inspire others, to take them on a journey and to deal with any obstacles and challenges you might face along the way.

Think about that for a second.

- What would your team be like if they could navigate change and transformation better than the competition can?

- How successful could your organisation be if challenges

didn't put a halt to or slow your productivity and the delivery
of outcomes?

- And finally, how much could you increase your bottom line
if your team was built to innovate to overcome industry and
global challenges?

The sky is the limit, but it all starts with you. As a leader, you must
decide to enhance your ability to bounce back and remain optimistic
in order to ensure that you can consistently deliver a transformational leadership style to your team and to your organisation. So, the
key question is: how do I go about developing my leadership?

## 3.1 Leadership Development Research

While leadership is a widely researched topic, we have not made the
same strides in leadership development research (Day & Sin, 2009).
One thing we know is that leadership can be taught and improved
through effective developmental strategies. In fact, with all the information available, you and your organisation have access to resources
and tools to enhance leadership, increase productivity and gain a leg
up on the competition ladder. However, while a lot of research is out
there, an interesting observation is that ongoing global concern still
exists over the lack of effective leadership development, along with
significant questions on the positive impact of leadership development (Howard & Wellins, 2009). Gaps remain in our understanding
of how to develop the capacity of individuals to deliver inspirational
leadership. Even though businesses are investing significant amounts
of money in developing leaders, we do not have a clear and definitive
strategy that consistently delivers results.

Research on leadership development has significantly trailed behind
the broader leadership research and has not received the attention it
deserves (Avolio et al., 2013; Howard & Wellins, 2009). In an attempt

to respond to the issue of leadership development, the research focus has increased on what aspects of development deliver the best results (Gilley, Dixon & Gilley, 2008). Day and Sin (2009) suggested that a lack of a consistent scientific theory and a lack of quality research exists in this area. Riggio (2008) also noted that leadership skills are both abstract and complex and are therefore challenging to develop and evaluate. Within most organisations, however, leadership development is still the main strategy utilised to enhance leadership and improve leadership outcomes (Howard & Wellins, 2009). Beer, Finnstrom, and Schrader (2016) estimated that organisations spend upwards of $160 billion in the US and over $350 billion globally on leadership development each year. Despite this investment, results are mixed concerning the effectiveness and outcomes of leadership development strategies.

In their review of global leadership development practices, Howard and Wellins (2009) observed that leadership development is not achieving the desired organisational outcomes. For example, some evidence indicates that the effects of leadership development interventions are relatively short-lived and do not achieve the desired change in behaviours (Creed & Davies, 2009). Conversely, other evidence shows positive short- and long-term outcomes related to leadership development (Burke & Day, 1986). Some meta-studies have confirmed that significant changes can occur as a result of leadership development, although the desired outcomes are not always achieved (Burke & Day, 1986; Morrow et al., 1997).

Clearly, traditional leadership development strategies are not working as effectively as they should. These traditional development programs have generally been designed to include a variety of skills-based topics, such as marketing, strategy, managing change and managing performance. The choice of subjects has depended on the individual business challenges and requirements deemed to be important aspects of organisational success at that point in time (Barling, Weber & Kelloway, 1996). These traditional leadership programs have shown mixed results for their impact on leadership outcomes (Russell & Kuhnert, 1992).

Day (2001) noted a greater focus and investment in leadership development as opposed to leader development. These differences may play a part in the mixed results of leadership developmental practices (Day, 2001). Landy and Conte (2016) also separated leadership development and leader development. They view leadership development and the more traditional leadership programs as focusing on developing leadership skills and organisational leadership deliverables. Conversely, leader development focuses on developing the intra-personal attributes of a leader and their internal capacity to lead (Landy & Conte, 2016). The studies outlined in chapter two focused on enhancing the attribute of leader resilience, which is leader development and not leadership development. This research offers exciting possibilities for the future of organisational development practices in the leadership domain.

A growing body of research now describes ways of enhancing the impact of leadership development (Button, Mathieu & Zajac, 1996; Day & Sin, 2009; VandeWalle, 1997; Wasylyshyn, 2008). Wasylyshyn (2008) found that including behavioural dimensions in leadership development significantly increased the impact of training in the work context. Research has also found that enhancement of a leader's personal identity and self-regulation had a greater impact on leadership development (Day, Harrison & Halpin, 2009; Hall, 2004). Day and Sin (2009) found that developmental interventions focused on improving clarity around leadership identity resulted in enhanced levels of leadership effectiveness.

One body of research shows that developing aspects of resilience within leadership programs has a positive impact on developmental outcomes (Boyatzis, 2008; Button et al., 1996). Using an intentional change theory (ITC) framework can enhance the outcomes and longevity of leadership development programs (Ballou, Bowers, Boyatzis & Kolb, 1999; Wheeler, 2008). An ITC framework focuses on developing resilience as a core part of the program (Wheeler, 2008), and leadership development can be enhanced by a mastery approach to the learning experience (Button et al., 1996; Day & Sin, 2009; VandeWalle, 1997). This approach is related to aspects of the cognitive characteristics and the self-determination aspects of resilience (Button et al., 1996). These enhancements in leadership development offer a new perspective on building leadership competence and the capacity to cope with the complexity of today's business context.

This aligns with research into dispositional attributes that has indicated the need to develop the internal leadership attributes of the individual prior to developing leadership style. This is new research that is pushing the boundaries of leadership and redefining our focus for leadership development.

## 3.2 Development of the Leader Resilience Training Program

The need to develop more resilient leaders to achieve enhanced levels of transformational leadership is very clear. In Study 2, a resilience training program was developed for leaders that was specifically designed to develop resilience and enhance leadership capacity. This program focuses on the three dimensions of resilience. The curriculum is centred on working to enhance leaders' abilities to effectively transform themselves first and then to build resilient teams and resilient organisations.

The workshops were comprehensively assessed to ascertain their impact in terms of a change in behaviours and attitudes of the attendees. The workshops had a significant impact on the levels of resilience of individuals as well as their ability to deliver a transformational style. This was measured by self-analysis and by boss-analysis, both of which showed a significant shift in leadership capacity following the workshop review.

Transformational leadership has never been more essential in the context of a volatile and changeable business environment. In the present economic climate, organisational success relies on leaders inspiring their people to meet the challenges while maintaining a focus on the long-term vision and direction of the organisation. Consistently using a transformational style of leadership is key to achieving success. The findings of the research outlined in Chapter 6 align with recent studies in suggesting that leaders striving to deliver a transformational leadership style should focus on enhancing their resilience. This is essential to ensure that the leaders have the capacity to truly lead in the VUCA world that we live and work in. Enhancing an individual's transformational leadership capacity requires a focus on building that person's resilience. I would go as far as to say that unless the persons in the position of power are prepared to develop their resilience, they should not be entrusted with the role of leader. The reason for this is that if they are not prepared to build their internal leadership capacity, they are highly likely to have a negative impact on the engagement and motivation of the people they are managing and this, in the long term, will negatively impact their organisations' outcomes.

## 3.3 Leadership and Dispositional Attributes

While Bass (1985, 1989) has provided us with greater clarity on leadership style and how this impacts organisational outcomes, his work only hints at the internal aspect of leadership and does not elucidate the importance of the internal attributes necessary to deliver a transformational style of leadership. Therefore, while Bass has moved this discussion forward with a comprehensive style-based framework of leadership and defined a full-range leadership model, the model does not make a clear link to resilience (Avolio, Bass & Jung, 1999; Bass & Riggio 2006). Bass's full-range leadership model has captured the attention of business communities worldwide; however, a gap is still apparent in terms of understanding and limited guidance for organisations on how individuals can change their internal attributes to ensure they deliver a consistently effective leadership style in the workplace (Ashford & DeRue, 2010; Day & Sin, 2009). The research has shown that, when it is demonstrated, a transformational leadership style will deliver positive outcomes. However, the research does not give any clarity regarding the internal capacity of the leader that is required for the delivery and sustainment of this style.

The good news is that Bass's model sparked a resurgence of interest in investigating the relationship between leadership style and the internal attributes of the individual. This has provided a platform for investigations into the internal capacity of the leader and has offered new insights into the attributes that influence the capacity of leaders to deliver an effective style of leadership (Garbowski, 2010; Sylvester, 2009; Wasden, 2014).

As already discussed, early leadership research commenced with the 'Great Man' theories of leadership and focused on identifying personal traits that support great leadership (Landy & Conte, 2016). This research was dominantly focused on personality traits and has generally shown inconsistent correlations between a specific set of personality traits and leadership effectiveness (Hollander & Julian, 1969). This correlates with what you would have experienced in working life: people with vastly different personality traits can be and are successful. This research area confirmed that traits alone are not enough to define the internal attributes that support a trans-formational leader. The deficits in these theories have prompted debate on whether 'dispositional attributes' might provide a more insightful approach for investigating individual differences in a leadership context (Garbowski, 2010; Offutt, 2011; Sylvester, 2009). Dispositional attributes, unlike traits, are personal attributes that have the capacity for change and development. Unlike personality traits, which are fixed and don't change over a lifetime, dispositional attributes have the capacity for enhancement.

The study of dispositional attributes—resilience, in particular—is a relatively new field of research in organisational psychology. Much of the research on resilience has remained largely within the realm of clinical, social and community psychology over the past three decades, with some more recent research having developed in the organisational arena (Garbowski, 2010).

So where does that leave us today? In authoring this book and working with leaders across the globe for thirty-five years, I have learned three key things. This learning is both from academic research and from organisational experience.

- **A consistent, transformational leadership style makes a positive difference for individuals, teams and organisations, regardless of the type of organisation.** It doesn't matter if you sell cars, work on the mines, run hotels, work in politics or develop tech products—the positive impact of transfor-mational leadership is evident in all these organisations' outcomes.

- **In all organisations and industries, ongoing stressors, chal-lenges, obstacles and ever-present hurdles present them-selves.** No sector, industry or organisation is challenge-free or challenge-neutral. Thus, a key part of effective leadership is the ability to navigate in what researchers describe as a VUCA world (Bennis & Nanus 1985), a world that is volatile, uncertain, complex and ambiguous.

- **In order to deliver a transformational leadership style in a VUCA world, you first need to develop the internal attributes that support leadership. Specifically, you need to develop your resilience.** The internal attribute of resilience allows us to bounce back from adversity and challenge and to maintain psychological, emotional, physical and mental health. This, again, is not specific to industries or organisations.

The truth is that research on leadership is constantly evolving and developing, and while we have made significant strides forward, new frontiers will always be there to investigate. Based on recent research, we have clearly found a new frontier of leadership research that is significantly shifting our understanding of leadership.

By leveraging one of the most researched models of leadership style, my research has taken a look below the surface of leadership style to investigate what allows one individual to deliver a transformational style, while another individual with the same training, development and experience is unable to deliver this style. This offers the opportunity to push the envelope and redefine the requirement for leadership. We need to change our focus and look at how dispositional attributes support an individual in delivering a transformational leadership style. In the pages to come, you will find that we have established a very strong correlation between the dispositional attribute of resilience and the ability to lead with a transformational leadership style. This correlation opens up the debate on what comes first: the dispositional attribute of a leader or the leadership style they deliver. You will be provided with the research evidence that supports the development of your dispositional attributes, in particular your resilience, as a prerequisite to your ability for effective delivery of a transformational leadership style. When you get on an aeroplane, you are given instructions that, in the case of an emergency, you should put on your own oxygen mask first before attempting to put on someone else's mask. Fundamentally, this is the same instruction that we should be issuing to leaders: 'In the VUCA world, you need develop the attribute of resilience before attempting to lead others.' In the coming chapters, we will discuss what resilience is, its importance for leadership and how to develop it.

Leadership matters. In today's ever-changing environment, a transformational leadership style is essential, but you need resilience before you can consistently deliver this style. I am comfortable in sharing with you that I believe, more than ever, that resilience is the single most important attribute for strong, sustainable and successful leaders and the key to transforming leadership outcomes. Not only do I believe this personally, I have also shown this to be true from a research basis, and I have also had the opportunity to observe leaders transform their leadership style by developing their resilience. These transformations are dramatic and bring about team and organisational shifts that make a significant difference. Throughout the pages to come, I am confident that you will be inspired to take action to build your resilience and enhance your leadership capacity.

"If your actions inspire others to dream more, learn more, do more and become more, you are a leader."

John Quincy Adams

# CHAPTER 4

# TRANSFORMATIONAL LEADERSHIP IN A VUCA WORLD?

Transformational leadership is by no means a new topic, as its origins have been a point of conversation in the leadership world since the late 1970s. However, as we look to a new and contemporary understanding of leadership that has the capacity to navigate challenging times, our consideration of substantive leadership theories as a foundation for our discussions is now more important than ever. Also essential is our exploration of aspects that influence leadership, including those that might seem out-of-the-box and revolutionary. The transformational leadership model is a well-established framework that offers organisations and their leaders a clear approach for achieving effective leadership in the present day. However, as this model has been around for some time, something is clearly missing if we still have a global deficit in effective leadership. In defining Bass's (1985) model, we will focus on its origins, its modern-day applications, and how we can leverage these concepts in connection with research on dispositional attributes. This will offer us a new and contemporary approach to leadership that will redefine how we recruit, develop and build leadership in organisations.

## 4.1 The Origins and Foundational Concepts of the Transformational Leadership Model

Burns (1978) was one of the first to articulate the concept of transformational leadership. He formed this description in a political setting and included the distinction between ethical/moral leadership and dysfunctional leadership. Bass (1985), as one of the first organisational psychology theorists to take up this line of research, built on Burns's (1978) notion of transformational leadership and further developed this into the full-range model of leadership that we see today. Bass's (1998) conceptualisation separated transactional and transformational leadership and defined the transformational aspect as building on transactional capacity. In this model, leadership is defined as having three elements (Bass et al., 2003): internal (intra-personal), relational (interpersonal) and organisational.

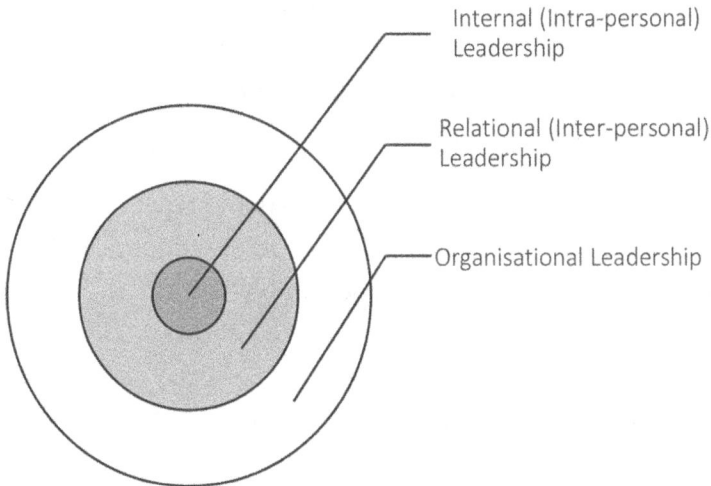

Internal (Intra-personal) Leadership

Relational (Inter-personal) Leadership

Organisational Leadership

*Figure 2: Levels of leadership*

Internal leadership (intra-personal) is the ability of leaders to maintain themselves and respond adaptively to the environment to make effective decisions. In Bass's (1985) approach, internal leadership is given very little attention, and leaders are assumed to somehow arrive with this capacity. Bass does not focus on what it might look like from a developmental perspective. His dominant focus is on the interpersonal leadership aspect, which includes measuring and developing a transformational leadership style to impact organisational outcomes.

In the present VUCA world, this internal leadership is paramount, and if it is undeveloped, it will hinder the ability of the individual to deliver transformational leadership. This lack of focus on internal leadership is why we still see people in positions of power who are unable to lead and yet have been trained and developed to deliver an effective style of leadership. As noted previously, this is a bit like the instructions you get on an aeroplane in relation to putting on oxygen masks. The instructions are always the same: you need to put on your own mask before attempting to assist others. The same applies to leaders: they need to develop their internal leadership before attempting to deliver a transformational leadership style. Without their own mask in place, leaders will be ineffective in assisting and working with others.

The second aspect of the model, the relational aspect of leadership, focuses on the capacity of the leader to energise, engage and develop followers to respond adaptively and flexibly (Bass et al., 2003). This involves the essential ability of leaders to develop healthy relationships with followers that result in them being inspired to find creative solutions to challenges (Bass & Riggio, 2006).

The third element of leadership is the organisational aspect, which extends to the broader corporate context and the ability of the individual to guide an organisation through a changing and dynamic business environment (Bass, 1985; Bass et al., 2003; Sylvester, 2009). This broader organisational leadership is impossible without first developing the internal (intra-personal) leadership and the relational (interpersonal) leadership. Organisational leadership requires that the individual is able to assimilate information constructively and make objective decisions that strategically guide the people within the organisation towards an enhanced future. Organisational leadership outcomes also incorporate the ability to respond to external factors in the business environment (Saunders & Barker, 2001).

The transformational model of leadership provides clarity on the importance of each of these aspects of leadership; however, it does not fully articulate what is necessary to develop in the internal leadership aspect. This is the new frontier of leadership and provides the platform for understanding the importance of resilience. The research that precipitated the writing of this book shows that a very defined link exists between resilience and the transformational leadership. This research shows that the key attribute of internal leadership is resilience. Therefore, without resilience, the ability to lead is significantly hindered, and the individual will not likely be able to deliver a consistent transformational style.

## 4.2 Transformational vs Transactional Leadership

For many organisations, the focus of leadership development is on enhancing the interaction between leaders and their teams (interpersonal leadership) and the organisational aspects of leadership (organisational leadership), such as building culture and enhancing collaboration. However, we know that this developmental focus does not make a difference in all instances. In fact, this focus is likely to result in short-term changes that are not sustainable. For subordinates, this focus can be annoying, as they get their leader back from a leadership workshop with a whole lot of new skills and initiatives that they want to try out. Then, within a month, all the new initiatives and skills have been forgotten and things are back to how they were before. The reason this happens is that the leader has not made a substantive shift in their internal attributes. Without this, the interpersonal and organisational changes are unlikely to be sustained. If this fantastic model of leadership is going to deliver sustainable results, the focus needs to be on first developing internal leadership capability. However, before we focus on the internal leadership aspect, let's first understand what this model of leadership requires in terms of interpersonal and organisational leadership capability. Let's tackle the question: What does transactional and transformational leadership look like?

Transactional leadership entails exchanges between leaders and their subordinates that involve defining role requirements, offering rewards for action and delivering corrective action when required. This exchange aims to ensure that followers can produce the necessary business outcomes.

There are four levels of transactional leadership:

**1. Laissez-faire**—the manager abdicates responsibility and avoids making decisions, resulting in a lack of direction and a requirement for followers to step up and make decisions. These are managers who abdicate their leadership responsibility. While Bass (1985) does not discuss narcissistic leaders, they sit alongside the laissez-faire leaders because they also make a decision to abdicate the responsibility to lead effectively.

**2. Passive management by exception**—the only time the leader intervenes is when performance expectations are not met or when standards are not achieved. Resorting to punishment is likely when performance is unacceptable.

We have all worked for or seen these first two styles in action in organisations. This is very often the person that has landed in a management role and really does not want lead or is actively refusing to lead. They have become comfortable in receiving the remuneration but abdicate all responsibility for leadership and simply deliver the bare minimum in their interactions. Under times of pressure and stress, these leaders are either nowhere to be seen or are barking out commands that demoralise and disengage their teams.

**3. Active management by exception**—the leader actively monitors work standards, watching for mistakes or deviations from the rules and taking corrective action to ensure mistakes are minimised.

**4. Contingent reward**—the leader sets mutually agreed-upon and well-constructed goals, clarifies expectations, provides necessary resources and offers rewards for satisfactory performance. These two aspects of transactional leadership are an important foundation and often the basis of a lot of frontline management programs.

These transactional aspects sound familiar, don't they? That's because a lot of managers in organisations never move beyond this level of exchange with their teams. For many old-school leaders, this style has worked for as long as they could remember, so why change it now? In the VUCA world, this is a recipe for disaster. If we do not move beyond the transactional exchange, we will fail. However, these transactional exchanges are still part of what managers are required to do. If we are going to create leaders who can respond to the VUCA world, we have to develop a different form of leadership. Transformational leadership is different, as it entails an exchange between the leader and their subordinates that involves a higher level of interaction and engagement. Bass and Avolio (1997) proposed that transformational leaders utilise four key strategies to deliver a transformational style:

**1. Idealised influence**—these leaders display and articulate clear and positive values. They act as role models for followers by behaving in ways that are admirable, showing conviction, and causing followers to identify with and follow them.

**2. Inspirational motivation**—these leaders articulate a vision and direction that appeals to and inspires optimism in their followers, leading to the achievement of goals that contribute to delivering the vision and offering a sense of meaning in the delivery of the work.

**3. Intellectual stimulation**—these leaders challenge assumptions, encourage creativity and help followers to overcome obstacles that get in the way of success.

**4. Individualised consideration**—these leaders connect with individual team members and understand and attend to their needs while acting as coaches and mentors. These leaders display respect for everyone and appreciate both the individual and the team contribution, thereby resulting in the inspiration of followers towards achievements.

I imagine that just reading about the differences in transformational leadership excites you. Visualise a leader who incorporates all four aspects of the transformational style. If these four strategies are utilised by leaders, they engender trust, loyalty and respect from their followers. This results in their followers moving beyond self-interest to the delivery of organisational objectives (Bass, 1985, 1998). However, as already noted, consistent and effective delivery of this style of leadership requires that the leaders first put on their own 'oxygen masks.' That is why, in the research that was carried out, internal leadership is incorporated into a holistic framework for leadership (Folan, 2019).

The leadership framework illustrated in Figure 3 identifies the relationship between internal leadership (resilience) and interpersonal (transformational) leadership. Research shows that internal leadership should be the priority focus and that only once this is developed will the individual be able to deliver effective interpersonal leadership (Folan, 2019).

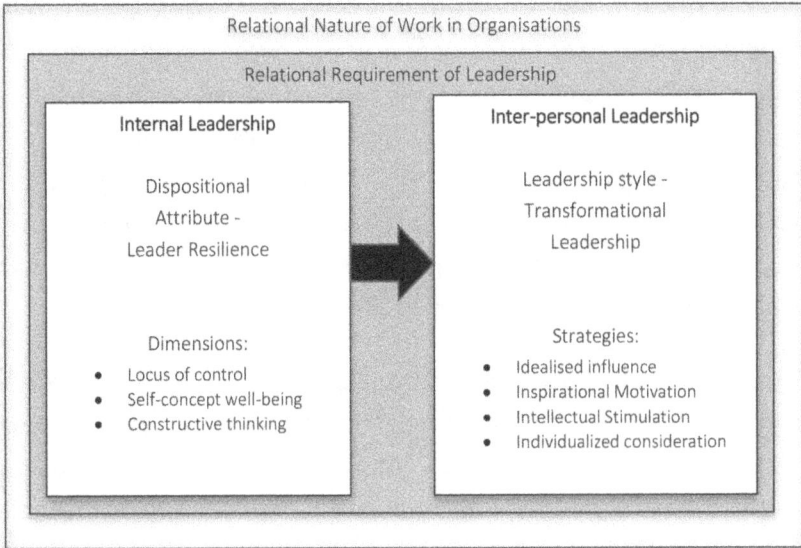

Figure 3: A framework for leadership effectiveness (Folan, 2019)

## 4.3 Research on Transformational Leadership

The conceptualisation of transformational leadership outlined in the previous section has attracted a lot of interest over the years. A substantial volume of research evidence has confirmed the construct of transformational and transactional leadership and the factors that make up the model (Bycio, Hackett & Allen, 1995; Piccolo et al., 2012). This has been replicated through research that confirms the six-factor model of transformational leadership (Antonakis et al., 2003; Avolio et al., 1999).

Research on the impact of transformational leadership in organisations has consistently shown the positive impact of this style of leadership in various domains. Transformational leaders have been found to inspire higher levels of motivation, engagement, loyalty and increased social identification in their followers (Lowe et al., 1996; Shamir, Zakay, Breinin & Popper, 1998). Transformational leaders' followers are also shown to develop enhanced job attitudes, better performance at work and self-concordant work goals (Bono & Judge, 2003). Transformational leaders have been shown to offer greater levels of recognition of teams and enhanced responses to the emotional needs of followers, resulting in increased motivation and productivity (House & Shamir, 1993). Increased self-efficacy and the overall satisfaction of followers have also been linked to transformational leadership (Bono & Judge, 2003; Fuller, Patterson, Hester & Stringer, 1996; House & Shamir, 1993).

Transformational leadership has been empirically linked to research on effective organisational culture (Denison & Mishra, 1995). During the 1990s, studies showed that cultural orientations that focus on transformational qualities are conducive to higher levels of business performance (Denison & Mishra, 1995; Gordon & DiTomaso, 1992; Smart & St. John, 1996). Bass and Avolio (1993) argued that leadership and culture are so interconnected that one can describe an organisational culture characterised by transformational qualities. Similarly, Xenikou and Simosi (2006) defined transformational leadership as a key component in creating healthy organisational cultures that deliver enhanced outcomes. Transformational leadership has been shown to underpin a culture of ethical organisational behaviour (Ciulla, 2009; Gardner, Avolio & Luthans, 2005; Karakas, 2009). Another body of research also shows the relationship between transformational leadership and leaders' enhanced ability for the effective management of organisational challenges (Gilley, 2005; Lawler & Worley, 2012). Research has shown that transformational leadership results in enhanced business outcomes, such as financial and business performance (Bass et al., 2003; Walker, Smither & Waldman, 2008; Walumbwa, Wang, Lawler & Shi, 2010).

Clearly, direct links exist between a transformational leadership style and the engagement of subordinates, the culture that develops and the success of the organisation's outcomes. Particularly in the context of a VUCA world, the research clearly shows that survival in a constantly changing environment requires transformational leadership. The research-based links between the levels of leadership and outcomes are outlined in Figure 4 below.

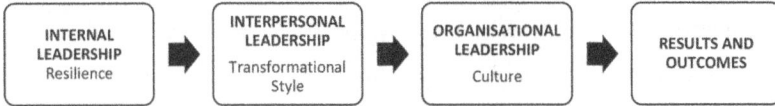

*Figure 4. Relationship between levels of leadership and outcomes*

Research shows that forty-six percent of the variance in transformational leadership can be explained by the resilience of the leader (Folan,2019). Research also shows that fifty percent of the variance in organisational culture can be explained by the leadership style delivered by the leadership team. Up to thirty percent of the variance in organisational outcomes and results can be explained by the differences in cultures.

### 4.3.1 The Critics of Transformational Leadership

Criticism has been levelled at all leadership research over the years, and the transformational leadership model is no exception. While much of the criticism has been answered with further research providing clarity on issues and enhancing aspects of the models, some of the criticism does have validity. Much of the valid criticism tends to be common to the majority of leadership research and simply attests to the challenges of effective research controls.

One of the dominant criticisms of research in leadership is that making use of single-source measurements is a common practice. Lowe et al. (1996) found different results for self-assessment and follower-assessment, highlighting the challenges of relying on a single-source measurement strategy. They found that although a strong correlation was present for both measures on the transformational leadership scale, a difference was evident between the leaders' self-evaluation scores and the followers' evaluation scores. Hunt and Conger (1999) noted an opportunity to broaden the research in this area and utilise a broader range of research techniques. However, to make this a reality, some challenges to using other methods in an organisational context will need to be overcome. A broader range of measures, inclusive of boss, subordinates and business responses, has been suggested to balance the issues around common method variance (Brannick et al., 2010; Lowe et al., 1996). The research that forms the foundation of this book makes use of both the leaders' self-ratings and their bosses' ratings in an attempt to overcome this limitation of research in this space.

Criticism has been levelled at the focus on the outcomes of transformational leadership and the lack of focus on how a leader might go about developing these capabilities or even the nature of the underlying skills or competencies that align with a transformational leadership style (Hunt, 1991; Parry, 1998). This has been a gap in the research, with a lack of exploration of the developmental activities likely to enhance a leader's personal capacity to deliver transformational leadership. A leader's underlying capabilities, and the development thereof, were among the primary objectives of the research on which this book is based. The two studies that form the foundation of this book sought to identify the dispositional attributes of individuals that enable a leader to consistently utilise a transformational style (Folan, 2019).

Yukl (1998) argued that the level of emphasis in the transformational model is limited, noting that its focus is predominantly on dyadic relationships. Although much of the research maintains this focus, the model itself conceptualises leadership in the broader context of organisational leadership. An opportunity arises within the leadership debate to broaden the research to look at the impact of leadership on teams and businesses. A new area of research is now developing that looks at the interplay between transformational leadership research and leader–member exchange research; this may go some way to bridging this gap (Dienesch & Liden,1986; Liden, Erdogan, Wayne & Sparrowe, 2006).

Within the field of leadership research, focus on the dysfunctional attributes of leaders has been limited (den Hartog, Van Muijen & Koopman, 1997). This is a valid criticism and indicates a potential challenge to the concept of a full-range leadership model (Bass, 1985). Some of the very serious ethical and moral issues that have arisen in organisations in the past would indicate that the full-range model may not be sufficiently extensive to incorporate these negative aspects of leadership (Pendse, 2012).

Bass (1998) did define laissez-faire leadership as a less functional style. However, no definition is yet in place for truly unhealthy leadership, such as unethical or narcissistic leadership, which is on the rise in organisations (den Hartog et al., 1997). The theoretical models that have dominated leadership research have tended to focus on a range of styles from slightly less than optimal to highly functioning. From an organisational and leadership perspective, the issues around dysfunctional leadership have become more relevant as a result of some of the business disasters that have occurred in recent times (Pelletier & Bligh, 2008). This has given rise to a new wave of research examining narcissism and corporate sociopaths and investigating these issues of dysfunctional leadership more fully (Boddy, 2014; Henning, Wygant & Barnes, 2014; Twenge & Campbell, 2009).

Taking cognisance of the issues of destructive and ineffective leadership is important, as this type of leadership is impacting organisations across the globe. While the research that underpins this book does not specifically look at the impact of narcissism and corporate sociopaths in organisations, individuals with these tendencies very clearly do not have resilience. Yes, they may be tough, and they may look like they can bounce back, but they are not healthy mentally or emotionally and would therefore not be capable of leading transformationally. During the recent issues around the COVID-19 pandemic, this has become obvious in the contrasting behaviours of individuals in positions of power. We have watched some individuals step up to lead respectfully and with courage and dignity. These individuals demonstrate the dimensions of resilience on a daily basis and seek to deliver positive solutions in a challenging context. Conversely, we have also watched some individuals with low levels of resilience resort to openly abusive and disrespectful behaviour. Their style includes blaming everything on others, accusing, throwing temper tantrums, inciting dysfunctional behaviour and displaying a range of other bad behaviours. Resilience requires the mental and emotional capacity to remain calm and rational to deal with challenges proactively and optimistically. Without this, providing leadership is impossible.

While some of the criticisms levelled at transformational leadership have validity, it still remains the most highly validated and researched model of leadership. This model has the scope to extend to include more depth of understanding of the internal attributes of a leader that play a part in leadership effectiveness. It is the only research-based full-range model of leadership that comprehensively defines effective leadership.

## 4.4 Transformational Leadership and Resilience Research

Strong research support is evident for Bass's (1985) model of leadership, and it remains the dominant model of leadership in research today. The research investigating the link between leadership and dispositional attributes, such as resilience, started to emerge about fifteen years ago. Much of this research has been carried out in combination with Bass's model of leadership. The organisational context of leadership with constant challenges and the changing nature of businesses is driving the demand for a more thorough investigation of this link (Draghici & Draghici, 2007). Some of the most critical components of effective leadership today are the ability to assess issues objectively, make balanced decisions, remain emotionally stable and adapt to the constant change that is a regular part of business life (Draghici & Draghici, 2007). This ability requires a level of personal leadership that comes from internal balance and the capacity to bounce back.

The transformational leadership model mentions internal or intra-personal leadership, but it does not fully explore the dispositional attributes that are the foundation of this internal leadership and key to individuals' abilities to lead themselves. The understanding of leadership must be broadened to incorporate the intra-personal capacity of individuals and the impact of this on leaders' abilities to deliver a transformational leadership style. Dispositional factors, such as resilience, offer a broader perspective and add to the breadth of understanding of effective internal leadership (Garbowski, 2010; Howell & Avolio, 1993; Sylvester, 2009).

A small number of recent research papers have specifically focused on the link between resilience and leadership. The research articulated in this book has found a significant association between these two constructs. This research is discussed further in Chapter 6, which builds on the examination of the broader resilience research in Chapter 5, while the proposed dimensions of leader resilience are presented in Chapters 10, 11 and 12.

For now, we can begin by clearly defining resilience and discovering what is really required at the intra-personal level to be an effective leader in our contemporary workplace. Now, more than ever, leaders have to deal with a diverse range of issues they never before faced. Adversity and challenge are around every corner, and the more resilient the leader, the better equipped they'll be to weather the storms.

"Do not judge me by my success, judge me by how many times I fell down and got back up again"

Nelson Mandela

# CHAPTER 5

# DEFINING WHAT RESILIENCE IS AND WHY IT MATTERS FOR LEADERSHIP

Now more than ever, in a business context, finding ways to separate yourself from the competition so that you stand out as unique is crucial for the delivery of sustainable organisational success. An effective leadership style is one of the greatest identifying and distinguishing factors amongst highly successful companies. Show me a company moving the needle and delivering sustainable results, and you will likely be able to point to a leadership team that is the driving force of this success. Show me a company that is failing, and this failure is highly likely to be attributable to the leadership. Over the years, we have all repeatedly read stories of companies that failed due to a failure in leadership. Transformational leadership is the driving force that carves out success for individuals, teams and organisations in the VUCA world, and resilience is the key attribute that enables the delivery of a transformational style of leadership.

In this chapter, we take a closer look at resilience and the complex relationship between the factors that determine our resilience. To better understand the symbiotic connection between resilience and leadership, we will look at resilience research from multiple disciplines and research areas, including clinical, educational, community, social and organisational psychology. After doing so, we will also take some time to define the research foundation for defining resilience as a dispositional attribute with adaptive capacity, rather than as a trait with limited capacity for change (Anthony, 1987; Rutter, 1999).

This chapter will conclude with an articulation of the model of leader resilience and the research that informed the development of this model (Folan, 2019; Garmezy, 1974; Keyes, 2007; Rutter, 1999; Wagnild, 2009).

## 5.1 The Origins and Definition of Resilience

Often times, the best place to start is at the beginning. The term 'resilience' did not originate within the field of psychology. Therefore, to go back to the beginning, we have to look to other domains in order to better contextualise its use within the field of psychology and leadership. Many researchers believe that Holling (1973) coined the term resilience in his landmark paper on system ecology. In that work, he described how natural ecological systems 'rebound from disasters' or change and display the ability to bounce back. Other early uses of the word resilience appeared in the physical sciences in descriptions of substances and materials. The term was used to describe their 'elasticity' or 'ability to bounce back' (Hollnagel, Woods & Leveson, 2006). Resilience was never meant to be a term used in describing our leaders. However, just like science and nature, it actually has substantial relevance and value.

In psychology, resilience was initially a term used in relation to individuals and their ability to cope with environmental circumstances and bounce back from adversity (Garmezy, 1991; Werner, 1982; Werner & Smith, 1992). As research has increased on the subject, the various definitions started to incorporate greater breadth and included the generative capacity of individuals to cope with disruptive events and maintain healthy physical, emotional and psychological functioning (Bonanno, 2004; Keyes, 2002).

Rutter, one of the key researchers in this area, defined resilience as 'reduced vulnerability to environmental risk experiences, the overcoming of a stress or adversity, or a relatively good outcome despite risk experiences' (2012, p. 336). Keyes (2002) defined resilience as a continuum of human capacity from languishing to flourishing, incorporating all aspects of well-being. Keyes (2002) also defined the determining factors of resilience as emotional, psychological and social well-being and identified the need for individuals to manage their levels of well-being to maintain their health, vitality and ability to flourish. As another key researcher in this area, Wagnild (2009) described resilience as 'the ability to adapt or bounce back following adversity and challenge, and [it] connotes inner strength, competence, optimism, flexibility and the ability to cope effectively when faced with adversity' (p. 29).

We have already discussed the importance of intra-personal leadership in the full-range model of transformational leadership. Effective intra-personal leadership requires the ability to respond adaptively and flexibly to the environment and to assimilate information accurately in order to take effective actions and make important decisions (Bass, 1998). In doing so, leaders have the capacity to become transformational on an interpersonal and organisational level of leadership, enabling them to effectively adapt to challenges and adversity (Hardy, Concato & Gill, 2004).

Thus, in the organisational context, resilience has now been defined as:

'The internal (intra-personal) capacity of the individual which enables them to bounce back from adversity and flourish in the face of challenges while maintaining healthy levels of psychological, emotional and cognitive well-being.' (Folan, 2019, p. 50)

In essence, the intra-personal capacity is what allows the leader to flourish in the face of challenges while also maintaining well-being. One important point to emphasise is that resilience is not simply keeping on going or bouncing back. We know that, on its own, the ability to keep going or keep bouncing back will result in dysfunction and that, in the end, it will impact both health and well-being. We can all attest to times when we have kept on going, then gone on holiday to recoup only to fall ill. This is not resilience. If you want to be resilient, you must maintain well-being alongside the ability to bounce back; this is what enables us to flourish.

Does this sound important to the overall success of the leader and the organisation? If you think so, that's because it is. Every organisation globally will face varying degrees of obstacles, challenges and pressure. The leadership's response to these inevitable challenges will be a distinguishing factor in the overall success of the organisation in navigating the VUCA world.

## 5.2 Resilience: Nature or Nurture?

Defining resilience is one thing. The big question that remains is: are you born with it (nature), or is it something that you can develop (nurture)? Within the framework of individual differences, debate continues regarding nature and nurture in relation to a construct such as resilience (Lee et al., 2013). Some researchers view resilience as a trait that is 'nature', has stability and is intransigent to change (Anthony, 1987). Conversely, others view it as a malleable dispositional attribute (nurture) that is adaptable, flexible and has the capacity for development, i.e. 'nurture' (Reivich, Gillham, Chaplin & Seligman, 2013; Robitschek & Keyes, 2009; Wagnild, 2009). This conversation is key, since, if resilience can be developed, then organisations should be focusing their efforts on building this essential attribute to enable their leaders to become effective.

In the early research on resilience, the definitions were aligned with the concept of a trait, with some of the early discussion using terms such as invulnerability (Anthony, 1987). This means we have fixed qualities that make us either susceptible or resistant to adversity. More recent research suggests resilience is a dispositional attribute, rather than a stable trait (Rutter, 2012; Wagnild, 2009). Wagnild (2009) argued that resilience has an adaptive quality that can be developed to bring about improved health and vitality. Rutter (2012) concluded that resilience is a process and provides evidence of how this process can be modified with interventions to enhance it. Consequently, if resilience is a dynamic and malleable dispositional attribute that can be 'nurtured', then it can almost certainly be influenced by developmental strategies designed to enhance this key capability (Garbowski, 2010; Keyes, 2002; Wagnild, 2009).

A meta-analysis of research in this area by Lee et al. (2013) found that certain factors, such as self-efficacy and positive affect (dispositional attributes), have a greater influence on resilience than personality factors (traits). Interestingly, both self-efficacy and positive affect are also described as dispositional attributes that are adaptable and amenable to change (Bandura, 1978). Similarly, organisational resilience research shows that individual difference factors, such as age, personality and gender (fixed and unchangeable attributes), do not have a significant impact on people's coping capacities in the context of adversity, whereas resilience (a dispositional attribute) has a significant positive impact on the coping capacities of individuals (Offutt, 2011; Sylvester, 2009).

A growing body of research now recognises resilience as a dispositional attribute with the capacity for adaptation and development over time and across circumstances (Reivich et al., 2013; Rutter, 2012; Wagnild, 2009). This conceptualisation of resilience as a malleable dispositional attribute highlights the possibility that we can enhance resilience and bring about change in an individual's capacity. Research has also demonstrated the capacity of individuals to change and increase their levels of resilience through a range of developmental strategies, such as training, coaching and mentoring (Cohn & Pakenham, 2009; Griffith & West, 2013; Varker & Devilly, 2012).

The most up-to-date research clearly shows that resilience is a dispositional attribute that has the capacity for change and can be enhanced using developmental strategies. I have also come to know, from practical experience in organisations, that people can transform their resilience and their leadership style through programs and developmental strategies designed to support them. Obviously, as with most dispositional attributes, some people are born with a more natural level of resilience or have developed this in their younger years. Research evidence supports the idea that adversity and challenging life experiences build resilience in some individuals. However, this clearly can also be developed further to enable enhanced coping strategies and to develop intra-personal leadership capacity. This is a game-changer in the leadership space. If you don't have resilience or are not actively working to build your resilience, then you are effectively limiting your ability to lead.

The great news is that resilience can be developed. Having worked with leaders from across the globe for over thirty-five years, I am one hundred percent convinced that a leader's resilience can be altered as a result of well-designed developmental strategies. The one caveat that I would place on this is that the individual has to make a choice to do the work that is required to build their resilience. Resilience will not change by attending a course or having a coach; it requires that the individuals take action to build their internal capacities. This is the same as getting physically fit; you can't and won't get fit if you go to the gym just once or occasionally. Regular fitness activities are required to build and maintain physical fitness. The same holds for resilience; the individual needs to put consistent effort into maintaining their resilience.

Waiting until adversity hits is also ineffective for building your resilience. It needs to be built in advance if you want to flourish and maintain well-being. I hear lots of people telling me that they are resilient because they keep going and they bounce back from adversity. Then, in the next breath, they describe their levels of stress, and often distress, as a result of the challenges in the workplace. This is not resilience; this is simply coping. Demonstration of true resilience means that we are able to flourish under any level of pressure and find challenges energising and engaging.

In simple terms, what we are saying is that resilience can be developed. Therefore, if you want to be able to lead effectively in a VUCA world and flourish under pressure, you need to put in the work to develop and maintain your resilience. This also means that if you don't develop your resilience, you will not have the intra-personal capacity to sustain a transformational leadership style. If leaders were only born, just a few people would be capable of moving these mountains. However, that is not the case, as leadership can be developed in everyone. The choice is yours: if you want to lead, then build and maintain your resilience.

## 5.3 The Evolution of Resilience Research

Over the last two decades, a significant paradigm shift has occurred within the field of psychology, and this has defined a new direction for research into human difference and its impact on an individual's capacity (Richardson, 2002). The deficit- and problem-orientated frame of reference in psychology has given way to a strength-based approach. This exciting change of focus has signified a new era in psychology that was long overdue. The focus has shifted from finding problems to fix to developing attributes that enhance outcomes. While this is not apparent across all areas of psychology, a strong movement is evident towards this positive, strength-based approach. The construct of resilience falls within the broad strength-based approach and adds to the body of knowledge developing within the world of psychology (Wagnild, 2009).

As resilience is a relatively new area of research in organisational psychology, exploring a breadth of research across all the psychological disciplines and domains is necessary to obtain a fuller understanding of this important construct. Resilience research has evolved within a multidisciplinary framework that falls into four distinct domains. The following section summarises these four domains. Each domain has had a specific focus and direction and provides different insights into the construct of resilience.

### 5.3.1 The First Domain: Early Identity Research

The first domain of resilience research predates the use of the term resilience in the human sciences. Early research looking at individual differences investigated certain constructs, such as emotional well-being and identity, in an attempt to understand the differing reactions of individuals to adversity. These constructs are now described as underlying factors in the ability to bounce back and remain resilient (Adler, 1979; Erikson, 1950). The early researchers acknowledged and investigated the impact of these constructs on human behaviour (Adler, 1979; Erikson, 1950).

The work of early researchers, such as Erikson (1950, 1968, 1980) and Adler (1979), around identity and well-being formed the foundations of the research that now influences the resilience debate. These early researchers did not utilise the term 'resilience'; however, their research aligns closely with modern resilience research and gives some early indications of the importance of dispositional attributes to human functioning. Their conversations focused a great deal on the topics of identity and well-being. Erikson (1950, p. 203) stated that a 'sense of identity provides the ability to experience oneself as something that has continuity and sameness and to act accordingly.' To that end, the evolution of identity is a crucial developmental stage through which individuals must move before establishing meaningful and intimate relations with others (Erikson, 1980).

This focus on identity influenced some of the early thinking around the importance of developing the self-concept to maintain well-being and enhance an individual's ability to interact healthily with others (Baumgardner, 1990; Campbell, 1990). Further research supported Erikson's (1980) perspective, showing that a strong sense of identity promotes a sense of control over outcomes and generates positive affect and confidence in oneself and towards others (Baumgardner, 1990). This strong identity is closely related to some of the constructs associated with resilience, such as psychological well-being and self-concept well-being (Campbell, 1990; Keyes, 2004).

The work by Stephen Covey (1989) also falls within this domain; his work focused on effectiveness. At the time of his writing, the term resilience had not yet been used in relation to human functioning. His book, *The seven habits of highly effective people*, significantly influences the work that I do with individuals, teams and organisations, and it has provided amazing insights for my research on leadership and resilience.

## 5.3.2 The Second Domain: Resilience in a Broad Societal Context

The second domain of resilience research falls within the community and cultural context and focuses on the factors that assist in the adaptation of a community to challenging contexts (Tajfel, 1981; Trickett, 1996). Challenging environments and the need to adapt have been shown to enhance resilience within some communities (Norris et al., 2008). Sonn and Fisher (1998) reviewed the implications of resilience in the context of oppressive social systems. They noted that communities cope with oppression and display resilience, even though others may describe this as capitulation (Sonn & Fisher, 1998).

Elsass (1992) investigated the impact of resilience on ethnic minorities and found that resilience levels had a significant impact on their ability to cope with external factors. These studies broadened the resilience debate and have paved the way to studying resilience in groups, with significant implications for broader organisational research in the future. One of the aspects of the work that I do involves building team and organisational resilience, and the impact of this is significant. The idea that groups can develop resilience and be able to bounce back from adversity is another exciting area of focus for organisational resilience research.

## 5.3.3 The Third Domain: The Effect of Resilience on Human Capacity

The third domain of resilience research—and probably the most dominant to date—is research focused on the human capacity to withstand adversity and to maintain well-being (Garmezy, 1974). This domain has had a significant impact on the conceptualisation of the resilience construct, and much of the organisational research draws heavily on the learning from this domain (Werner, 1982). The research in this area initially focused on the conceptualisation of these individual differences as fixed traits that allow individuals to respond differently to stress and adversity; however, it was later broadened to explore the dispositional aspect (Werner, 1995).

This domain initially focused on children and then broadened fairly quickly to include adolescents, adults and the ageing (Garmezy, 1974; Werner, 1982). Garmezy's (1974) research showed that some children exposed to mothers with mental illness were healthy and functioning, despite their adverse environmental circumstances. Another foundational study within this domain was the work of Werner (1982). Werner and Smith (1992) investigated the resilient qualities in young people that allowed them to do well despite environmental risk factors. Studies examining qualities that mitigated environmental risk factors reiterate these findings at various developmental stages and in various contexts (Benson, 2006; Richardson, 2002). The qualities are described as protective factors that help individuals bounce back from adversity and/or stress (Rutter, 1985).

The focus on understanding individual differences in responses to adversity has led to definitions of a process of resilience with implications for human capacity (Rutter, 2012). Although early research in this domain tended to describe resilience as a trait, many of the key researchers moved to conceptualise resilience as a malleable, dispositional attribute.

Resilience studies in this domain have shown strong positive correlations between resilience and adaptive capacity and healthy functioning (Keyes, 2007; Rutter, 2012; Werner, 1982). An association is evident between resilience and positive outcomes in various areas: positive life outcomes for individuals, adaptive patterns of social behaviour in teenagers, the adaptive functioning of children raised in high-stress environments and developing competence and autonomy (Bleuler, 1978; Brockner, 1988; Garmezy, 1993b; Madzar, 2001). Research has also revealed correlations with increased academic attainment in school, reduced internalisation of disorders in children with anxiety and depression, the ability of children to maintain balance and cope with adversity and misfortune and improved wellness in trauma survivors (Harvey, 2007; Lipsitt & Demick, 2011; Reivich et al., 2013; Rutter, 1999; Wagnild & Young, 1993). This third domain of resilience research has had a significant impact on the literature in organisational psychology.

### 5.3.4 The Fourth Domain: Organisational Resilience

The fourth domain of resilience research is the newest and investigates resilience in an organisational setting. At first, researchers looking at resilience in organisations focused on the capacity of individuals to cope with business challenges and change. More recently, this area of research has evolved to look at how resilience may influence the enhancement of capacity and capability to deliver business activities, particularly in relation to the impact on leadership (Wagnild & Young, 1993; Folan, 2019).

Organisational research shows that individuals with high levels of personal resilience respond more positively to challenges in work and produce enhanced outcomes for both the individual and the organisation (Fugate, Kinicki & Prussia, 2008; Kerber & Buono, 2009; Lawrence & Callan, 2011; Tvedt & Saksvik, 2012). For example, we now know that optimism, a construct closely aligned to resilience, has a positive impact on general success at work (Seligman, 1990).

A fairly consistent body of research now links personal resilience to an individual's ability to cope with organisational change and disruption (Van den Heuvel et al., 2009; Wanberg & Banas, 2000). Individuals with low levels of resilience have been shown to withdraw and to display high levels of distress in the context of organisational change

(Fugate et al., 2008). Research aimed at creating sustainable organisational change has repeatedly found that an individual's ability to enhance their resilience by changing their personal mindset is key to enhanced organisational outcomes (Lawrence & Callan, 2011; Van den Heuvel et al., 2009). Furthermore, one of the key elements in achieving change readiness within organisations is developing individuals' resilience and adjusting their mindsets (Kerber & Buono, 2009). Resilience positively enhances individuals' abilities to develop their capacities to perform in their job roles, to access greater numbers of personal growth opportunities, to improve their levels of relational effectiveness and to enhance social connections (Cowdrey & Walters, 2013; Reivich et al., 2013; Seligman, 2011).

From a leadership perspective, the research shows that resilient individuals have a greater capacity to deliver positive organisational outcomes in situations of change (Tvedt & Saksvik, 2012). Research evidence supports the idea that resilient leaders deliver enhanced outcomes and have greater relational capacity (Kobasa, 1979; Wagnild & Young, 1993). This area of emerging organisational research has found that resilience influences a leader's ability to deliver transformational leadership (Garbowski, 2010; Offutt, 2011; Sylvester, 2009). These findings all align with the research that formed the basis of this book (Folan, 2019).

## 5.4 Important Related Research: Hardiness and Optimism

When discussing resilience as a whole, another important consideration is research that is closely aligned with resilience research. Two areas of interest are research on hardiness and on optimism. Hardiness is described as a combination of coping strategies, attitudes and beliefs that assist individuals in coping positively with life stressors. People with a hardy personality—which includes the traits of challenge, control and commitment—are more likely to have coping strategies that assist them in overcoming challenges and stress (Kobasa, 1979).

Kobasa (1979) conducted the initial research into the trait of hardiness, and research has continued on this construct since then. A number of studies have looked at ways to develop hardiness and to enhance individuals' ability to cope (Bossick, 2008; Kobasa & Puccetti, 1983). Maddi (2011) described a hardy personality as having developed through learned attitudes and skills that support higher levels of effectiveness. Hardiness has been shown to enhance performance, health and well-being. The hardiness construct has been empirically linked to the ability to cope with stress and stressful life situations, enhanced levels of satisfaction, improved levels of self-confidence and increased ability to deal with challenges (Rush et al., 1995; Solcova & Tomanek, 1994). In the organisational context, hardiness has been shown to have a moderating impact on severe corporate disruption, to increase executives' capacity to cope with stress and to enable a greater commitment to tasks (D'Arienzo, 2010; Folkman, 1984; Kobasa, 1979). More specifically, Maddi (2011) showed that hardiness is associated with increased levels of resilience that result in higher levels of performance under pressure.

Research into hardiness describes it as both a personality character-istic and a learned set of attitudes and skills (Bossick, 2008; Maddi, 2011). Some evidence indicates that hardiness may be a dispositional attribute similar to resilience (Kobasa, 1979; Rush, Schoel & Barnard, 1995; Solcova & Tomanek, 1994). While confusion exists on whether it is a trait or a dispositional attribute, the research in this area has very similar findings to the research on resilience.

Optimism, another key construct linked to resilience, is described as an attribution style that allows individuals to perceive positive events as permanent and personal, while assessing negative events as short-term and external (Seligman, 1990). The optimist tends to see the positive aspects of any situation and therefore has an easier time seeking solutions to challenging situations (Carver & Scheier, 1998). Seligman (1998) conducted extensive research into the constructs of optimism and its antithesis, learned helplessness. Optimism is associated with enhanced well-being, while helplessness results in maladaptation, ineffective functioning and ill health (Reivich et al., 2013; Seligman, 1990). Enhanced levels of optimism have been shown to prevent depression in youth, assist in the development of natural defences against the impact of stress and aid in recovery from trauma (Di Sipio, Falco & De Carlo, 2012; Hand, 2004; Reivich et al., 2013). In the organisational context, optimism has been shown to increase work performance, job satisfaction and organisational commitment (Luthans et al., 2005; Youssef & Luthans, 2007). However, optimism has been suggested to possibly lead to overestimations of capability and result in a failure to take the necessary precautions a situation may require (Maddi & Hightower, 1999). Epstein's (2014) work on constructive thinking outlined a distinction between realistic optimism and unrealistic optimism. The use of constructive thinking as a dimension of resilience therefore includes the realistic aspects of optimism from the work by Seligman. The findings from research on optimism have informed the research on resilience and continue to provide insights into the intra-personal capacity of the individual. Optimism and helplessness are easy to observe in an organisational setting, and if you have ever led a team of people, you will know that the team achieves more if the individuals are optimistic.

Research describes optimism within the frame of a dispositional attribute, and evidence indicates that it has the capacity to develop and change over time (Luthans, Avolio, Walumbwa & Li, 2005; Seligman, 1998). Seligman (1998) went so far as to define optimism as a required capability of a resilient person.

## 5.5 Developing a Contemporary Model of Leader Resilience

The creation of a model of leader resilience required the review and integration of the multidisciplinary research on the attributes of resilience and leadership. This review and integration have provided guidance on the dimensions of resilience and the links to leadership style.

### 5.5.1 Dimensions of Resilience

So...............what are the dimensions that allow the prediction of an individual level of resilience in an organisational context?

And what are the aspects of resilience that will allow us to enhance our capacity to lead if we build them?

The existing research in this arena clearly shows that resilient leaders have an enhanced capacity for transformational leadership. But is it enough to tell leaders that they need to have resilience? For many years, we have simply told leaders that they need to deliver a transformational style of leadership, without any definition of how to develop their intra-personal attributes to do so. Therefore, if we simply tell leaders they need to be resilient without any definition of how to achieve this, we are back to square one. It is imperative that we provide practical and pragmatic guidance to leaders on how to build their resilience and maintain this over time. As we look into the existing research, we learn there is a range of dimensions that have been identified in the research as playing a part in building resilience. The research on resilience that formed the foundation of this book identified three areas of focus from the multidisciplinary research. Based on this, a contemporary model of leader resilience was developed. The focus areas that were highlighted were:

## 1. Well-being and Locus of Control

Strong evidence, both in the workplace and in research, supports the impact of the overall well-being of leaders on their abilities to be resilient (Keyes, 2002). Keyes's (2007) model of resilience incorporated all aspects of well-being in a continuum from languishing to flourishing. This model defined three underlying factors or dimensions of resilience, namely emotional well-being (satisfaction and happiness with life); psychological well-being (the extent to which people are thriving in their personal lives, self-acceptance and a sense of purpose); and social well-being (an individual's ability to build and maintain relationships and give and receive support from others).

Research evidence also supports the importance of both self-concept well-being and locus of control as determinants of resilience (Seligman, 2011; Wagnild, 2009). Seligman (2011), for example, defined some of the determinants of resilience as being positive emotions, meaning and a sense of accomplishment. Ryff (1989) defined resilience as being determined by a combination of factors, including self-acceptance, autonomy, environmental mastery, purpose in life and personal growth. Wagnild (2009) listed the determinants of resilience as purpose, perseverance, equanimity, self-reliance and existential aloneness. Jayawickreme, Forgeard and Seligman (2012) noted that the research indicates three important internal capacities of an individual to maintain resilience: positive affect, cognitive evaluations and self-control. This requirement to maintain the well-being of the self and utilise an effective locus of control is defined as a key determinant of resilience.

## 2. Cognitive Processing

Numerous studies on resilience have highlighted the importance of healthy cognitive processing in relation to an individual's capacity to bounce back and cope in the context of challenge (Epstein, 1998; Rutter, 1999). As part of his concept of resilience, Rutter (2012) included mental evaluations, planning, self-control, self-agency, self-confidence and determination, all of which are connected to cognitive processing. Epstein's (2014) constructive thinking model views the cognitive aspects of health and well-being as necessary for maintaining resilience. This aligns closely with Rutter's (2012) views on the importance of cognitive assessment. Epstein (2014) conceives of two minds—a rational mind and an experiential mind. In his view, these two minds jointly deliver our experience of the world around us and predict our reactions and actions. Epstein's (2014) constructive thinking research identified the existence of six cognitive processes that either support or damage well-being. These include emotional coping, behavioural coping, categorical thinking, superstitious thinking, naive optimism and negative thinking. Each of these is an aspect of our cognitive processing system and has implications for our ability to bounce back and maintain well-being.

### 3. Family and Societal Support

While family and social support were not included in the organisational model of resilience described in this book, acknowledging these as key dimensions of resilience, as defined in research, is important, particularly in the clinical arena (Garmezy, 1974; Werner, 1982). Garmezy (1991) defined the dimensions of a nurturing family and societal support as crucial in enhancing the resilience of the individual. However, in the organisational context, although family and social support remain factors in an individual's ability to bounce back, they are not considered factors in a leader's intra-personal capacity to bounce back and maintain resilience. Within the transformational leadership framework, leader resilience is the intra-personal aspect of leadership. Social support is considered an element in interpersonal leadership and is therefore not included as a dimension of leader resilience (Bass & Avolio, 1997). This does not in any way denote that a nurturing and supportive family, social support and strong interpersonal relations don't play crucial roles in an individual's resilience. They are just not factors in the intra-personal aspect of leader resilience. In fact, one of the things that is important to acknowledge is that every leader needs to have strong social support, and nurturing this is important, particularly in the presence of long-term work pressures.

If you feel that many different scholarly schools of thought are conveyed regarding the dimensions of resilience, you are correct. However, in reality, these dimensions fall into distinct categories and are highly correlated. To help summarise these categories and understand the differences and similarities, consider this breakdown of dimensions associated with key researchers:

| Study | Dimensions of resilience |
| --- | --- |
| Rutter (1999) | Planning, self-control, self-agency, self-confidence and determination |
| Epstein (2014) | Emotional coping, behavioural coping, categorical thinking, superstitious thinking, naive optimism and negative thinking |
| Keyes (2002) | Emotional well-being, psychological well-being and social well-being |
| Ryff (1989) | Self-acceptance, autonomy, environmental mastery, purpose in life and personal growth |
| Wagnild (2009) | Purpose, perseverance, equanimity, self-reliance and existential aloneness |
| Seligman (2011) | Positive affect, cognitive evaluations and self-control |
| Lamp (2014) (meta-analysis) | Self-efficacy, self-esteem, positive affect, optimism, locus of control and social support |

TABLE 1. FACTORS THAT ARE DEFINED IN RESEARCH AS DIMENSIONS OF RESILIENCE

Where does that leave us today? How do we make sense of all these differing yet valuable opinions? To start, let's look at some of the similarities amongst the group and the common threads that run through the dominant conceptualisations of resilience.

### 5.5.2 The Contemporary Model of Leader Resilience

Based on the comprehensive multidisciplinary research outlined above, a contemporary model of leader resilience was developed. This model conceptualises resilience as a malleable, dispositional attribute that is part of the intra-personal aspect of leadership.

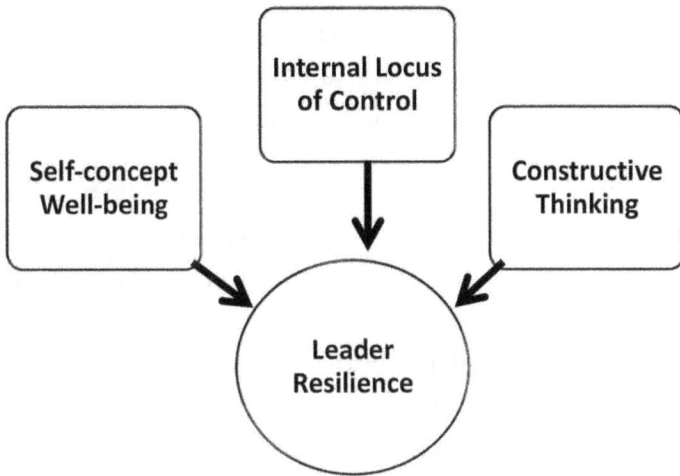

*Figure 5: A contemporary model of leader resilience (Folan, 2019)*

The three dimensions of leader resilience are:

1. **Self-concept well-being:** leaders who have a clear and stable sense of self with healthy psychological functioning and adjustment are able to maintain their emotional stability and well-being in any context.

2. **Internal locus of control:** leaders with the capacity to assess

that their decisions, actions and outcomes are within their control will take action in any context. They understand that their choices and actions have an impact on their results and experience, and this gives them the ability to bounce back in any context.

3. **Constructive thinking:** leaders who have the ability to assess external and internal stimuli constructively and to utilise clear, well-reasoned and balanced judgements in their decision-making are able to maintain their mental and emotional stability in any context.

These dimensions are interrelated and work together to enhance a leader's ability to cope with the challenges that arise as part of the responsibility of leadership. They support the leader in maintaining well-being and flourishing through challenge and adversity.

Although the constructs of self-concept well-being, locus of control and constructive thinking have been studied separately to date, they are clearly related to one another (Abouserie, 1994; Anazonwu, 1995; Brockner, 1988). Research indicates that, when combined, they are likely to offer a greater depth of understanding of leader resilience (Judge et al., 2002). Research has clearly shown that they are interdependent constructs. For example, Brockner (1988) shows that an unstable self-concept results in an individual being more susceptible to unhealthy cognitive processing strategies. Anazonwu (1995) linked self-concept and locus of control by incorporating both elements in a study of the enhancement of performance in an academic environment. Abouserie (1994) found a correlation between having an unstable self-concept and an external locus of control, showing that these, together, resulted in higher levels of stress. Judge et al. (2002) demonstrated a strong empirical relationship between the measures of locus of control and self-esteem.

The dimensions of leaders' resilience defined in the model are all conceptually associated with each other, and their inclusion as dimensions adds to the depth of the discussions on resilience. As we expand our discussions on this model, you will begin to see just how important these dimensions are in supporting modern-day leaders. In the end, you will discover that becoming a transformational leader requires that you develop each of these dimensions.

It is not the strongest of the species that survive, nor the most intelligent, but the ones most resilient and responsive to change"

Charles Darwin

# CHAPTER 6

# YOUR ABILITY TO LEAD IS DETERMINED BY YOUR RESILIENCE

The world around us is moving ever faster, resulting in a constantly evolving context, with changing demands being placed on businesses and their leaders. We are seeing unprecedented levels of challenge, uncertainty and ambiguity in the workplace and in society in general. In a leadership context, the impact is fundamental and is demanding a change in how leaders behave, think, respond and act. To deliver effective leadership in today's world, the leadership styles of the past are simply not good enough. We can no longer accept or tolerate 'old-school leadership' if we are going to meet the challenges facing organisations in these unprecedented times.

The shift happening in the global economy and in society in general is changing the role of leadership and demanding an entirely new way of working. Protecting and delivering the bottom line is not enough, nor can we simply maintain the status quo; if businesses are to survive and thrive, they need to take a very different approach. The key areas that leaders need to take ownership of in today's world are: building effective organisational cultures, delivering sustainable employee engagement, creating purposeful connection, delivering transparent and engaging communication, navigating ongoing digital transformation, manoeuvring through the complexity of social media and globalisation, confronting the ongoing challenges of diversity and building and delivering a sustainable service model. Just blink, and an otherwise successful company moves in the wrong direction.

In today's world, success can be achieved overnight, but failure is also lurking in the shadows. We can easily look across industries and see failures of leadership and the demise of once highly successful organisations. If businesses want to maintain effectiveness and sustainability, then they must focus on building and maintaining leadership and organisational resilience. Resilience is, without a doubt, the new frontier of leadership. Without it, we will not be able to meet the challenges we face in business and society. With resilience, our leaders, teams and organisations will thrive and survive.

The VUCA world is both exciting and challenging, and to meet this world, organisations need to be on the lookout for the next generation of leaders to lead them through these times of change. What is required of leaders has changed so substantially that, once organisations find a great leader, they need to do all they can to cultivate, develop and keep that person in place. Stealing great leaders away from the competition is not easy, as great leadership is still a rare commodity (Howard & Wellins, 2009). Therefore, we must focus on building the resilience of leaders and organisations to fully mitigate the impact of the VUCA world we live and work in.

The most recent research and the history of leadership support the requirement for resilience as the focus in hiring, firing and developing leaders. As you can tell from everything that has already been said, this is not merely a suggestion. Building resilience is a necessity for successful organisations and transformational leaders.

## 6.1 Research Linking Resilience and Transformational Leadership

The potential to lead, to succeed and to win in a highly volatile context requires resilience. Resilience is the barometer or measuring stick for the success of a leader. Show me poor leadership, and I will show you low levels of resilience. Show me great resilience, and I will show you a transformational leader in action. Most importantly, preserving a high level of performance while navigating the business and economic challenges requires a sustainable level of resilience that is maintained on an ongoing basis.

The requirements of leadership in today's world can't be explained by looking at the traditional leadership and individual difference research, including areas such as IQ and personality (Goleman, 1995; Judge & Bono, 2001; Judge, Bono, Erez, & Locke, 2005; Lefcourt, 1992). We need to shift our attention to the contemporary research that is evolving in the dispositional attribute domain, with its implications for enhancing the capacity of individuals (Folan, 2019; Garbowski, 2010). This offers a truly contemporary way of looking at the issue of individual differences and the internal capacity required for effective and sustainable leadership.

In the past decade, a developing body of research has shown that dispositional attributes, such as resilience, positively contribute to leadership capacity. They enhance a leader's ability to successfully navigate complex environments while maintaining the overall well-being of a company and its employees (Garbowski, 2010; Sylvester, 2009). This capacity is an essential underlying attribute that supports leaders in their ability to maintain healthy relationships and to deliver a transformational leadership style (Howell & Avolio, 1993). A transformational style enables leaders to encourage, inspire and motivate employees to innovate and create change that will help grow and shape the future success of the company. Who wouldn't want to be capable of delivering this style of leadership? This capacity lives at the intersection of resilience and leadership.

A number of recent studies have shown that personal attributes offer a contemporary perspective on individual difference research, in particular by explaining the capacity of an individual to deliver a transformational leadership style (Garbowski, 2010; Howell & Avolio, 1993; Kinman & Grant, 2011; Sylvester, 2009). For example, Howell and Avolio (1993), show that leaders who successfully manage their mental processing and emotions have the capacity to enhance relationships with their employees, team members and co-workers, while maintaining an effective leadership style. Kinman and Grant (2011) found that, in a social work environment, emotional and social competencies explained forty-seven percent of the difference in levels of resilience. They also found that these competencies significantly mediated the effects of stress and enhanced a leader's ability to maintain well-being and effective leadership. Recent studies have also shown that improved levels of resilience enable leaders to deliver a transformational leadership style (Garbowski, 2010; Offutt, 2011; Sylvester, 2009; Wasden, 2014). Garbowski (2010) found a strong correlation between transformational leadership behaviours and the personal qualities of hope, optimism and resilience. The study showed a stronger correlation between resilience and transformational leadership than with the other attributes. This research offers support for a significant link between resilience and leadership. In short, the two go hand-in-hand. If you want to develop as a transformational leader, then you recognise the importance of working to develop the intra-personal attribute of resilience.

Sylvester (2009) investigated correlations between a range of variables and transformational leadership. Of all the considered variables, Sylvester concluded that resilience explained approximately twenty-three percent of the variance in transformational leadership. These findings show that resilience within leaders is significantly related to transformational leadership style. Offutt (2011) linked resilience and leadership, with findings showing a strong positive correlation between resilience and effective leadership practices. Wasden's (2014) study found a strong correlation between resilience and transformational leadership, in support of the findings of Offutt and Sylvester.

So, what can we conclude from these studies? These studies provide consistent evidence of the relationship between resilience and leadership style (Garbowski, 2010; Offutt, 2011; Sylvester, 2009; Wasden, 2014). In fact, the research supports the view that becoming a transformational leader is extremely challenging without first being resilient.

## 6.2 A Research-based Model of Leader Resilience (Folan, 2019)

The research (Folan, 2019) which prompted this book investigated the link between resilience and the ability to deliver a transformational leadership style. This research provides clarity on the strength of the relationship between these two constructs, as well as a research-based model of resilience (Folan, 2019). The model of resilience was structured to align with the framework of Bass's (1985) transformational leadership model. This paves the way for a new way of thinking about leadership and resilience and a contemporary approach to leadership and leadership development practices. The research incorporated two separate studies that sought first to establish the relationships between resilience and transformational leadership, second to define the dimensions of resilience, and third to determine the developmental impact of resilience on leadership styles (Folan, 2019).

Traditional research has focused predominantly on the external expression of leadership, rather than on the internal dispositional attributes of leaders. This focus has provided clarity on the styles and behaviours leaders are required to deliver; however, it has not identified the internal attributes that are core to a person's ability to deliver a specific style. The traditional focus has therefore limited the efficacy of leadership development practices. Contemporary leadership research focuses on the intra-personal attributes of leaders as a prerequisite for effective delivery of a transformational style of leadership. The research that provoked this book and the conclusions drawn are based on a comprehensive review of related constructs from multiple psychological disciplines, an in-depth look at the relationships, a rigorous statistical analysis of the relationship constructs and practical application of the constructs in a learning environment.

The model of leader resilience brings together a range of constructs— resilience, self-concept, locus of control, constructive thinking and transformational leadership—all of which have previously been treated as independent constructs from a range of different disciplines. This model, along with structural equation modelling, allowed us to define the relationships and their strengths and then to further test these relationships with a workshop-based intervention. The model of leader resilience defined the intra-personal dimension of resilience in a work-based setting and is the first of its kind in organisational psychology.

The articulation of a model of leader resilience in the business context provides the opportunity for evolving discussions on the measurement and development of leadership. The focus of the research that has informed this book was very different from traditional approaches. The focus was on dispositional attributes that enable the leader to deliver a specific style of leadership. This is a new and evolving area in the field of psychology, and the two studies that formed the foundation of this research are leading the way in redefining how we go about developing leaders and enhancing organisational outcomes (Folan, 2019).

If I were to ask you about leaders with whom you have worked and suggested that you evaluate their competence, you would intuitively agree that the leaders who are resilient (i.e. who have the ability to bounce back from challenges while maintaining emotional stability, effective mental processing and personal balance) are more effective in working with others and maintaining focus and direction. While we have known this intuitively for years, no research has validated this. The reason that I took up the challenge of completing this research was to validate what we already intuitively know and understand in relation to leadership. We can now make sense of why someone can attend all the leadership development programs on offer and still not deliver good leadership; it allows us to understand how someone can go from being a successful leader one day to crashing and burning the next day. Most of all, however, what it has allowed us to do is to define a clear set of developmental strategies that are guaranteed to enhance resilience and enable transformational leadership.

This sounds so easy, you say, and it is. However, as with any change, it is not going to happen without discipline and focus. You are not going to become resilient by doing something once; it requires a change in focus and a discipline around managing your mind, emotions and reactions. What I can guarantee is that if you put in the work to develop your resilience, you will improve your ability to lead others.

This break with traditional approaches to leadership research, with a focus on developing dispositional attributes, is unique, and it will pave the way to re-evaluating our practices in leadership and leadership development. Figure 6 outlines the framework for the research. This framework was developed from the multidisciplinary review of research and aligns with the transformational leadership model defined by Bass (1985).

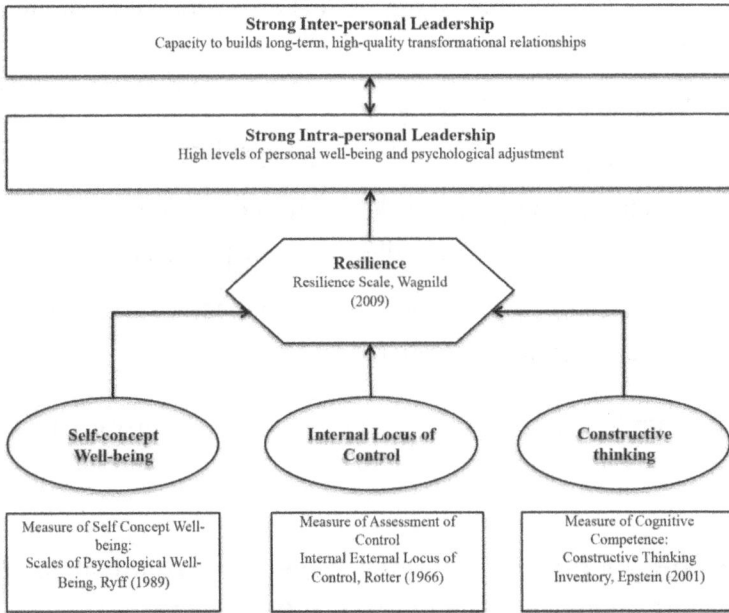

*Figure 6: The research framework for the two studies (Folan, 2019)*

Leader resilience is conceptualised in this framework as the intra-personal component of leadership. Building resilience at the intra-personal leadership level is necessary as a prerequisite for leadership effectiveness (Bass et al., 2003). Stronger levels of leader resilience in the intra-personal aspect of leadership will support a leader in the consistent delivery of a transformational leadership style in the interpersonal aspects of leadership.

Based on my years of experience in working with leaders across the globe, a number of questions were uppermost in my thinking as I set out to research the link between resilience and leadership:

1.  What is the relationship between resilience and leadership and how do they impact each other?

2.  Is there an organisational-based model of resilience that

will aid us in understanding this dispositional attribute in a business context?

3. What are the underlying dimensions of resilience that can be developed to enhance leadership capability?

4. Can a training program designed to develop resilience bring about a change in the resilience of the participants?

5. Can a change in resilience be used to predict a positive change in transformational leadership?

The two studies were designed to investigate the answers to these questions.

### 6.2.1 Study 1: Defining and validating an organisational model of resilience and assessing the link to transformational leadership

Study 1 focused on finding the answers to the first three questions; therefore, it had two main purposes:

1) To test the association between resilience and the dimensions of self-concept well-being, locus of control and constructive thinking (Campbell, 1990; Epstein & Meier, 1989; Rotter, 1990; Wagnild, 2009); and

2) To investigate the relationship between resilience, the dimensions of resilience, and transformational leadership style (Bass, 1985; Wagnild, 2009).

A model of leader resilience was first developed from a multidisciplinary review of relevant research. This model was then described in a structural equation model for statistical analysis purposes. Figure 7 shows the structural equations model that formed the foundation of the statistical analysis in Study 1.

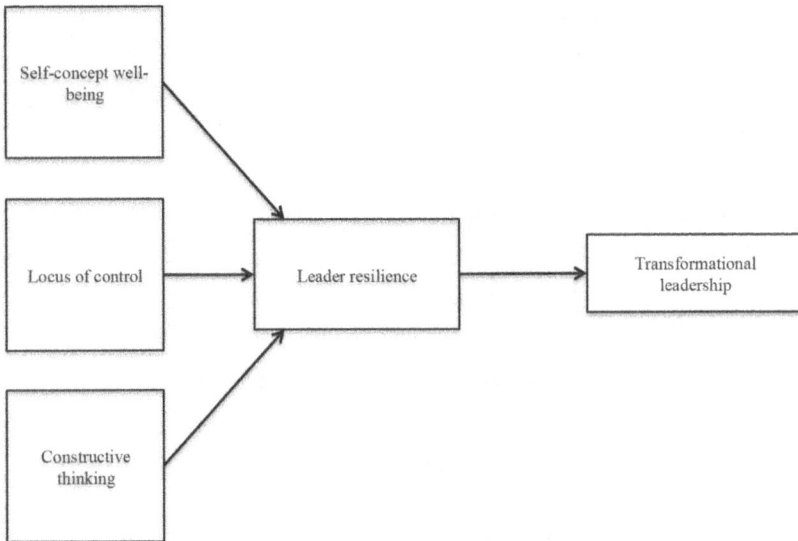

*Figure 7. The structural equations model of the research relationships for Study 1 (Folan, 2019)*

Upon establishment of the model, the research was carried out to statistically analyse the relationship between resilience and the dimensions of resilience defined in the model. This study made use of a quantitative, non-experimental research design, which is a robust methodology for deductive field-based research involving a moderate number of respondents (Kelemen & Rumens, 2012). This research design allowed access to a range of participants from a variety of organisations across all sectors. Much of the research focusing on organisational resilience has utilised participants from one organisation, with attendant limitations in terms of environmental bias and lack of generalisability (Garbowski, 2010; Offutt, 2011; Sylvester, 2009).

The target population for this research included individuals holding a leadership position involving responsibility for managing staff and delivering organisational outcomes. The participants were drawn from a range of organisations in the private, public and not-for-profit sectors. Data analysis established the relationship between transformational leadership, leader resilience and the dimensions of resilience.

The statistical analysis using the structural equation model (SEM) showed a good fit for the data, providing support for the model of leader resilience and the dimensions of resilience (self-concept well-being, internal locus of control and constructive thinking). The SEM also confirmed the hypothesised relationships between leader resilience and leadership style. These results show that leader resilience is a significant predictor of transformational leadership.

This study makes a significant contribution to the research on leadership and offers interesting insights and opportunities for those involved in leadership and leadership development. As only a small number of studies have focused on leader resilience, this study makes an important contribution to the debate (Garbowski, 2010; Offutt, 2011; Sylvester, 2009). No previous attempts have endeavoured to define a model of the intra-personal resilience of leaders (Garbowski, 2010; Offutt, 2011). This study validates the model of leader resilience and provides an exciting opportunity for enhancing outcomes in the leadership space. With the strength of the established relationships, it makes clear that achieving enhancements in leadership developmental practices requires a focus on resilience. Based on the model developed, a measure of leader resilience in an organisational setting has been developed and is discussed in the next chapter. The measurement tool will pave the way for a clearer assessment of leader resilience and the opportunity to target developmental strategies for leaders.

## 6.2.2 Study 2: Developing resilience to bring about enhanced levels of resilience and transformational leadership

Study 2 involved the development of a training program designed to enhance resilience and to assess whether resilience levels can be shifted though developmental interventions. The purpose of Study 2 was two-fold:

1) To establish whether resilience can be enhanced through a three-day workshop-based intervention designed specifically for the purpose of enhancing leader resilience; and

2) To assess whether a change in leader resilience can be used to predict a shift in leadership style.

The training intervention used in this study was aligned to the model of leader resilience developed and validated in Study 1.

A quasi-experimental, field-based research design was used with a before-and-after cohort assessment. The impact of the workshop was investigated through pre- and post-measurements of leadership style, resilience and the dimensions of resilience. Leadership style was measured using both self-assessment and an assessment requested from the leader's boss. Two organisations were involved in the study and each offered a full commitment, from the commencement of the process, to allow their leaders to participate.

Not only did this provide evidence of the impact of development strategies, it also provided the opportunity to further validate the results from Study 1. A before-after assessment of the data provided statistical evidence that a three-day workshop can bring about a significant change in leadership style and resilience levels.

These findings afforded an important opportunity to review the focus of development for leaders. For all leaders, the focus of development should, first and foremost, be on developing the individual's resilience. These findings align with previous research indicating that enhancements can be achieved in resilience and leadership capability with developmental interventions designed to strengthen dispositional attributes (Maddi et al., 1998). An increasing body of research shows that developmental practices enhance well-being and that resilience enhances the outcomes of leadership development programs. This research indicates that the enhancement of resilience levels using well-designed interventions has a positive impact on leadership outcomes.

As noted previously over the last decade, the lack of leadership and the traditional focus of leadership development strategies have been sources of ongoing discontent. The results of Study 2 show that organisations will need to refocus their developmental strategies on enhancing resilience first if they are to improve leadership capability. The ability of organisations to effectively navigate the constantly changing circumstances of today's turbulent business environment clearly requires new leadership competencies and underlying attributes (Gilley, 2005; Gilley et al., 2008). The leadership capabilities that were deemed essential in the previous business context no longer support success in the present environment (Garbowski, 2010; Gilley, 2005; Offutt, 2011). The results show that developing leaders' intra-personal capacities enhances their resilience, which in turn supports adaptability, flexibility and maintenance of well-being.

So, you now have all the most recent research data needed for a fuller understanding of the relationship between resilience and transformational leadership. If you are reading this book as a leader, you are likely beginning to evaluate and assess just how resilient you are and, consequently, how transformational you are. If you are reading this book as a member of an organisation responsible for recruiting and training leaders, as a business owner or a senior executive, you are likely now reviewing your leaders and wondering just how resilient they might be. The next step is to look at this in a broader context of the organisation and assess if some lessons are available to learn regarding how to provide the right environment in which leaders can build their resilience and flourish.

"The organisations we admire are like
the people we admire, resilient, authentic,
personable, collaborative, ambitious,
and humble."

C. Conley

# CHAPTER 7

# REQUIREMENTS FOR A RESILIENT ORGANISATION

We have looked at the importance of building resilience and the impact on transformational leadership. We will now take time to investigate building resilient organisations to provide the environment to grow resilient leaders. The quote by George Bernard Shaw says, 'People are always blaming circumstances for what they are. I do not believe in circumstances. The people who get on in this world are the people who get up and look for the circumstances they want, and if they cannot find them, they make them.' There is beauty in this quote, as it empowers us all to be the change, become the difference makers and evolve ourselves and our organisations to their true potential. No longer do we have to settle for the status quo in our leadership or our business. We can set a direction, define our desired outcomes, plan our organisational change and realise our vision. We can create better leadership in ourselves and others and courageously lead better organisations that can healthily respond to the challenge of the VUCA world.

Understanding the importance of resilient leadership in influencing the broader organisational context is imperative. In a VUCA world, our leaders, their teams and the whole organisation must possess the capacity to bounce back and maintain well-being in the context of

challenge and change. In essence, we need our teams and organisations to be resilient. Without this, we will be building organisational
systems, practices and ways of doing things that do not support
success in the VUCA environment.

In this chapter, we will focus on the key strategies that will assist
you in evaluating and enhancing the resilience of your organisation
and then supporting its resilience development. If your organisation
focuses on enhancing resilience, everyone involved will reap the
rewards and experience exceptional outcomes. If your organisation
does not build resilience, don't be surprised if the team culture de-
teriorates and adversely impacts the team's ability to deliver results.

## 7.1 Organisational Culture and Measurement

Over the years, I have had more than one leader say to me, 'My organisation would be so much easier to manage if we did not have
to rely on people.' For many CEOs and executives, the people issues
are what create their biggest challenges. Culture and people aspects
of the business that are not effectively managed get in the way of
the organisational performance and create challenges for all those
involved. Clearly, without the people, the organisation can't operate.
People truly do make the difference, but whether that difference is
positive or negative is based on the choices the leadership makes.
If people are not engaged in the organisation's mission and vision
and doing the work they are required to do, the leader's job becomes
more challenging. Conversely, if the people are delivering above
and beyond, then the business will flourish and the leadership will
become easier.

For organisations to flourish, they require transformational leaders
that deliver a transformational culture with a strong foundation of
resilience across the whole organisation. This is not something that

occurs without focus; leaders need to be measuring and building this culture to support their teams to be successful and to deliver outcomes aligned with the organisation's mission, vision and values. In the context of leadership in a VUCA world, when things are changing at the pace they are, the leader has no option but to be building resilience at all levels of the organisation.

As a business leader, if you feel your organisation is not as resilient as you would like it to be, then the first place to start is to evaluate your resilience and that of the leaders who work for you. The diagnostics of the Folan Resilience Scale in Chapter 8 allow a self-assessment of the resilience of you and your people. The Team Resilience Scale diagnostic will allow you to assess the resilience levels of the individual teams.

A hugely important step is to take the time to evaluate the resilience of the whole organisation as well and to get below the surface of the cultural aspects that underpin it. Measuring this via traditional organisational engagement diagnostics is not sufficient, as these tools only provide you with an assessment of the surface level climate and do not go beneath the surface to look at the culture. A number of organisational culture measures are available; however, when selecting the measure, make sure that it is aligned with the culture you are seeking to create and not simply measuring the climate that exists on the surface of the organisation.

In simple terms, what you measure is what you get. If you only measure engagement, please don't expect your culture to be correct. Engagement is the climatic aspect of an organisation and is indicative of the underlying culture, but definitely not an accurate measure of culture. For example, we discussed Enron earlier in the book. Notably, twelve months prior to the collapse of Enron, a highly respected consultancy firm completed a culture survey on the organisation and deemed the organisational culture dysfunctional. The executive chose to ignore the data, as a previous engagement survey had shown very positive scores. They therefore refused to accept that the culture required work and realignment. Twelve months later, the business collapsed as a result of a toxic culture built on unethical behaviour, self-interest and financial embezzlement.

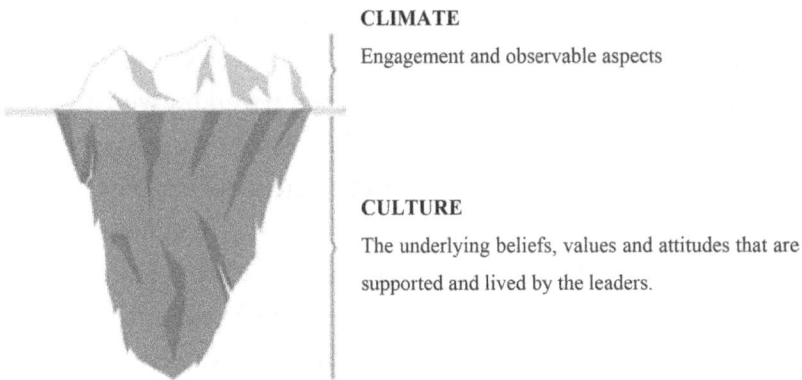

**CLIMATE**

Engagement and observable aspects

**CULTURE**

The underlying beliefs, values and attitudes that are supported and lived by the leaders.

*Figure 8: Iceberg model of climate and culture*

So, the question is: what does an organisational culture look like if it is resilient and transformational?

## 7.2 The Seven Habits of Resilient Organisations

The question is often asked: which came first—the chicken or the egg? When you are speaking about resilience and leadership, a completely fair question is: do resilient organisations create resilient leaders or do resilient leaders build organisations that can bounce back and flourish? From my perspective, this is a two-way street. Resilient leaders manifest the qualities that create resilient organisations, and resilient organisations help to sculpt resilient leaders. Since we have focused most of the book on how to craft resilient leadership, wrapping up our discussions by looking at the qualities or habits that are common in resilient organisations makes sense. In doing so, we can see the complementary, symbiotic relationship between the two. In this context, we are defining organisational resilience as: 'A resilient organisation has the capacity to bounce back from adversity and flourish in the face of challenge and change, while maintaining a healthy culture that supports the well-being of everyone involved.'

Part of the research carried out to investigate the relationship between resilience and leadership was a review of what creates resilient organisations. This review, coupled with experience in working with organisations for three decades, clearly revealed key aspects of an organisation's functioning that support the creation of resilience at this broader level. Based on this, we have defined the seven habits that enhance organisational resilience. Building organisational resilience requires that we build and maintain all aspects of organisational resilience. Figure 9 defines the seven habits or highly resilient organisations.

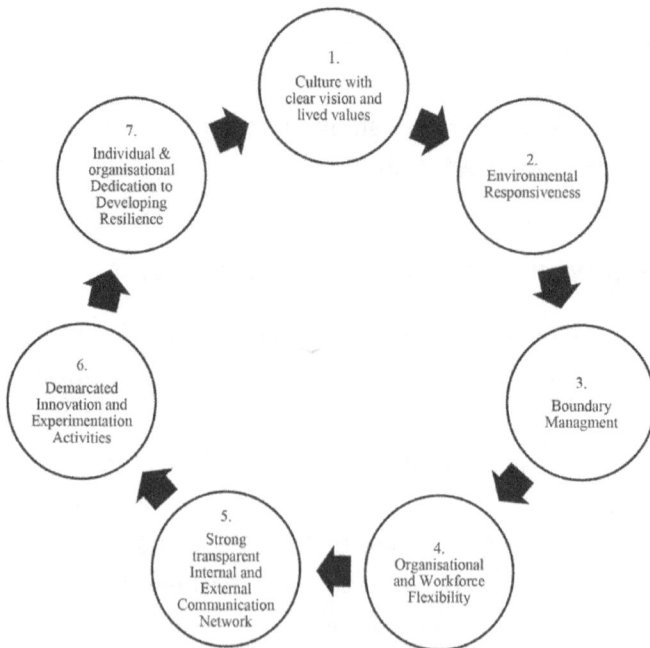

*Figure 9: Seven habits of highly resilient organisations*

## 7.2.1 A Culture with a Clear Vision and Strong Values

If an organisation is going to achieve resilience, first and foremost, the leader must first focus on setting the intention for the future and being clear about where the organisation is heading, from both a business perspective and a cultural perspective. A clear vision of the organisation's future, along with the strategy and goals that will support the delivery of the vision, are essential aspects for resilience.

A lot has been written about visionary and strategic leadership over the years, and a significant amount of research supports the need for clarity of focus with a clear vision and strategy (Kantabutra & Avery, 2010; Taylor, Cornelius & Colvin, 2014). However, in relation to broader organisational resilience, the issue is not whether a document is written with a vision and strategy. The issue is whether the vision and strategy are fully understood and that they are the driving force of everything that is done in the organisation. In a truly resilient organisation, everyone knows and focuses on delivering the vision. People in resilient organisations are clear on the key strategic pillars or drivers of the organisation and how their role aligns with its direction. They fully understand the importance of their contribution to the broader organisation. What we are talking about here is a vision and strategy that are collaboratively created, agreed upon and lived. As many people as possible must be involved in the creation of these. When a vision and strategy are effective, they will ensure that people are engaged and aligned with the organisation's direction. Each individual in your organisation needs to understand the vision and direction of the organisation and how they contribute to its overall success.

The vision, mission, values and strategy should not be a long-winded and complex document that is tucked away in the leaders' offices and never sees the light of day. We are talking about a live document that everyone in the organisation uses—it is the focus of everyone's working day. Organisations that are successful in this space have this information on one or two pages, and everyone, no matter what their role, knows the key aspects of the document. You will know when you have achieved success with this document if you can go up to anyone in the organisation and ask them what the organisation's vision and values are, and they are able to tell you without hesitation. This is as much about communication as it is about defining the vision, values and strategy.

'The only thing of importance that leaders do is manage culture' Edgar Shine (2010, p.2). With a constant flow of business news headlines talking about organisations whose "toxic culture" has led to their demise or resulted in business disruption, the time has arrived for leaders to take this issue seriously. Whether you choose to manage culture or not, you still have a culture. Unfortunately, if you don't manage your culture, it will be managed by the collective un-conscious of the organisation. One thing that you can be guaranteed is that if you leave the culture up to the collective unconscious of the organisation, you will end up with a toxic culture.

To ensure you are building a resilient organisation, a key aspect is to systematically build and maintain a values-based culture. Again, this is best done by engaging everyone in defining the desired culture and then developing the values. While it may take some time, engaging everyone in the process of building the organisational culture will result in a higher level of buy-in. Part of this process should be in building everyone's understanding of what culture is and how to manage it to achieve enhanced outcomes.

Again, this is not just a document that is hidden in a drawer, on your organisation's website or a poster on the wall that no one ever refers to or takes any interest in. Values that drive resilience are a living, breathing part of everyday working life; they influence the discussions and decisions you make in every aspect of the business. The values need to provide the guidelines for everyone on what is and isn't acceptable behaviour in the drive for resilience and excellence. They ensure that fences are placed around acceptable and unacceptable behaviour to guide people in the process of delivering their work. A truly values-led culture is the key to ensuring that resilience is maintained in the behaviours across the organisation.

The achievement and maintenance of organisational resilience requires that these two key aspects of the organisation's functioning are in alignment. The organisation's direction and culture must receive a balanced level of focus and be aligned with each other. Over the years, I have seen organisations that have not got this balance right and this has led to challenges. If your organisation is too focused on the values, with not enough focus on the strategy, you will end up not delivering results and constantly missing key business milestones. If you focus only on strategy, then the behaviours and culture will deteriorate and, in the end, they will get in the way of your organisation's ability to deliver results. We need to keep the balance, as per Figure 10 below. We must invest in both aspects.

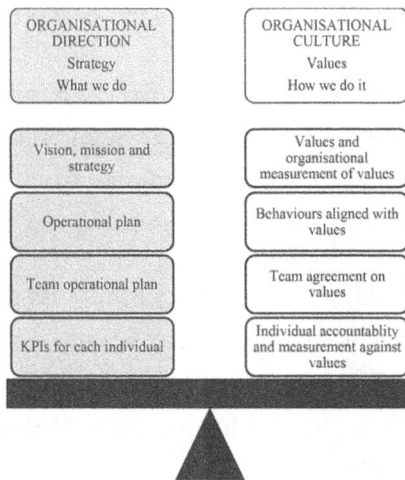

*Figure 10: Organisational alignment—direction and culture*

An understanding of both strategy and culture should be live and active in the organisation, and people should have these embedded in their minds and driving their decision-making and their actions. This is the foundation of organisational resilience; without this in place, the organisation will not develop and maintain resilience.

### 7.2.2 Environmental Responsiveness

Resilient organisations keep a watchful eye on the external and internal environments so that they can realign their strategy and focus to be responsive to changes. Simply responding to the pressures for change is no longer possible; we must be closely attuned to the changes in the external environment and able to respond successfully to the requirements for change and evolution. Charles Handy (1995) suggests that the best time to start the next wave of success for your organisation is not after you have reached the peak of success, but before you reach it. If organisations are not systematically assessing their environment and aligning to these changing dynamics, they will eventually end up in decline or become irrelevant to their clients, customers, consumers or the community. We have seen enough businesses go through this cycle and end up irrelevant to know the importance of staying ahead of the curve. Now, more than ever, we must stay attuned to the external environment and have the agility to meet the demands we are facing. The Sigmoid Curve in Figure 11 below articulates Charles Handy's sigmoid curve, which defines the importance of environmental responsiveness.

Charles Handy (1995) says that if organisations do not evolve and change, they will eventually become irrelevant or go out of business. All organisations have a starting point, and if they want to flourish, they have to be constantly looking for the next stage of evolution to stay ahead of the curve.

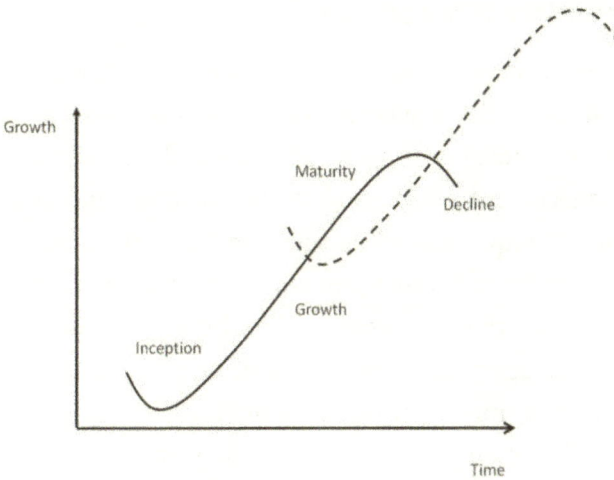

*Figure 11: Sigmoid Curve (Handy, 1995)*

By being responsive to your environment, you are pre-empting the need for change before it is forced on you. This pre-emption is only possible if you keep up to date with the external environment and ensure you are aligning with the changes before they are forced onto you. Take, for example, the taxi business, Globally, it was not keeping up with the pace of change in the technology platforms, and Uber took the industry by surprise, crippling taxi companies' revenue and profit base.

Unfortunately, people often think of making a change or doing something different only when they have reached a crisis, such as a financial decline, declining market share or funding cuts. Successful resilient businesses reinvent themselves while they are still successful and on an upward trajectory. Truly resilient organisations no longer talk about 'managing change'; rather, they talk about building organ-isational resilience for successful incorporation of the requirement for ongoing change and evolution.

### 7.2.3 Boundary Management

In my years of working with organisations across the globe, I found that the single most neglected aspect of organisational resilience is effective boundary management. This is the systemic and disciplined management of acceptable and unacceptable attitudes and behaviours. It requires, on the one hand, a regular and consistent celebration of attitudes and behaviours that align with the values and direction of the organisation. On the other hand, regular and consistent management of unacceptable attitudes and behaviours is needed. Each is important in terms of consistent management and requires a disciplined focus. Together, they are key to building and maintaining resilience in teams and organisations.

The repercussions of not managing unacceptable behaviour impact strongly on the resilience levels in a team and organisation. Porath and Pearson's (2009, p. 1) research found that the inability of leaders to manage boundaries on unacceptable behaviours resulted in the following:

o   48% of people intentionally decreased their work effort

o   47% of people intentionally decreased the time spent at work

o   38% of people intentionally decreased the quality of their work

o   80% of people spent time at work worrying about the incident

o   63% of people wasted work time avoiding the offender

o   66% of people said that their performance declined

o   78% of people said that their commitment to the organisation declined

o   12% of people said that they left their job

o   25% admitted to taking their frustration out on customers

A test check of whether boundaries are being managed is to ask the following questions:

- Have I, as a leader, celebrated the positive attitudes and behaviours of my team today?

- Are there unacceptable attitudes or behaviours in my part of the organisation? And have I actively managed these attitudes and behaviours?

- Are unacceptable attitudes and behaviours being managed consistently across all teams in my organisation?

Boundary management is key to building and maintaining organisational resilience. Without this in place, every opportunity exists for people to damage their own resilience and that of other people.

## 7.2.4 Organisational and Workforce Flexibility

Traditionally, organisations have focused on consistency, length of service and longevity in role. In today's world, these are less of an issue. In fact, if you want to maintain the resilience of your organisation, you will need to focus on flexibility, regular changes and agility. Kinsinger and Walch's (2012) description of our world as a VUCA world of volatility, uncertainty, complexity and ambiguity gives us a clear indication of what we need to prepare for in our organisations. To remain resilient in today's world, you must build flexibility into your organisation's framework and ways of working.

Some questions to ask about your organisation's flexibility:

- Have we got people who have been in their job for more than five years without a change in remit, focus or opportunity to refresh?

- Do we have a focus on continuous improvement in our teams?

- Do we review roles every time a vacancy arises to see if the role is still necessary or needs to be realigned?

- Are people multiskilled to take on different roles if and when required?

- Do we move people to different roles or projects to refresh their experience and broaden their knowledge?

- Are there silos in the organisation that stop people from gaining new experiences?

- Do we support people to develop and learn new skills?

- Do we actively support people to manage their careers though a range of roles and functions?

- Do we encourage secondments to other parts of the business to develop people's expertise?

- Have we got a cross-functional mentoring program?

- Do we promote people who actively choose to learn other functions and roles?

- Can all our leaders step into another leadership role in a different function should they be required?

If you have said 'no' to any of these, then your organisation has an opportunity to further build on this aspect of organisational resilience. Over the years of working with organisations, I have seen both ends of the spectrum, ranging from some organisations with people who have been in the same role for forty-five years to those who require a commitment from leaders to only keep people in roles for a maximum of five years. My observation is that, in the VUCA world, organisations need to ensure that people remain flexible and agile. Where no possibility exists for people to change roles with some level of regularity, then other strategies must be in place to refresh individuals and ensure they remain agile and flexible. At a senior leadership level, the leaders must shift around and take on different roles. Rotating the leadership team through different roles or functions is good practice.

Organisations that maintain flexibility have a range of ways to ensure that people remain flexible and continue to learn and grow. The following programs are some of the ones that support flexibility and stop people from becoming intransigent to change.

o  Succession planning and succession development programs

o  Highflyers programs

o  Graduate programs

o  Student placement programs

o  Developmental roles

o  Job rotation programs

o  Job experience programs

o  Job shadowing opportunities

o  Multiskilling

o  Multidisciplinary project teams

o  Management rotation systems

o  Regular reinvigouration for those in long-term roles

o  International placement programs

o  Opportunities to act up

o  Continuous improvement programs

o  Cross-functional mentoring programs

This flexibility must be maintained at all levels of the organisation. My challenge to you is this: if you are a leader who has been in your role for more than five years and you have not refreshed yourself, then please understand that the change starts with you.

### 7.2.5 A Strong and Transparent Internal and External Communication Network

When asked to rate an organisation on engagement, one of the areas that comes up as a standard is communication. This is often the aspect that gets one of the worst ratings and the most comments about requiring improvement. To be given feedback, both as a leader and an organisation, that there is room for improvement in communication is not uncommon. To ensure resilience is maintained in your organisation, you will need to rise to the challenge of creating effective and transparent communication processes. When the culture is right, people will take responsibility for communication, while also expecting it from their leaders.

Very recently, and for the first time in my years of working with organisations and teams, I was delighted to find a team that rated their team communication as 'exceptional'. The broader organisation had recently had an organisation-wide engagement survey completed, and they had been rated very poorly as an organisation. So, what did this team do that we can learn from?

Was it that they had the best office environment to provide effective communication or the best systems or the best organisational newsletter? No, they had the opposite. They were a team that all worked remotely, with no office base; getting people together was a challenge. They were contracted to work with clients daily; their online tool was Microsoft teams; the organisation did not have a newsletter; and they had to meet up in coffee shops if they wanted to catch up in person. So, what is their secret? It is simple: the team all made a commitment to ensure they communicated, and they actively used the communication channels that were provided. Yes, they had meetings in the diary; yes, they had an online platform for disseminating information; and yes, the leader made sure they sent out organisational information. The key was not the systems and processes; it was the intention of every team member and their commitment to providing and accessing the communication they needed to deliver a great service to their clients. As much communication occurred between team members as from the top down, and if someone did not get the information they needed, they asked for it without blame or accusation. This became a truly resilient team with a leader who led the way to providing communication that is valued and sought out.

The basic team strategies that need to be in place to improve team communication are:

o   A weekly formal meeting structure that is in the diary (just because it is formal does not mean it needs to be boring)

o   Regular informal meetings away from the normal office environment, where work is not the main topic of conversation

o   Some teams prefer quick daily catchups

o   Bi-weekly meetings with individual team members—this supports effective boundary management

o   An online platform for disseminating information that is accessed easily and efficiently for everyone, even those who are not office-based

o   Team development sessions on a quarterly basis

o   HAVE FUN together.

However, the only way that these strategies will work is if everyone makes a commitment to communicating and accessing the communication available. The role of leaders in this scenario is to provide the information, to follow up with people and to check that they are accessing the information. The leader needs to create a buzz in the team about communication so that the team starts to own it and drive it.

Organisationally, many ways are available for enhancing the broader communication strategy. However, the key to enhancing communication is to use multiple platforms and types of communication to get the message across. Never opt for one strategy, as it won't work. I often hear leaders say, "But I send a regular newsletter and they don't read it". In today's world, this is simply not enough, and from a leadership perspective, it is abdication of responsibility. If you believe that sending a newsletter is effective communication, then you are missing a trick. Your people want to hear from you in a range of ways, including face to face.

Our job as leaders is to communicate, communicate, communicate, and then communicate some more. If one type of communication is not working, try other methods or communication channels. The more variety in the communication, the more chance you have of getting the messages out. Communication is closely linked to culture, so if the culture is strong and positive, then communication becomes easier, and people want to find out what their leaders are saying.

External communication is about effective networking and staying attuned to what is going on outside of the organisation. Cross, Ernst and Pasmore (2013) note the importance of 'boundary spanning' for leadership and organisational effectiveness. The ability to boundary span is fundamentally the capacity to build relational-based networks to stay ahead of what is going on in the external environment. If organisations are to effectively maintain their resilience, then they need to have effective communication and relationships with external stakeholders, businesses and key players in the industry.

Every leader in the organisation should be responsible for their own networking and building of relationships with external entities. Being insular and remaining cocooned in your organisation is no longer acceptable; you need to be regularly networking with people external to the organisation so that you can bring knowledge and experience back to your team. The more senior the leader, the more time they should be allocating to this external networking and to focused external communication. If senior leaders are not maintaining a consistent commitment to networking and external information gathering, this will impact the ability of the organisation to foresee challenges and be agile enough to bounce back when they are hit.

## 7.2.6 Demarcated Innovation and Experimentation Activities

Innovation is one of the buzzwords that few organisations fully understand, and most organisations make very poor attempts at delivering. For an organisation to become effective in this space, demarcated time must be allocated to the process of innovation and creative thinking.

Tacking innovation onto a meeting agenda is not enough. In my experience, attempting an innovation discussion at the end of a meeting that is focused on operational issues is ineffective. Innovation occurs when you make time to explore and experiment, without restraints and timelines. This is most effective if it occurs outside the normal linear frameworks of the business and outside the environmental context of your organisation.

If you are going to effectively deliver innovation, you need to have time dedicated to the activity and the right people in the room. Your organisation will have some people who are more easily able to create and explore, and any activity aimed at innovation needs to have a percentage of creative people involved. One key to the success of these strategies is to block out time and space for this to happen.

### 7.2.7 Individuals Developing Their Personal Resilience

Well-designed development strategies are key to unlocking the potential of your people. Strategies designed to enhance personal resilience levels are essential for building the resilience of the organisation. Organisations can play their part in enhancing resilience; however, if individuals do not build their own resilience, they will remain less effective than their potential.

All the aspects that have been defined as enhancing a leader's resilience can be applied to those in a leadership role and those that are leading themselves. Individuals must be dedicated to their own development for a sustainable change to occur in the organisation.

Each of these habits of resilient organisations is both independent and interdependent. They are all crucial aspects of organisational behaviour and generate an environment that nurtures and supports resilience and allows resilient leaders to flourish. While related, they each play their own distinct and vital role. You can find resiliency in executing a few of these very well, but the best practice for you and your organisation should be to take a deep look into the fabric of your business and assess if you feel that these habits are an accurate description of your business practices and daily business functioning.

If not, then there is work to be done. This is, at least in part, why you are reading this book. In our constant effort to grow and evolve, these are the place markers that allow us to accomplish just that. Now, you might be wondering exactly how resilient your organisation might be. If so, start by rating yourself on each of these seven habits and take the time to think about the questions posed on specific habits. If you are finding yourself with lots of low scores, then you have some work to do. If you are happily giving yourself higher grades, celebrate and then focus on improving those areas which might still be lacking. No one organisation effectively executes this one hundred percent of the time. However, the most successful organisations are willing to work consistently on those areas that need improvement, while doing everything they can to maintain the good habits already in place.

## 7.3 Resilient Leaders, Resilient Organisations

Resilient leadership is truly the culmination of the intra-personal competence and practices of the leaders, as well as the habits of the organisation. Sure, you can have a resilient leader in a non-resilient organisation, but how much more powerful would it be to have both in the same organisation? Over the years, I have often seen struggling organisations hire exceptional leaders to help turn things around. Unfortunately, this does not always work, as the new leaders often simply get beaten down by the unhealthy culture and either leave or acquiesce to the culture. Just hiring someone new does not guarantee a new culture. We have to take action to build a positive and resilient culture.

In those unique situations when the two paths intersect—when resilient leaders meet resilient organisations—something truly special occurs and they are unstoppable. Both the leaders and the organisation flourish and can reach their true potential. We can identify these businesses as the market leaders and innovators. They lead the pack and often set the bar for the rest of the competition. I can think of many examples of organisations with both resilient leadership and organisational habits that support their leaders. Personally, I was lucky enough to have worked in one such organisation early on in my career, and this set the framework for my own thinking and ultimately drove the research behind the book that you are reading. *The making of Tesco* (Ryle, 2013) tells the story of an organisation with no resilience that was built into a highly resilient giant in the retail industry. This was an amazing journey, and one that I will always be grateful to have been a part of. What was created in four years was a highly flexible, agile and resilient organisation that was innovative and leading the market. During that time, 140,000 staff were taken on a journey of development and evolution that delivered an unimaginable organisational outcome, moving the organisation from number 3 to number 1 in a cutthroat and highly competitive market.

A company like Delta Airlines, which started as a humble little aerial crop-dusting operation called Huff Daland Dusters in 1925, has now grown into one of the world's largest global airlines, helping more than 180 million travellers get to the places they want to go to each year. Delta CEO Ed Bastian (International Business Times, 2018) emphasises that his primary focus as CEO is Delta's people. 'My schedule is based around our people, which occupies an enormous part of my time,' Ed said. 'One of the most important things I do, if not the most important thing, is to spend quality time with our people—not just at the management level, but with our frontline personnel.' Ed highlights the importance of prospective candidates embodying servant leadership, noting that service and selflessness are core attributes of the company's values. 'We're looking for people who love to serve, and we look for it in various ways—in terms of the jobs they hold outside of school and their work experiences,' Ed said. 'We can teach people about the airline business, but you can't teach people to serve unless they have a real passion for it.' Delta has set itself apart by building a resilient and responsive organisation.

Delta is a values-led company, with a focus on honesty, integrity, respect, perseverance and servant leadership. Their Rules of the Road define who they are and provide a solid foundation for Delta's culture. Their family of 80,000+ employees takes great pride in the success of their company, and they put their money where their mouth is. In 2019 alone, Delta was paying employees $1.3 billion, the airline's second largest profit-sharing pool in company history. To fuel Delta's commitment to communities and to celebrate five years of paying out over $1 billion, the airline has introduced a paid day of service for all 80,000 employees during which they can volunteer and give back to the community. The program put up to 640,000 additional hours of service into communities, on top of the thousands of hours of time Delta employees already give.

In just this small snapshot of the second largest airline in the world, we see many of the habits of resilient organisations. A culture with a clear vision and strong values, environmental responsiveness, flexibility in the workforce and individuals developing their own resilience. In turn, we find not only a fantastic internal structure, but an airline that delivers the most on-time records, at a staggering 83%. From the outside in and the inside out, Delta is flourishing, in part because of the makeup of the organisation, but also because of tremendous leadership.

Resilient leadership and resilient organisations are evident in all sectors and all organisations. Whether we recognise them or not, they are absolutely part of our everyday lives. However, we should also acknowledge that organisations that were once resilient may later fail. In most cases, this is a result of a change in leadership and therefore a change in focus. Unfortunately, a deviation from the focus on building habits that sustain resilience and agility will result in a decline in the organisation's outcomes. However, as we look towards organisations that build and maintain the seven habits of resilient organisations, we can begin to gain insight into what makes these wonderful businesses maintain a high quality of performance and constantly push the industry bounds. We can also see that resilient organisations are a breeding ground for resilient leaders.

If we are going to build resilient leaders and resilient teams that provide a breeding ground for effective leaders, then we need to talk about measurement. Things that can be measured can be monitored and improved! The next chapter will help you assess and evaluate your resilience and provide you with tools that individuals and teams in your organisation can use to review their resilience levels.

"What you measure affects what you do. If you don't measure the right thing, you don't do the right thing."

Joseph Stiglitz

# CHAPTER 8

# MEASURING RESILIENCE

Are you starting to question the quality of your own and others' resilience and leadership style?

My hope is that you are beginning to wonder if your leadership style is leaving a positive mark on your team, supporting their engagement and enhancing your organisation's outcomes. Sadly, for many of us, an external force is needed to get us to look at ourselves and evaluate our leadership and resilience. My hope for you is that this book is the tool that will support you in taking a long hard look at yourself, your resilience and your leadership, and that you won't have to have a major event to get you to shift your focus. You own your resilience and your leadership, and both require a level of inward focus to achieve excellence in external outcomes.

In organisations, leaders often miss a trick by not focusing on this key area of development; thus, we achieve compromised outcomes. Some companies measure leadership competence in relation to the delivery of task-related functional outcomes. They don't recognise the importance of leadership and the additional discretionary effort that can be achieved with an effective leadership style. Other organisations allow leaders to become comfortable, even complacent, settling for reduced results and not rocking the boat. If organisations want to remain ahead of the curve in today's VUCA world, they are going to have to stop avoiding the issue of leadership and start focusing on building capacity. Now, more than ever, we cannot understate the remarkable value of a great leader. Great leadership is capable of shifting markets, outperforming the competition and transforming organisations. Just look at the most successful companies in the world. They not only share a great brand identification and top-notch product or services, but they enjoy visionary leaders that constantly work to lead the charge and show the rest of the organisation the way.

Do you want to lead in this way, making a difference to your organisation and industry? Do you want to set the pace? Do you want to inspire a workforce to give it their all every single day of the business year? If the answer to these questions is yes, then read on. If your answer is no, then please don't choose to lead others; step aside to allow others who are passionate about leadership to take up the challenge. If you stay on without change, you will negatively impact the people you are leading and, in the long term, damage your organisation. Be honest with yourself here. Don't rest on your laurels or feel comfortable in the sense that you have the right to lead. All leaders and leadership styles can be improved upon. The aim of this short, yet profound, part of the book is to help you shine the bright light of reflection onto your personal attributes that contribute to your leadership. Leadership is a choice; make the decision to lead and find enhanced success by developing your capacity and building your leader resilience.

To do so, we have developed two questionnaires. They are designed to evaluate and analyse your resilience as a leader and to assess the resilience level of your team. If the past few chapters haven't demonstrated the importance of this characteristic, then let me reiterate—resilience is a key predictor of transformational leadership and organisation success. It cannot be ignored, and it has to be measured. Only then can you, the reader, begin to take steps to improve or maintain it. If the seeds are already planted, then these evaluations should help you nurture them further. If not, then let's get to planting.

The first evaluation, *The Folan Resilience Scale*, was created to allow both the leader and team members to assess their level of resilience. Ideally, the leader will take this simple yet effective questionnaire first. Once some honest reflection has been completed by the leader, it will then be time to ask your team to get involved. Having each team member reflect on their own resilience by completing this scale is useful. Then, to assess the team and whether resilience is embedded in the team and its ways of working, the team, as a whole, needs to complete the *Team Resilience Scale*. The individual scores will be mirrored in the team score. Show me a resilient leader and I will show you a resilient team. The converse is often true as well: low levels of individual resilience will produce a team that lacks resilience. Just to be clear, even if a team is part of a highly dysfunctional organisation, the team can build resilience. After completing the assessment, the next important step is to take some time to reflect on the results. If nothing else, this should offer you some valuable insight into exactly where both you and your team stand.

Please be aware that all self-assessments have limitations, as each is based on your views of your own internal processing. If your levels of self-awareness are low, or if you have significant blind spots, then your responses in a self-assessment will naturally be skewed. If you have assumed that resilience means simply keeping on going, then you might also be surprised at your scores when you measure your resilience against all the dimensions. If your assessment of yourself is in some way skewed, either positively or negatively, don't be surprised if your personal assessment is not reflected in your team scores. This does, however, provide you with some very useful information for self-reflection and analysis.

The Johari window is a tool used in developmental discussions to discuss the level of self-awareness of an individual. As part of the reflection on the scores, it is useful to keep this tool in mind as you assess your level of resilience and your team's level of resilience.

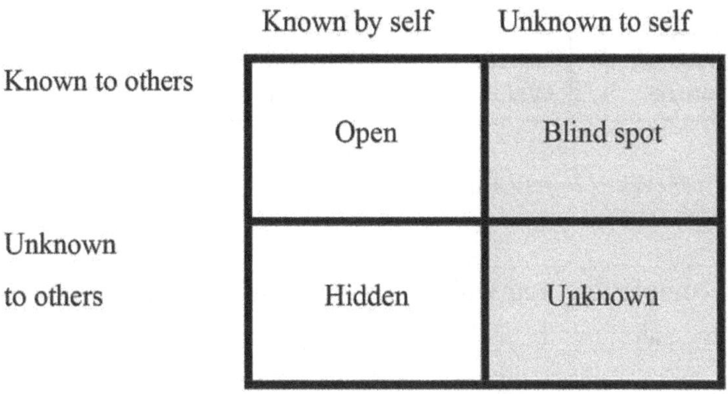

|  | Known by self | Unknown to self |
|---|---|---|
| Known to others | Open | Blind spot |
| Unknown to others | Hidden | Unknown |

*Figure 12: Johari Window Model (Luft & Ingham, 1955)*

If you have significant blind spots, then you will likely need more than a self-assessment tool to uncover your development needs. A 360 tool, which provided feedback from your team, your peers and your boss, would be useful for this purpose; 360 tools are available that assess transformational leadership and emotional intelligence of leaders and would be useful in further exploration of your areas for development.

But first let's start by measuring your resilience.

## 8.1 The Folan Resilience Scale

The first step in making a change in your resilience is to review your present level of resilience. You can either complete this scale by accessing the Inspired Development Solutions Pty Ltd. website at www.inspireddevelopment.net or by completing the paper version in this book. This questionnaire will assist you in assessing your resilience in alignment with the Folan model of resilience (2019).

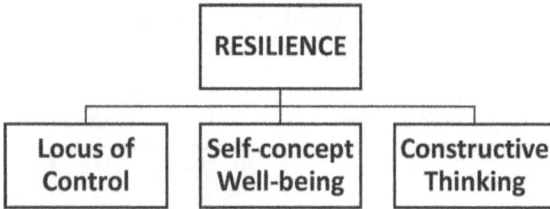

*Figure 13:: Model of resilience (Folan, 2019)*

After completion, you will be able to identify your overall level of resilience along with:

- Areas of resilience that are strengths
- Areas of resilience that are potential vulnerabilities or blind spots.

The questionnaire is designed to provide you with insights on your resilience against an organisational model of resilience (Folan, 2019).

### 8.1.1 Directions for Completion of the Questionnaire

Please read each statement carefully and then rate the degree to which you agree or disagree with the statement. It is important not to overthink your responses, and your first reaction is usually the most accurate.

# FOLAN RESILIENCE SCALE

| 1 = Strongly disagree | 2 = Disagree | 3 = Agree and disagree | 4 = Agree | 5 =Strongly agree |
|---|---|---|---|---|

| | | |
|---|---|---|
| 1. | I feel that my life has meaning. | |
| 2. | I know my personal strengths. | |
| 3. | I am aware when my thinking becomes persistently negative. | |
| 4. | I am fully aware of my emotions when they occur. | |
| 5. | Life is what you make it. | |
| 6. | I believe I can influence the direction of my life. | |
| 7. | When facing tough times, I keep on seeking solutions to problems. | |
| 8. | I share my feelings and concerns with people whom I trust. | |
| 9. | I have clear life goals. | |
| 10. | I know my personal vulnerabilities or weaknesses. | |
| 11. | When I experience unwelcome recurring negative thoughts, I can stop them and focus on positive thoughts. | |
| 12. | In stressful times I manage my emotional reactions. | |
| 13. | I can accomplish whatever I set out to achieve. | |
| 14. | I believe I can solve the challenges I experience in my life. | |
| 15. | When problem-solving, I use a range of approaches. | |
| 16. | I find it easy to ask for and accept assistance and support from others. | |
| 17. | There are significant people, causes and beliefs in my life. | |
| 18. | I am realistically optimistic about my capabilities and limits. | |
| 19. | When I find myself dwelling on negative thoughts, I deliberately change my thinking to positive thoughts. | |
| 20. | In tense situations, I express my own emotions in ways that others can understand and accept. | |

| 21. | If there is something in my life that I am not satisfied with, I will make the necessary changes. | |
| --- | --- | --- |
| 22. | In my life, I choose to be positive rather than negative. | |
| 23. | When needing to deal with tough problems, I deliberately open myself to different ways of viewing the problem. | |
| 24. | During tough times, I am sensitive to the feelings, needs and motivations of others. | |
| 25. | I am taking steps to achieve my life goals. | |
| 26. | I draw strength from having overcome previous challenges and tough times. | |
| 27. | I avoid getting into persistent negative thinking patterns. | |
| 28. | When I experience intense feelings, I rationally choose my actions and behaviours, rather than being driven by my emotions. | |
| 29. | I am always prepared to admit my mistakes. | |
| 30 | During stressful and challenging times, I choose to persevere rather than give up. | |
| 31. | When problem-solving, I listen to people with views different to mine. | |
| 32. | I respond sensitively to the feelings of others, by acknowledging them and showing understanding. | |
| 33. | I view experiencing tough times in my life as having some higher purpose and meaning. | |
| 34. | I accept myself for who I am. | |
| 35. | I consistently maintain a positive point of view in my thinking. | |
| 36. | When I experience powerful negative emotions, I take action to deal with the issue/s which are causing them. | |
| 37. | I don't believe that luck plays an essential role in my life. | |
| 38. | When experiencing challenges and tough times, I create balance in my life by doing things that are enjoyable, relaxing and recharging. | |
| 39. | I take considered risks to solve problems. | |
| 40. | I easily assist and support others. | |

| 41. | I am clear about the legacy that I want to leave. | |
|-----|---------------------------------------------------|---|
| 42. | I am aware of the impact I have on others. | |
| 43. | I actively manage my thinking to remain constructive. | |
| 44. | I actively manage my emotional reactions, ensuring that my emotions are effectively processed. | |
| 45. | What happens to me is my own doing. | |
| 46. | I am consistently optimistic but not unrealistic. | |
| 47. | I take ownership of my outcomes and choose not to be a victim of circumstances. | |
| 48. | I maintain healthy relationships based on honesty and transparency. | |

## 8.1.2 Scoring the Resilience Questionnaire

Instructions:

Transfer the scores you have given for each item to the appropriate box below. Then add the scores for each row to calculate your scores for each resilience principles and write this in the box at the end of the row. Finally, add the scores for each of the principles to give the total score of your resilience.

| RESILIENCE | Item no. | Your score | Item no. | Your score | Item no. | Your score | Item no. | Your score | Item no. | Your score | Item no. | Your Score | Totals |
|---|---|---|---|---|---|---|---|---|---|---|---|---|---|
| -concept well-being sonal clarity) | 1 | | 9 | | 17 | | 25 | | 33 | | 41 | | |
| -concept well-being f-Awareness) | 2 | | 10 | | 18 | | 26 | | 34 | | 42 | | |
| structive thinking naging thinking) | 3 | | 11 | | 19 | | 27 | | 35 | | 43 | | |
| -concept well-being f-management) | 4 | | 12 | | 20 | | 28 | | 36 | | 44 | | |
| structive Thinking imism) | 5 | | 13 | | 21 | | 29 | | 37 | | 45 | | |
| us of control (Influence outcomes) | 6 | | 14 | | 22 | | 30 | | 38 | | 46 | | |
| us of Control ice) | 7 | | 15 | | 23 | | 31 | | 39 | | 47 | | |
| lience outcome lthy relationship) | 8 | | 16 | | 24 | | 32 | | 40 | | 48 | | |
| 'AL RESILIENCE SCORE | | | | | | | | | | | | | |

### 8.1.3 Interpreting the Scores

**Score range 220 to 240: Very resilient**

You are consistently able to deal with change, challenges and tough times. You deal with the change and challenges effectively and can find fun and enjoyment in ambiguity and disruption. You have meaning in your life, know yourself well and are aware of and able to control and choose your thoughts, feelings and attitude.

**Score range 190 to 220: Fairly resilient**

Most of the time, you can cope and deal positively with tough times, challenge and change. You have strategies to cope that also enable you to experience joy and fulfilment in your life from time to time. To be able to bounce back from adversity quicker and with less difficulty, and also to live your life filled with more joy and fulfilment, you should consider developing your resilience in the lower-rated principles of resilience.

**Score range 130 to 190: Partially resilient**

You do have some strategies, which you use to deal with tough times, change and challenges. These strategies, however, do not enable you to consistently and effectively cope and thrive in demanding circumstances. You would, therefore, benefit from working on the principles of resilience to develop your resilience plan. The place to start is enhancing your stronger aspects and then focusing on the lowest scoring principles of resilience.

**Score range 90 to 130: Somewhat resilient**

You have limited strategies, which you use to keep going in tough times. These strategies, however, do not enable you to consistently and effectively cope, and you are likely to be undermining your health and well-being. You would, therefore, benefit from consistent work on developing your resilience plan. The place to start is the lowest scoring Principles of Resilience.

**Score range below 90: Not very resilient**

Change, adversity and tough times often seem to upset your equilibrium, and you struggle to cope with the uncertainty and the lack of stability they bring. At times like this, you do not experience much joy and vigour in your life, as you often struggle to get through the day. To cope and bring perspective, fun and enjoyment back in your life, start by developing resilience through a personal resilience plan. Begin this by reviewing your lowest scoring principles of resilience and work from there to determine what would be most effective for you.

## 8.2 Team Resilience Scale

The first step in making a change in your team's resilience levels is to identify the aspects of team resilience and effectiveness that require a shift. After completion, you will be able to identify your overall level of team resilience along with the aspects of team resilience that are strengths and those that are weaknesses. The questions are designed to assess your team's resilience against a research-based model of team resilience developed by Dr Lynda Folan.

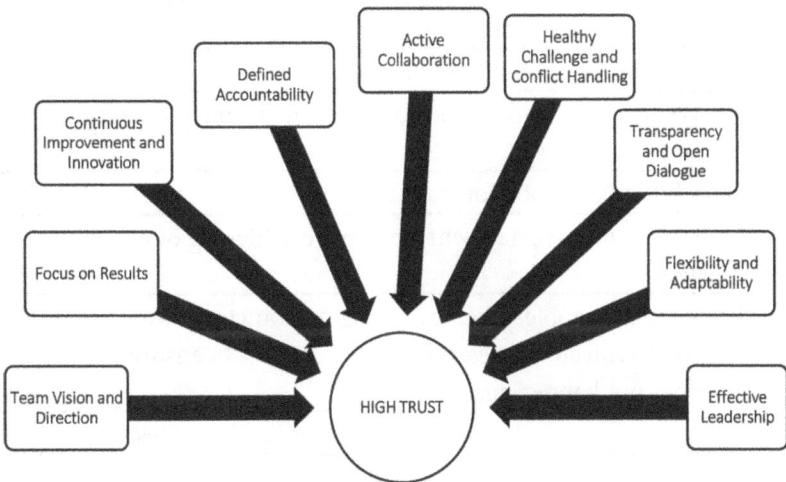

*Figure 14: Dimensions of resilient teams (Folan)*

You can either complete this scale by accessing the Inspired Development Solutions Pty Ltd website at www.inspireddevelopment.net or by completing the paper version in the book.

| 1 = Not at all | 2 = A little | 3 = A moderate amount | 4 = A lot | 5 =A great deal |
|---|---|---|---|---|

| | |
|---|---|
| **TEAM VISION AND DIRECTION** | |
| 1. We have a shared vision of what success looks like for our team. | |
| 2. We have a set of agreed behaviours that ensure we work effectively together. | |
| 3. We align our actions to our agreed behaviours. | |
| 4. We have a set of agreed team goals. | |
| 5. Each person has individual actions plans that they deliver. | |
| 6. We work collaboratively to achieve team outcomes. | |
| Total for Vision and Direction | |
| **FOCUS ON RESULTS** | |
| 7. Our team focuses on delivering results that support the organisation's strategy. | |
| 8. We support each other to achieve team outcomes. | |
| 9. We take personal responsibility for achieving planned actions. | |
| 10. We regularly look for ways to improve our results. | |
| 11. We regularly review whether we are achieving our goals. | |
| 12. If we are unable to achieve an agreed outcome, we communicate the reasons and review this to ensure it does not happen again. | |
| Total for Focus on Results | |

| | |
|---|---|
| **CONTINUOUS IMPROVEMENT AND INNOVATION** | |
| 13. We set aside time to brainstorm creative solutions to challenges. | |
| 14. We are continually finding ways to improve our systems and processes. | |
| 15. Every member of the team makes time to develop their expertise and improve their performance. | |
| 16. We regularly look for ways to improve our effectiveness. | |
| 17. We find new and innovative ways of doing things. | |
| 18. We seek feedback from our customers/clients and make changes based on their input. | |
| Total for Continuous improvement and innovation | |
| **DEFINED ACCOUNTABILITY** | |
| 19. All team members maintain their resilience and manage their stress levels. | |
| 20. All team members deliver high-quality results in alignment with agreed timelines. | |
| 21. Each team member communicates their progress to the team. | |
| 22. Where there are overlaps between roles, both parties ensure that accountability is maintained. | |
| 23. When things go wrong, we find solutions. | |
| 24. As a team, we deliver high-quality results in alignment with the organisation's strategy. | |
| Total for Accountability | |
| **ACTIVE COLLABORATION** | |
| 25. Team members actively work on developing their emotional intelligence. | |
| 26. Team members build strong relationships with each other. | |

| | |
|---|---|
| 27. Team members come prepared for and actively contributes to team meetings. | |
| 28. Team members go out of their way to support each other. | |
| 29. Team members don't judge each other. | |
| 30. We regularly allocate time to collaborate. | |
| Total for collaboration | |
| **HEALTHY CHALLENGE AND CONFLICT HANDLING** | |
| 31. We constructively resolve differences and conflict. | |
| 32. We celebrate diversity. | |
| 33. Team members constructively challenge each other. | |
| 34. The team make time to debate and discuss issues for enhanced understanding and decision-making. | |
| 35. We don't talk behind each other's backs. | |
| 36. When there is conflict in the team, we all actively support the resolution of this. | |
| Total for Healthy challenge and conflict handling | |
| **TRANSPARENCY AND OPEN DIALOGUE** | |
| 37. We regularly give positive and constructive feedback to each other. | |
| 38. We seek out feedback and reflect on it. | |
| 39. Our meetings are open and transparent and get to the heart of the matter. | |
| 40. Team members are transparent and open in their communication with each other. | |
| 41. We openly discuss things that are getting in the way. | |
| 42. Team members are comfortable having tough conversations when required. | |
| Total for transparency and open dialogue | |
| **FLEXIBILITY AND ADAPTABILITY** | |
| 43. Team members are flexible and able to adjust to changing priorities. | |

| | |
|---|---|
| 44. Team members are continually learning new things to remain adaptable. | |
| 45. We respond quickly to changing requirements. | |
| 46. We remain optimistic in the context of change. | |
| 47. We can deliver each other's roles if required. | |
| 48. We change responsibilities and take on other projects to ensure we don't become inflexible. | |
| Total for flexibility and adaptability | |
| **EFFECTIVE LEADERSHIP** | |
| 49. Our leader/s provide clear direction and support us to keep on track. | |
| 50. Our leader/s regularly provide feedback, both positive and constructive. | |
| 51. Our leader/s provide regular business and industry updates. | |
| 52. Our leader/s effectively communicate organisational changes. | |
| 53. Our leader/s effectively manage bad behaviour in our team. | |
| 54. Our leader/s are role models and walk the talk. | |
| Total for effective leadership | |
| **HIGH TRUST** | |
| 55. We trust each other. | |
| 56. We do not allow anyone to talk in a derogatory way about another member of the team. | |
| 57. We deliver on our commitments to each other. | |
| 58. Team members demonstrate trustworthiness. | |
| 59. We actively work to build trust. | |
| 60. When trust is damaged, we work to resolve this. | |
| Total for high trust | |
| **Your overall team resilience Score (add up all the scores)** | |

### 8.2.1 Interpreting the Scores

The maximum team resilience score is 300, and the lowest possible score is 60.

**Score range 250 to 300: Very high level of team resilience**

The scores indicate that your team is highly resilient and well placed to deliver excellent outcomes for your organisation. When the team faces challenges or adversity, they will bounce back, maintain momentum and continue to achieve results. To retain this level of resilience, the team will have demarcated and protected time for their continued development as a team and as individuals.

**Score range 200 to 250: High level of team resilience**

The scores indicate that your team has a high level of team resilience. However, there is an opportunity to keep developing your capacity as a team to reach excellence. The focus for your team enhancements should be the specific aspects where you have scored lower.

**Score range 150 to 200: Moderate level of team resilience**

You do have some strategies for maintaining resilience as a team, and you are likely to be achieving acceptable results. However, when faced with challenges, you have the potential to take longer to bounce back and maintain momentum. The team will need to dedicate time and focus on developing their resilience as a team. The starting point for your team enhancements should be the specific aspects where you have scored lower.

**Score range 100 to 150: Low level of team resilience**

These scores indicate that your team is demonstrating low levels of resilience and these are likely to be having an impact on the team's ability to perform to an acceptable standard. While individuals may still be achieving good outcomes, the team outcomes are likely to be compromised. Shifting the resilience levels and enhancing results will require a focus on all aspects of team resilience.

**Score range below 100: Very low level of team resilience**

These scores indicate that your team is functioning as a group of individuals and not as a team. The individual contributors are unlikely to have a focus or understanding of the team requirements. Making a change in this context will require a significant shift in all aspects of team resilience. The team will likely need to be tightly managed through this process, with an explicit requirement that everyone will need to change their behaviours.

## 8.3 Reflection and Looking Forward

We have established resilience as a dispositional attribute that has the capacity for change. Having taken the opportunity to self-reflect on your resilience at this moment in time is an important starting point for making a change. Once you have taken up the challenge to build your resilience, you must go back and look at the shift in your resilience and assess which specific areas have improved and which have not changed.

Self-reflection is key to change in any aspect of your life. In particular, if you want to enhance your resilience and your leadership, you first have to honestly reflect on where you are now.

Remember that your resilience changes over time and can be shifted with the strategies that are outlined in Chapters 10, 11 and 12. However, even if you are highly resilient now, don't assume that you don't need to work on your resilience. Over a lifetime, you will have ups and downs. If you have good resilience strategies, then you will be able to meet the challenges that you face in our VUCA world and bounce back healthily when adversity hits.

Let's take the time now reflect on the effect of challenge and adversity and discuss pressure and stress in connection to our resilience.

"The greatest weapon against stress
is our ability to choose one thought
over another."

William James

# CHAPTER 9

# PRESSURE VS STRESS! THE WAY YOU SEE THE SITUATION

Together, our goal is to build resilient leaders. We do that by nurturing resilience and enhancing the dimensions of resilience outlined in the previous chapter. Chapters 10, 11 and 12 will focus on how to go about building and maintaining resilience. Before we move in the direction of exploring how to develop resilience and build the dimensions of resilience, we must first work at understanding some of the barriers that get in the way of a leader's ability to maintain resilience.

Pressure is a natural part of organisational life and is very prevalent in the present business context. Pressure pervades all aspects of our existence and can, if not managed, wreak havoc on our ability to maintain resilience and deliver transformational leadership. At times, we sense pressure everywhere, following each of us around like an inescapable raincloud. We also tend to combine pressure and stress and see them as one and the same thing. This is not necessarily the case. What great leaders will tell you is that pressure is there all the time; it is inherent in all work contexts of all organisations, but it only tips over into stress as a result of our personal perspective.

So, while pressure is present for everyone, stress is a result of how an individual perceives a particular situation or set of pressures; it is not the situation itself. Individuals who have truly learned this and built their resilience to a sustainable level find a way to process pressure so that it does not turn into stress. These individuals take the sunshine with them; they remain optimistic even in the most challenging contexts.

In his book, *Man's search for meaning*, Victor Frankl (1946) describes how he observed these individuals in the concentration camps in Germany under Hitler's rule. He describes how some individuals, even in the most extreme circumstances of the prison camp, demonstrated their ability to make optimistic choices. We have recently seen the same demonstration of this in the context of the COVID-19 challenges. The actions of people like Captain Sir Tom Moore, who raised millions for the NHS by walking around his garden in the year he turned one hundred, demonstrates this same optimism. Frankl also describes the opposite end of this in individuals who, in his description, became as 'bad as their captors'. Again, in the context of COVID, we have seen behaviour that mirrors this in incidents like punch-ups over toilet rolls and people openly violating lockdown requirements.

In simple terms, there is absolutely no reason why pressure should convert into stress. Building your resilience will enable you to manage pressure and ensure you do not tip over into stress. Rather than allowing pressure to lead to stress, you can manage your response to pressure and embrace the strategies for developing your resilience. Let's spend a bit of time outlining in more detail what we mean.

## 9.1 What is Stress?

Most people, if asked, will attest to feeling stress at some point in their recent past. In fact, in my experience in working with leaders, 100% of people acknowledge that they have, at some point in the recent past, been stressed. However, they often find it hard to describe with any clarity what caused the stress, and the causes are vastly different for each individual. Stress is the group of non-specific responses of the mind, body and emotions to pressure. It is the unique reaction of the individual to the way they perceive or understand a situation. Stress usually arises when a perception of imbalance exists between our resources (physical, emotional, psychological and coping strategies) and the demands (pressure) placed upon us. Unfortunately, this is largely an unconscious assessment that results in the individual tipping over into stress without any conscious evaluation of the situation.

Stress is a subjective experience, in that the sources of pressure do not determine stress; it is the conscious or unconscious assessment of the pressure that defines an individual's response. In essence, each of us reacts differently to pressure. What is distressing for one person may be pleasurable or have little effect on someone else. For example, for person A, being promoted to the role of manager may be experienced as stressful for one or more reasons (e.g. anxiety about meeting expectations, fear of failure, no experience, etc.). By contrast, for person B, a similar promotion may be exciting and challenging and not stressful at all.

So, it isn't so much the pressure that is placed on us that causes stress; rather, it is what influences the experience of that pressure in our perception and interpretation of the situation. In becoming stressed, you must make two main judgements:

1. First, you must feel some level of threat (consciously or unconsciously) due to the situation or the pressure that you are experiencing;

2. Second, you must doubt your capacity and/or resources (consciously or unconsciously) to meet the threat.

These judgements may be conscious or unconscious. How stressed someone feels depends on how much damage they perceive the situation or pressure can do them, and how closely their resources meet the demands of the situation. In today's world, this sense of threat is rarely physical, and most of the time it is unconscious. It may, for example, involve perceived threats to our social standing, to other people's opinions of us, our opinion of ourselves, to our career prospects or to our own deeply held beliefs and values.

In particular, in working life, much of our stress is subtle and occurs without obvious physical threat or threats to our survival. Sources of pressure can be external (e.g. loss of a job opportunity or excessively high volumes of work) or internal (e.g. an individual's internal perceptions of the world, negative thinking patterns, perfectionism). In a work context, much of our pressure comes from things like work overload, conflicting priorities, inconsistent values, over-challenging deadlines, conflict with co-workers, toxic work cultures, poor leadership and so on. Not only do these have the potential to tip us over into stress, but they reduce our satisfaction and our performance as we divert mental effort into handling them. They can also cause a great deal of emotional distress.

To further break this down, take a look at an overview of how stress and pressure can impact the different aspects of your functioning:

### 9.1.1 Impacts of Stress

When you are stressed, a range of indicators may be evident. You will be aware of some of the indicators that you are likely to exhibit, and being able to observe these in yourself and in others is important for making a shift. Table 2 shows some of the stress indicators that you may experience.

| Physical indicators | Mental indicators |
|---|---|
| Lack of energy to perform normal aspects of life | Negative thinking |
| Feeling tired all the time | Catastrophised thinking—everything becomes a major issue |
| Sleep disturbance | Uncontrolled thinking that wakes you at night |
| Ill health | |
| Heightened physiological reactions to minor issues | Fear based thinking—becoming threatened by difference, e.g. racism and sexism |
| Needing external sources of physical energy, e.g. coffee and other stimulants | Fight and flight responses, e.g. road rage |
| Undiagnosed physical pain | Inability to shut off your thinking |
| Heightened colour or skin irritation | Mental illness |
| Self-medication to cope, e.g. use of painkillers, uppers, etc. | |
| Physical tremors or shaking | |
| **Self-concept indicators** | **Emotional indicators** |
| Inability to see value in things that used to be important | Inability to accurately self-reflect |
| Inability to focus on the things that are really important | Overly emotional or emotional flatlining (inability to show normal emotional responses) |
| Questioning of self | Inability to see one's own impact on others |
| Keeping on going but not having the energy to give back to yourself | Emotional reactions inappropriate to the situation |
| Values erosion | Suppression of emotions |
| Not caring about things that were once important | Aggression or withdrawal |
| Not doing things that help support your energy levels | Inability to be emotionally present |
| | General emotional management issues |
| | Overly caught up in emotions of others |

TABLE 2: INDICATORS OF STRESS

Stress is essentially an internal response or reaction to an external pressure. The internal response could include mental, emotional, physical and spiritual factors and can result in external attitude, mood, behavioural or physiological changes. According to Hans Selye (1956), one of the founding fathers of stress research, pressure is not necessarily bad—it all depends on how you respond to it. The pressure of exhilarating, creative work can be highly beneficial, while that of failure and humiliation can be detrimental.

Pressure isn't necessarily a bad thing. In fact, a certain level of pressure can be highly beneficial and useful in keeping us motivated to perform. Problems arise when we experience excessive levels of pressure over an extended period, coupled with a sense that we do not have the resources (physical, emotional, etc.) to effectively cope with the pressure. Of course, the 'optimal' level of pressure varies from individual to individual, depending on coping strategies, personality, resources, etc.

## 9.1.2 Warning Signs of Stress

If you lack the coping strategies, resources and skills to effectively cope with pressure, this may result in stress, which could eventually result in physical, mental and emotional reactions. In a work context, if this is not effectively managed, it can lead to what has been described as 'burnout'. Stress impacts our emotions, thoughts, behaviours and physiological responses. Consequently, performance and decision-making abilities decline, interpersonal relationships deteriorate and poor physical and emotional health ensue.

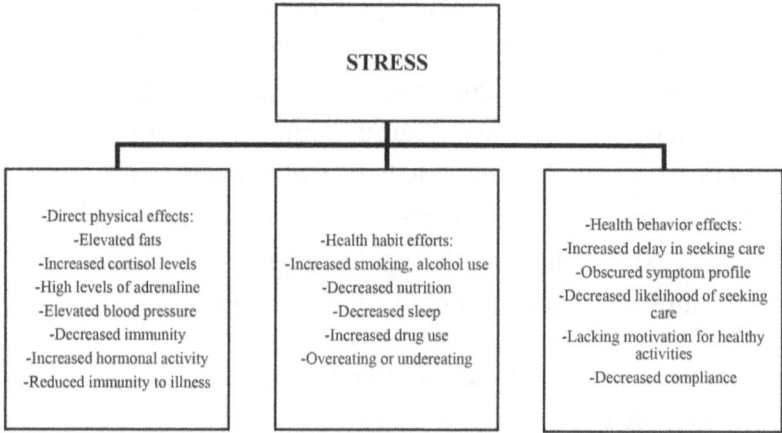

*Figure 15: Stress and physical health deterioration*

Here are some of the warning signs of stress:

**Physical:** Heart rate, blood pressure, stomach ulcers, gastric, breathing faster, shallow sweats, rashes, dry mouth, tiredness, fatigue, insomnia.

**Emotional:** Negative moods and feelings; bursts of anger; anxiety; depression; disinterest and apathy towards work and life in general; low job motivation; questioning of own ability (self-confidence).

**Behaviours:** Decline in work performance, decision-making becomes challenging, number of errors increases, accidents increase, absenteeism, avoidance of dealing with the basic requirements of the job, interpersonal relations decline, alcohol and drug use.

As I am sure you can tell, these conditions can often become a recipe for disaster at both a personal and a professional level. Thus, taking meaningful steps becomes important, not only to reduce stress, but also to recognise warning signs of stress in the first place. In a business environment, you are unlikely to be able to reduce the levels of pressure; therefore, the only option is to focus on managing that pressure to ensure that it does not tip over into stress. The following tool can help you to identify where you are right now in relation to stress and pressure.

Read through the following questions and respond accordingly:

| Physical Responses | | | Intensity or Frequency? |
|---|---|---|---|
| Heart | Examples: increased heart rate and blood pressure; diversion of blood to the muscles and away from the gut and skin (i.e. pale skin colour) | | |
| Stomach | Examples: gastric; ulcers, etc. | | |
| Breathing | Examples: faster breathing; hyperventilation, etc. | | |
| Others | Examples: 'cold sweat'; rashes or skin disorders; dry mouth; allergies; constantly tired or fatigued; insomnia | | |
| Emotional Responses | | | |
| Negative moods, feelings/ emotions | Examples: sudden burst of anger or violence; anxiety; low mood or depressed, etc. | | |
| Negative attitudes towards work, life, and re-lationships | Examples: disinterest/apathy; sense of hopelessness or despair; low job motivation and satisfaction, etc. | | |
| Low self-esteem and confidence | Example: questioning own abilities, etc. | | |

| Behavioural Responses | | | |
|---|---|---|---|
| Work role and performance | Examples: decline in job performance; morale; decision-making; increase in number of errors or accidents, etc. | | |
| Anti-social behaviour at work | Example: theft, etc. | | |
| Withdrawal behaviour | Examples: absenteeism and turnover from job; avoiding, ignoring stressor, or pretending nothing has happened. | | |
| Degradation of other life roles | Examples: spouse abuse or neglect; decline in interpersonal relations with family, friends or colleagues, etc. | | |
| Self-damaging behaviours | Examples: alcohol and drug use at work; over-eating or under-eating | | |

Do the results surprise you? Are you more stressed than you thought?

If so, then the next section will help you to understand your pressures and transform your internal response so that you build up your capacity and not tip over into stress.

## 9.2 Self-Talk and Stress

As easy as identifying and recognising pressure and stress might sound, determining its origins is actually quite difficult. Once you have moved from pressure into stress, stopping the impact on your emotions and reactions is extremely challenging. Stress can be triggered by myriad things, and most of the time it is not one single pressure that causes it, but rather a combination of things. The origins could be a reaction to a pressure today, emotional links to previous experiences, your beliefs, values, culture, upbringing or simply previous emotions that you have not resolved. The tipping point into a stress reaction is not as simple to diagnose as the external pressures or the warning signs that indicate the presence of stress. Accurate identification of the origins of stress is a challenge and moderating the behaviours that result once stress has taken over is just as difficult. That being said, if you have well-developed strategies for regularly 'cleaning up' your emotions and your mental processing and you have good self-awareness, you will have a much easier time identifying and managing the precipitators of stress. If you are effectively managing yourself and not carrying unhelpful historical emotions and mental structures, then identifying the internal responses to pressures will be easy and this will ensure you don't tip over into stress.

Your internal reactions to pressure are managed by the most amazing piece of equipment you have: your brain. One of the key aspects of the brain activity that supports or undermines your ability to manage pressure is your internal chatter or self-talk. The self-talk happening inside your head is influenced by everything that is stored in your cerebral cortex. Your cerebral cortex is a bit like the hard drive of a computer. It houses all of your memories, your personal attributes, your personality, your experiences, your values, your cultural heritage, etc. In simple terms, it is the coding that defines your uniqueness. This internal chatter is a constant factor in your mental processing system, and researchers indicate that the average person has about 60 to 200 thoughts per minute. Much of the time, you are totally unconscious of this self-talk, and it continues impacting your reactions without any involvement of conscious processing. Think about a time when you have driven somewhere and you simply don't remember how you got there because you were thinking about other things; this is your self-talk in action. Sometimes self-talk and inner mental processing is helpful, sometimes it is neutral, and sometimes it is destructive. When you become stressed, your self-talk is often one of the factors that exacerbates your stress, as it normally becomes negative, adding more internal pressure. In order to better understand the mental processing involved in stress, you must become conscious of your self-talk. The starting point is to observe it. The ability to monitor your self-talk provides you with insights into the unconscious internal processing of your brain.

For example:

- If your self-talk is making statements like, 'what an idiot', 'how stupid can you be', 'why can't you do better', then, over time, you will develop a belief that you are incompetent. This will then generalise to all areas of your life, and the outcome will be low self-esteem.

- If your self-talk is telling you, 'I did the best job I could in the circumstances', then, over time, this will result in a belief that 'I always do my best even if I don't always succeed'. Over time, this will enhance your self-esteem.

You need to be able to observe two key aspects of our self-talk:

1. You need to be able to identify situations, peoples, places or experiences that activate negative self-talk. When you are able to identify what has activated your self-talk, you then have the opportunity to manage it more effectively and prepare positive thinking patterns in advance of the stimulus presenting itself.

- You need to be able to observe the self-talk itself. Your self-talk describes your reaction to external stimuli in the form of internal chatter. This can be challenging, as, for many of us, this talk is mainly unconscious and we have taught ourselves to ignore it. This unconscious aspect of your self-talk means that, for the majority of the time, you are not even aware of what is going on in your mind. When something happens and you suddenly feel unsettled, you assume that it is the situation itself that has made you feel this way; you don't necessarily attribute it to your self-talk.

One important point to reiterate is that it is not the situation that causes stress; rather, it is the way we perceive and react to the situation that causes our stress. Our self-talk provides us with insights into our internal processing and what is happening in our brains that is creating stress and causing us to feel the way we do. Our feelings, emotions and behaviour are only triggered once we have internalised pressure into stress. Therefore, our self-talk gives us direct insights into our mental processing, and if we choose to listen to it, it will give us the ability to manage our reactions to pressure. Adjustment of our internal processing can very quickly change our reactions and deliver a change of emotions.

### 9.2.1 Self-talk and Presence

To be effective as leaders, we must have the capacity to manage our self-talk and remain present when we are working with people. One of the key things that prevents us from being in the present is the continuous stream of self-talk that is happening in our brains. To be truly present, we need the capacity to shut off our self-talk, thereby allowing ourselves to become fully aware of the nuances of the situation, rather than unnecessarily processing unconscious thinking that has no direct relevance to the present moment. If we want to be effective in responding in the present moment, we need to learn how to turn off our self-talk and be fully present in the issues at that moment. This is not to say that reviewing things from the past or visualising things in the future is unhealthy. This is still important; however, if we want to get the best out of a situation or a person, we need to be fully present to that situation or person, and to do this requires control over our minds.

If we allow our unconscious self-talk to dominate our mental functioning and define our actions and reactions, this will have an unmanaged impact on our emotions. This will hinder us from being truly present in the here and now. Our self-talk has a direct impact on our ability to live in the moment. When it is unmanaged, it clouds our judgement and negatively influences our moods and emotions. The three major negative emotions that are stimulated by negative self-talk are anger, sadness and fear. If these or other emotions are regularly being stimulated by our self-talk, we will notice a reduction in our ability to cope. Fear, anger, sadness or any other negative emotion will focus our energy on negative reactions and actions. This interferes with our ability to focus our attention on the actual cues in a situation and can lead to distorted reactions. This is not to say that anger, sadness and fear are bad, but if we become captured by these negative emotions, they can start to erode our ability to function effectively.

People may develop negative self-talk when faced with specific situations, people or events. This can be because they have a predisposition or reactivity to these factors. Another reason might be that they have developed self-talk that was learned through past interactions with social connections, such as with parents, friends, siblings, etc. Whatever the reason for the negative self-talk, it will cause ongoing damage to the individual and will reduce their resilience and effectiveness over time. The only way that these negative thinking patterns can be shifted is:

1. To become aware of your negative self-talk and start to observe it.

2. To evaluate what has created this negative self-talk—this is tough work, as it requires a high level of self-reflection and honesty.

3. To clean up the negative self-talk by finding out the under-lying reason for the negative self-talk (to be discussed further in Chapter 12, in constructive thinking).

4. To keep cleaning up your self-talk on an ongoing basis.

5. To develop constructive thinking strategies (to be discussed further in Chapter 12).

When it comes to leadership and stress, remember that your ability to lead is directly related to your ability to manage your stress and maintain your resilience. This is the difference between effective and ineffective leadership, and it also has significant implications for your impact on the people around you and their ability to achieve outcomes. If you become mindful of your self-talk and develop strategies to enhance your mental processing, you will reduce the negative impact on yourself, your team, your organisation and your family (who often bear the brunt of your stress). This requires a high level of self-awareness and the discipline to observe your self-talk and then go deeper to really assess what is driving that self-talk.

## 9.2.2 Managing Blind Spots

Being self-aware is key to managing your self-talk and involves recognising your strengths and weaknesses and your blind spots. If you have blind spots in your self-awareness, these could influence your internal chatter and cause emotional triggering. As a leader, you must become aware of your blind spots so that you can minimise any potential negative impact they may have on your effectiveness.

These are some of the blind spots that get in the way of effective leadership:

**Blind ambition:** has to win or appear 'right' at all costs; competes instead of cooperates; exaggerates one's value and contribution; is boastful and arrogant; sees people in black and white terms as allies or enemies.

**Unrealistic goals:** sets overly ambitious, unattainable goals for oneself, the group or the organisation; is unrealistic about what it takes to get the job done.

**Perfectionist tendencies:** expectations of perfection that are not achievable and result in unrealistically high expectations of self and others.

**Relentless striving:** compulsively hard-working at the expense of all else in life; runs on empty; is vulnerable to burnout.

**Drives others:** pushes other people too hard, burning them out; micromanages and takes over instead of delegating others; comes across as abrasive or ruthless and insensitive to the emotional harm to others.

**Power hungry:** seeks power for one's own interest, rather than the organisation's; pushes a personal agenda regardless of other perspectives; is exploitative.

**Insatiable need for recognition:** addicted to glory; takes credit for others' efforts and puts blame on them for mistakes; sacrifices follow-through in pursuit of the next victory.

**Preoccupation with appearances:** needs to look good at all costs; is overly concerned with public image; craves the material trappings of prestige.

**Need to seem perfect:** enraged by or rejects criticisms, even if realistic; blames others for one's own failures; cannot admit mistakes or personal weaknesses.

Adapted from D. Goleman (1998), *Emotional intelligence*

How would having any one or more of these blind spots impact your effectiveness as a leader/manager/supervisor?

These are just some of the blind spots that might be driving our internal chatter and self-talk, and once we are aware of them, we are able to readjust them and become more effective as leaders. If we are able to make our self-talk conscious, it provides us with important insights into these blind spots. If we actively work on developing our resilience and, in particular, our constructive thinking, we will start to realign our self-talk so that it becomes more uplifting and positive.

## 9.3 Coping with Stress

A variety of strategies are talked about in the media and popularist books. However, if you want to effectively manage your stress, the only guaranteed way to do this is to develop a high level of resilience and maintain it on an ongoing basis. This will allow you to effectively manage all aspects of your mental processing and ensure your emotions and reactions remain mostly positive. While plenty of strategies may assist at a particular moment, the effect of these will only last for a limited time. If you do not systematically develop your resilience, stress will simply return. The extent to which a strategy will be successful varies from individual to individual and for each situation. You must first be able to identify which strategies you currently use to deal with stress, and you can then evaluate whether these strategies are getting to the core of the issues or are simply a short-term fix. If you want to eradicate your susceptibility to stress, you will need to develop your resilience across all three dimensions: your locus of control, self-concept well-being and constructive thinking. Once you do this, you will be able to manage the pressure so that it does not result in stress, even in highly pressurised environments. That is a big statement, but let me qualify it. To achieve this requires discipline and ongoing work. It is not something that you do once and suddenly you are resilient and have no stress; it requires regular discipline in managing your mental processing and your emotions.

## 9.4 Avoid Stress by Developing the Three Dimensions of Resilience

Research identifies a number of qualities and skills that support resilience; in particular, the research outlined in the previous chapter identifies three key dimensions required for resilience. Each of these is essential for the eradication of stress responses. Each of these dimensions is the product of hundreds of years of research and expert guidance. They are the secret ingredient or quick fixes to ensuring your health and well-being. You will require resilience to be a leader who is in control of yourself and your emotions and reactions.

As you work through each of these dimensions, start by evaluating and analysing if you, as a leader, are consciously executing them. If not, then the next few chapters of this book will help you to develop strategies to enhance each of the dimensions. This is the holy grail of resilient leadership, and in studying and implementing these, I am confident that you will take leaps and bounds in your journey to transforming into a resilient leader who has the capacity to deliver transformational leadership.

1. **Self-concept well-being**—this requires that you know yourself and understand all aspects of who you are. It also incorporates effective emotional management that supports your health and well-being.

2. **Internal locus of control**—this requires a belief that what you do makes a difference and that your outcomes are within your control. It includes the capacity to separate your reactions

from the stimulus or situation you are experiencing and to make healthy choices.

3. **Constructive thinking**—this requires management of your thinking and control over the way you process your experiences. It necessitates the ability to effectively manage your mind and not be managed by your mind.

Robert Collier (2013, p.188) reminds us that 'Success is the sum of small efforts, repeated day in and day out.' If you dedicate yourself to focusing on and improving each of these three dimensions of resilience, then you will begin to see results. Each of these acts as a guiding light that will help you to see the way through the tough times, while excelling and maximising your outcomes in the good ones. Over the next three chapters, we will unpick each of these and provide strategies for developing each of the dimensions.

"Knowing yourself is the
beginning of all wisdom"

Aristotle

# CHAPTER 10

# DEVELOPING YOUR SELF-CONCEPT WELL-BEING

As already noted, if we are going to build remarkable leaders, we first need to build resilience. Developmental strategies focused on self-concept well-being, locus of control and constructive thinking will build resilience and allow transformational leadership to blossom. Enhancing resilience paves the way for leadership and opens the doors for greater success as individuals and as organisations. In the previous chapter, we took a look at the role that stress and pressure play in reducing our effectiveness and well-being. In this chapter, we are shifting our focus to look at proactive strategies that develop resilience and provide an antidote to the effects of pressure. Developing resilience builds our capacity to flourish in the VUCA world, allowing us to successfully navigate the challenges we face without the need for stress reactions.

The choice is yours! You can keep stepping over the edge and finding yourself stressed. Or you can build your resilience to support you in coping with the pressures of life and thrive in the VUCA world. If you choose to take up the challenge to build and manage your resilience, you will develop the capacity to consistently deliver a transformational leadership style. This chapter outlines the research associated with the first dimension of resilience: self-concept well-being.

As self-esteem and self-concept well-being are frequently treated as interchangeable concepts in research, the conceptual links between these two will be discussed. This will assist you in understanding why self-concept well-being is defined as a dimension of resilience. After outlining the research, practical analysis interprets the requirements from a broad range of information. The chapter will wrap up with some strategies that can be used to develop your self-concept well-being and enhance your intra-personal leadership.

## 10.1 Defining Self-concept Well-being

The degree of external stimulation experienced by individuals in everyday life is far greater than their ability to absorb, process and respond. There is, therefore, a need to understand the internal strategies that manage the processing of external stimulants to ensure that health and well-being is maintained (Bandura, 1997; Blascovich & Tomaka, 1991; Markus, 1977). To cope, individuals develop a range of self-knowledge and self-belief strategies that they construct on an ongoing basis in their internal structure. These are described as self-concept or self-esteem and the two are often used interchangeably (Cantor, Markus, Niedenthal & Nurius, 1986; Seligman et al., 1988). When this internal structure (self-concept/self-esteem) is working well, it allows individuals to function effectively within a range of contexts, respond to their external world and maintain well-being (Markus & Wurf, 1987; Tharenou, 1979; Wells & Marwell, 1976). Self-concept and self-esteem both have a long research history in psychology, and a significant body of research is associated with each construct, along with their contribution to resilience and well-being (Campbell, 1990; Markus & Wurf, 1987; Sowislo & Orth, 2013). One of the reasons for the ongoing interest in these constructs is that they have consistently been shown to have a positive impact on people's well-being and behaviours in a range of contexts (Pierce, Gardner, Cummings & Dunham, 1989; Robinson, Shaver & Wrightsman, 1991; Wylie, 1979).

Much of the early research and theorising on self-esteem and self-concept originated in the field of clinical psychology, and many of the global measures of self-esteem evolved out of research into individual differences (Coopersmith, 1967; Rosenberg, 1965). In one of the earliest studies, James (1890) defined self-esteem as a sense of success in important life domains. Later researchers looked more at the social influences on self-esteem (Cooley, 1902; Goffman, 1959). Rosenberg (1965, 1989), the originator of one of the most validated clinical measures of self-esteem, the Self-Esteem Scale, described self-esteem as being related to feelings of personal worth. Recent conceptualisations of self-esteem have supported Rosenberg's (1989) definition. A number of researchers have separated self-esteem from other aspects of the self-concept, defining self-esteem as an affective, evaluative element of self-concept (Campbell, 1990; Leary & Baumeister, 2000). Researchers have shown that self-esteem is influenced by other aspects of the broader construct, self-concept (Baumgardner, 1990).

Self-concept is described as a combination of self-belief and the evaluation of the beliefs, along with the structure that supports the self-belief (Campbell, Assanand & Di Paula, 2003). It has also been described as a cognitive structure that organises and processes memories and abstractions about the self and assists in the development of a sense of self (Markus, 1977). A healthy self-concept facilitates an individual's ability to maintain psychological and emotional well-being (Baumeister, 1998; Markus, 1977). Based on these definitions, self-concept is clearly a broader construct that incorporates self-esteem.

Campbell's (1990) definition, which was used in the research outlined in this book, articulated two separate components of self-concept well-being: content and structure. Both have implications for developing self-concept well-being and resilience.

1. **THE CONTENT COMPONENT OF SELF-CONCEPT WELL-BEING.** This includes a knowledge aspect (who am I?) and an evaluative aspect (how do I feel about myself?). The knowledge aspect entails beliefs about one's personal attributes and the clarity of these, while the evaluative component is the evaluation of one's personal attributes and beliefs. Both aspects are intricately connected and work together to produce healthy or unhealthy levels of well-being. A well-established understanding of one's personal attributes (knowledge component) and a positive evaluation of these attributes (evaluative component) will result in higher levels of psychological adjustment and overall well-being. People with a low level of self-concept are more likely to have unhealthy aspects to their self-knowledge and/or maladjusted evaluations of the self. A healthy maintenance of the content of self-concept allows an individual to maintain a sense of self that is capable of responding healthily to life changes and events (Showers, Abramson & Hogan, 1998).

2. **THE STRUCTURAL COMPONENT OF SELF-CONCEPT WELL-BEING.** This is the way in which the content of the self is organised. The health of the structural aspect impacts self-concept well-being in the context of moods and emotions. The structural elements define how the content aspects are organised and require a level of coherence, unity and clarity to ensure that self-concept well-being is maintained. The structural component is the way the contents of the self are organised. The health of the structural aspect directly impacts moods, emotions and the ability to cope with pressure.

The changing nature of the self is associated with an evolution of both the structural and content components.

For example, when someone has always lived on their own and they have developed a sense of self that included a healthy adjustment to living alone, if this is destabilised, a fluctuation in the self will occur. Should they commence living with someone, they will need to take conscious steps to make a healthy adjustment of the self to this changed context. For most people, key moments arise when significant shifts take place in the self-concept: moving from the teenage years into adulthood, becoming a parent, getting married, getting divorced, becoming empty nesters, retiring, etc. These external adjustments require a healthy adjustment of the self-concept that allows the person to continue to function healthily.

For example, you have a belief that you are strong and capable (content) and this has been embedded in your structure and there is clarity around this. Should this belief be shaken, this will impact your self-concept well-being. When something happens that makes you feel vulnerable and incompetent, this will cause a shift in your content and structural aspects. If unmanaged, this will destabilise your structure and create a negative emotional reaction. Effective management of this requires that you make a conscious choice to integrate the new knowledge into the self and readjust your content and structure. This can be achieved in two ways:

- Readjusting your view on what strength is and incorporating vulnerability and failure into that view or,
- Observing how strong and capable people deal positively with their own vulnerability and failure.

These adjustments need to be made on a regular basis, and particularly at the time of significant life changes and life transitions. If you don't consciously manage these adjustments in your self-concept, your unconscious will incorporate potentially destructive patterns that will impact your health and well-being. This leaves you vulnerable to emotions and moods that are unconsciously driven. Over time, if you don't effectively manage these adjustments, they will start to develop into unhealthy and destructive patterns in your self-concept, which will damage your resilience levels.

Consider your day-to-day activities. I am sure you would agree that you often experience a degree of external pressure and that you have times when you feel overwhelmed and can't absorb or respond to the pressure. The mind works in mysterious ways, and researchers have uncovered the secret to managing this. To deal with these competing stimuli and effectively manage the pressure this brings, we have the capacity to develop an internal self-structure that maintains a sense of well-being even in the context of extreme pressure (Bandura, 1997; Blascovich & Tomaka, 1991; Markus, 1977). To cope, individuals must develop a healthy range of self-knowledge and self-belief strategies that they construct on an ongoing basis in their internal system, described as their self-concept (Seligman et al., 1988; Cantor, Markus, Niedenthal & Nurius, 1986). When this internal processing system is working well, it allows us to function effectively and maintain resilience.

Research shows that self-concept well-being is positively associated with resilience, psychological adjustment, achievement in academic domains, the ability to persist in the face of failure, improved coping skills and positive affect (Cheng & Furnham, 2004; DeNeve & Cooper, 1998; Heatherton, Herman & Polivy, 1991; Musser & Browne, 1991; Sawyer, Miller-Lewis, Oades-Sese, Cohen, Allen, & Lewis, 2014; Searle, Sawyer & Lynch, 2015). A healthy self-concept facilitates an individual's ability to maintain psychological and emotional well-being (Baumeister, 1998; Diehl, Hastings & Stanton, 2001; Donahue et al., 1993; Markus, 1977). Research shows that significant changes in the content of the self-concept are reflected in well-being levels, and they impact our ability to accurately maintain a clear sense of self. Variations in the structure of the self-concept are reflected in a shift in coping strategy to counteract stressful events and moderate the adverse impact of external factors (Showers et al. 1998). A coherent self-concept structure, along with clearly defined and healthily evaluated content, can enhance self-regulation and well-being, improve mental health and build the ability to deal with a broad range of life stressors (Baumgardner, 1990; Baumeister, 1998; Showers et al., 1998). Conversely, an incoherent, unstable self-concept structure is associated with lower levels of well-being, higher levels of anxiety and depression, a reduced ability to respond to daily stress and an increased negative affect (Baumeister, Tice & Hutton, 1989; Diehl et al., 2001; Diehl & Hay, 2010; Donahue et al., 1993).

The research outlined in this book defines self-concept well-being as a dimension of resilience and an important aspect in the individual's intra-personal ability to deliver a transformational leadership style. The research validates the importance of self-concept well-being as a key to unlocking your ability to cope and enhancing your leadership capacity.

## 10.2 Self-concept Well-being: Dispositional Attribute vs Trait

As with each of the concepts outlined in this book, some researchers believe self-concept well-being is a dispositional attribute that is adaptable over time, while others argue that it is a stable trait that is not amenable to change. Some experts argue for self-concept and its predictive power over long time periods, noting that it is likely to resist change and has trait-like qualities. Still others believe in dynamic conceptualisation of the self-concept, meaning it is an attribute that can be developed and honed.

Researchers who view the self-concept as adaptive describe it as dynamic, allowing for the constantly changing elements of the individual's life and the evolving contextual aspects (Markus & Wurf, 1987). In their review of self-concept, Markus and Wurf (1987, p. 299) stated that 'The unifying premise of the last decade's research on the self is that the self-concept does not just reflect ongoing behaviour but instead mediates and regulates this behaviour.' In this definition, the self-concept is seen as dynamic and active, with the capacity for change. They define a dynamic self-concept as an interpretive structure that houses a collection of self-representations that mediate between the intra-personal and interpersonal behaviours of the individual. This definition places the self-concept within the dispositional attribute domain and aligns with our definition of resilience as a dispositional attribute.

## 10.3 Self-concept Well-Being: Organisational and Leadership

As we apply this concept to organisations and leadership, note that self-concept well-being has a positive impact on job satisfaction, job performance, a stronger sense of task-based efficacy, organisational citizenship behaviour, levels of job satisfaction, motivation and effectiveness in the leadership and organisational change contexts (Bandura, 1997; Coopersmith, 1967; Hunt & Larsons, 1977; Judge & Bono, 2001; Markus & Wurf, 1987; Tharenou, 1979). In the organisational context, a leader's abilities to maintain the stability of their self-concept and manage their emotions and reactions have been shown to be important in defining their capacities to utilise a transformational style of leadership regardless of the organisational context. In fact, a high level of self-confidence arising from self-concept well-being is an essential characteristic of a charismatic/transformational leader.

Clearly, self-concept well-being is a prerequisite for the effective use of a transformational leadership style (Folan, 2019). Transformational leaders who have a healthy self-concept are not threatened by others or driven by ego; they therefore have a positive impact on their followers' sense of self and support them to develop a healthy self-concept, thereby enhancing motivation and commitment (Huebner, 2012; Mayfield & Mayfield, 2002). Although more research is still to be done in this area, the importance of the self-concept in the organisational arena is very clear when looking at the dimensions of leader resilience.

## 10.4 Self-concept Well-being Simplified

From a more practical perspective, having a clear understanding of what is required to maintain self-concept well-being is important. Achieving a healthy level of self-concept well-being requires that we work on the following:

- **Understanding who am I and what matters to me**

  This requires a deep knowledge of who you are that is grounded in reality and explores all aspects of the self—values, beliefs, attitudes, personality, strengths, weaknesses, cognitive processing capacity, cultural heritage, how you view yourself as a result of life experiences, your physical attributes, your triggers, your emotional makeup, etc.

- **How do I feel about myself?**

  This requires an optimistic and positive perspective about who you are. In simple terms, you must learn to love yourself, including your strengths and your shortcomings.

- **How is your self-concept structured?**

  Put simply, you need to clean up any negative and or destructive patterns that undermine your sense of self and how you feel about yourself.

## 10.5 Tools for Enhancing your Self-concept Well-being

Two key areas require focus when developing self-concept well-being:

1. **Developing the content aspect of your self-concept—** knowing who you are and having a healthy evaluation of who you are.

2. **Developing the structural aspect of your self-concept—** healthy emotional management based on how you structure the content of the self, delivering clarity and unity.

The tools outlined below are by no means comprehensive; however, they offer a range of options for the development of both the content and the structural aspects of your self-concept. While the tools are separated out, note that work done on either aspect of self-concept will enhance your levels of resilience. Another important point to realise is that this is not a one-off activity that suddenly enhances your self-concept. To maintain self-concept well-being, you must set aside time on a regular basis to develop the health and well-being of your self-concept. This is particularly true at the time of major life changes.

### 10.5.1 Tools for Enhancing the Content Aspect of Your Self-concept

#### 1. Journalling

Keeping a journal is a very powerful tool: it is the equivalent of you becoming your own therapist. Writing down your internal reactions and emotions that have occurred during the day allows you to consciously manage the content of your self-concept.

This is one of the most powerful strategies not only for managing your self-concept but also for maintaining an internal locus of control and enhancing your constructive thinking. It is not about keeping a diary of everything that happened in your day. Rather, it is a strategy for reflection which allows you to describe, evaluate and manage your mental and emotional reactions.

This reflection needs to be a regular activity and is best done at the end of your day. As a strategy, it is even more important in times of high pressure. This is an opportunity for you to reflect on your day and identify any emotional or mental processing that has been unhelpful or has produced a negative reaction. This not only helps with the processing of things that have occurred during the day, but it also supports healthy sleep. If you have unresolved issues from your day, they are likely to have an impact on your sleep, either waking you up or producing disturbing dreams.

### 2. Personality diagnostics

Complete a range of personality diagnostics and reflect on these with someone skilled in evaluating the tools.

Personality diagnostics allow you to reflect on your personality and your core traits and how they might affect your reactions and help you to develop a greater understanding of who you are. Some of the tools that are suggested are Myers Briggs, 16 Personality Factors, Herman Brain Dominance Instrument, OPP, FIRO-B, Occupational Personality Profile and Hogan Personality Inventory.

### 3. Personal strengths and weaknesses

Take time to clearly identify your strengths and your weaknesses.

We all have strengths and weaknesses; however, for some reason, we get bogged down by focusing on areas we struggle with and we neglect to develop and embrace our strengths. Knowing what you do best and how you can shine sets you up to succeed. Take inventory of your strengths by considering the following questions:

- When am I at my best?

- What ignites my passion?

- What are my natural preferences?

- What are the things that drag me down and de-energise me?

- What am I good at?

Continue to cultivate your positive attributes that make you feel confident and incorporate these into your daily life as much as you can. Be very clear on your weaknesses and manage them so that they don't negatively impact on your success. Another helpful task is to ask others about your strengths and weaknesses, as they may have a different perspective and see things that you aren't aware of.

## 4. Achievement and Accomplishments

Make a list of all the things you're proud of in your life.

A major factor in building a healthy self-concept is trusting and believing that you are able to achieve things. Those who believe they can accomplish a task are more likely to succeed, and those who feel uncertain will likely shrink away from a task at the first setback. Defining your achievements plays a role in motivating you to take action when setbacks happen. As you accomplish things big and small, you begin to trust that you can do more than you previously believed. It is as important to reflect on the big things you are proud of as it is to identify all the smaller things that have given you a sense of satisfaction when you have succeeded. Whether it's getting a project successfully completed or preparing a beautiful meal for your family or learning to surf, all these achievements are important and build your internal sense of motivation. Keep your list close by and add to it whenever you do something you're proud of. When you're low in confidence, pull out the list and use it to remind yourself of all the awesome things you've done and achieved.

## 5. Values alignment

A key aspect of understanding yourself at a deeper level is to reflect on your personal values. Your values drive your decision-making and influence every aspect of your life. Values are the things that you believe are important to you in the way you live your life. Consciously or unconsciously, they determine your priorities and influence your decisions. Deep down, they are the measures you use to decide whether your life is turning out the way you want it to. When the things that you do and the way you behave match your values, life is usually good—you're satisfied and content. But when these don't align with your personal values, that's when things feel . . . wrong and out of balance. If your life is out of alignment with your values, this can be a real source of unhappiness and stress. This is why making a conscious effort to identify your values is so important. Values exist, whether you recognise them or not. Life can be much easier when you acknowledge your values—and when you make plans and decisions that honour them.

For example, if you value family, but your job requires that you work a seventy-hour week, you are likely going to feel internal stress and conflict. And if you don't value competition, and your work environment is highly competitive, you are unlikely to be satisfied with your job. In these types of situations, understanding your values can really help. When you know your values, you can use them to make choices about how to live your life that will build your resilience.

## Core Values Worksheet

| | | | |
|---|---|---|---|
| Achievement | Ethical behaviour | Listening | Self-respect |
| Adventure | Excellence | Location | Serenity |
| Altruism | Fairness | Love | Service |
| Autonomy | Faith | Loyalty | Skills |
| Balance | Family | Leadership | Social responsibility |
| Beauty | Financial security | Making a difference | Spirituality |
| Belonging | Freedom | Meaningfulness | Stability |
| Challenge | Friendship | Money | Status |
| Change | Friendliness | Nature | Teamwork |
| Charity | Growth | Openness | Time freedom |
| Community | Happiness | Order | Tradition |
| Competence | Harmony | Partnering | Trust |
| Competition | Health | Peace of mind | Truth |
| Cooperation | Helping others | Personal growth | Unity |
| Country | Hobbies | Personal relationships | Wealth |
| Courage | Home | Power and authority | Wisdom |
| Creativity | Honesty | Privacy | Work |
| Culture | Honour | Professional growth | |
| Customer satisfaction | Independence | Professionalism | |
| Dedication | Influence | Public service | |
| Democracy | Inner Harmony | Purity | |
| Diversity | Innovation | Purpose | |
| Ecological awareness | Integrity | Quality of what I do | |
| Education | Intellectual status | Recognition | |
| Effectiveness | Involvement | Relationships | |
| Efficiency | Job satisfaction | Reliability | |
| Equality | Job security | Religion | |
| Ethics | Justice | Responsibility | |
| Fame | Knowledge | Respect | |

TABLE 3: CORE VALUES

a) Look at the list of values—if some important ideas are missing, add them.

b) Select the ten that are most important to you.

c) Delete five of the selected items, leaving the five that are most important to you.

d) Delete down to your top three.

e) Identify how these values affect your sense of self and what happens if these values are eroded or not honoured.

**6. Have, Do and Be Activity.**

Make a list of what you want to have in your life, what you want to do in your life and who you want to be.

This is a reflection that will assist you in defining what is important to you. It allows you to focus on those aspects of life that energise and engage you. A great way to obtain clarity on who you want to be is to imagine your one-hundredth birthday party and visualise what you would like important people in your life to say about you. This will help you to reflect on what it is that you want to be remembered for. The outer layers of 'have and do' are the external drivers; it is who you want to be and the legacy that you want to leave that is at the core of your resilience.

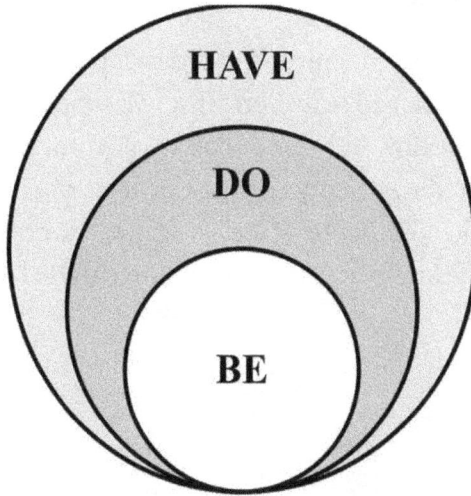

*Figure 16: Have, do, be, reflection model*

## 7. A Personal Mission or Vision of the Future

Take time to develop a personal vision/mission for yourself. This will provide clarity on what you want out of life and focus on the 'be' aspect of the previous activity. It defines what will bring meaning and purpose to your life and helps you to develop clarity on who you want to be and the contribution you want to make in the world. This should be refreshed each year to check that it is still in alignment with who you are and where you are going. This takes time and should not be rushed, and it is best if you have done the previous exercises prior to this.

Covey (2013), in his life-changing book *The 7 habits of highly effective people*, says that one of the starting points of personal effectiveness is to define your personal mission. This is not something that can be done in five minutes; it takes time and effort to reflect on how you have arrived at where you are today and then structure this into a clear definition of who you are and what you stand for.

## 8. Your Wheel of Life

Define your key roles in your life and develop your personal wheel of life that you can use to reflect on. This will support you to identify areas that are working and those that are not working and is a reflective tool that allows you to define the areas of your life that are important to you. The figure 13 below shows the areas of focus for your wheel of life however it is important to choose labels that work for you.

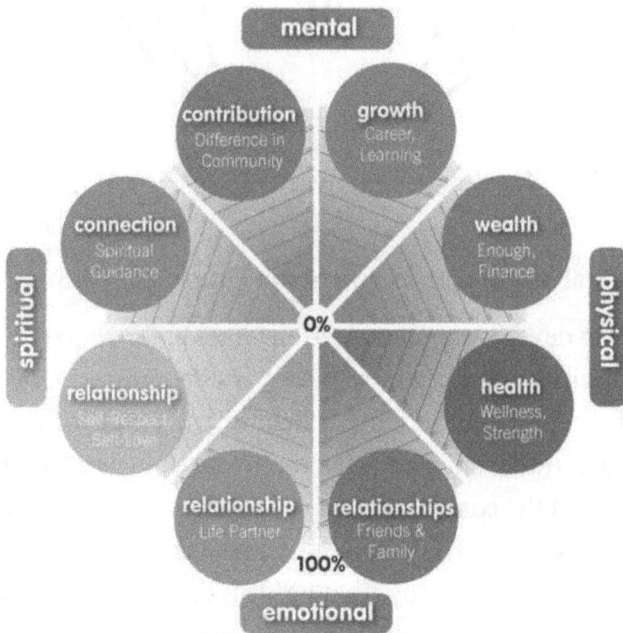

*Figure 17: Wheel of life*

Use the areas of balance—mental, spiritual, emotional and physical— to define the headings that you want on your wheel of life. It is important to use words that connect with you and have meaning in your life. Once you have these, place them on your wheel of life and complete the reflective process below. By completing the wheel, you will be able to identify what is going right in your life right now and what aspects require more attention.

a) Define the key aspects of your wheel of life under the headings mental, spiritual, emotional and physical;

b) Rate each aspect of your life as it is right now (10: you are satisfied with achievements and amount of time invested in this area, 1: you are dissatisfied with achievements and time invested);

c) Rate where you would like to be in the next 12 months on each area (1 to 10);

d) Identify the areas that you need to focus on and develop an action plan for achieving greater balance.

**9. Life Balance activity (similar to wheel of life; select which is appropriate for you).**

| MY LIFE BALANCE | | | |
|---|---|---|---|
| | WHERE AM I RIGHT NOW Score 1–10 | WHERE DO I WANT TO BE Score 1–10 | How will I know that I have achieved it? What will be happening? |
| 1. FINANCE | | | |
| 2. CAREER | | | |
| 3. FAMILY | | | |
| 4. FRIENDS | | | |
| 5. LOVE/ RELATION- SHIP | | | |
| 6. FUN/ RECREATION | | | |

| TAKING CARE OF YOURSELF | | | |
|---|---|---|---|
| | WHERE AM I RIGHT NOW Score 1–10 | WHERE DO I WANT TO BE Score 1–10 | Make a list of what you can do to take care of yourself for each of these categories. What could you do in the immediate future to raise your lowest scores? |
| 1. PHYSICAL WELL-BEING (To live) | | | |
| 2. EMOTIONAL WELL-BEING (To love) | | | |
| 3. MENTAL WELL-BEING (To learn) | | | |
| 4. SPIRITUAL WELL-BEING (To leave a legacy) | | | |

TABLE 4: LIFE BALANCE

Activity to complete this:

a) Give yourself an honest rating out of 10 for each of the areas.

b) Make a decision about where you want to be in the next 12 months for each dimension.

c) Pick 2 areas you want to focus on for the next 6 months.

d) Define what will be different as a result of focusing on these two areas.

## 10. Set some goals for the key aspects of your life

Set out your goals for the year, focusing on the things that are important to you. Use your reflections from your mission, wheel of life and or life balance tools to inform this.

For each of the goals, outline the steps you need to take to achieve your goals. They don't have to be big goals; they can even be things like baking a cake or planning a night out with friends. Just aim for some small achievements that you can tick off a list to help you gain confidence in your ability to commit to building your resilience.

| Areas of Focus | Goal for the next 12 months | Actions to achieve my goal | Date | My Achievements |
|---|---|---|---|---|
|  |  |  |  |  |
|  |  |  |  |  |
|  |  |  |  |  |

## 11. Leadership 360

In a business setting, a leadership 360 (obtaining feedback from your subordinates, your peers and your boss) is a very helpful tool for enhancing our understanding of self and developing a more stable sense of self, incorporating your strengths and weaknesses as a leader. A number of tools are available; some of the ones that are widely used are: Human Synergistics—leadership styles inventory (LSI); The Leadership Circle, Centre for Creative leadership—360 by Design; CPP—EQI 2.0; and the Transformational Leadership MLQ.

## 10.5.2 Tools for Enhancing the Structure of Your Self-concept

### 1. Positive Affirmations

Develop a set of positive affirmations that maintain alignment with your self-concept and use these to maintain clarity and unity.

Treat yourself like you would your best friend or someone you care about, and give yourself positive feedback. In the 1980s, this was a very popular method of assisting people to overcome negative self-concept issues. While it has lost some popularity in recent times, it is regaining its importance as people are faced with the challenges of a VUCA world. This process is a key to ensuring that your self-concept content and structure are aligned. In particular, it will help with re-aligning a structure when damage has been done by external factors. This realignment is very important when people have been subjected to bullying, trauma or abuse of any kind. Positive affirmations allow a person to reaffirm who they are when they have had consistent external messaging that has damaged their self-concept structure.

Some examples of positive affirmations:

| | | | | |
|---|---|---|---|---|
| Life doesn't have to be perfect to be beautiful | I am more than enough | My needs matter | Peace and happiness are inside of me | I am kind to myself |
| I follow my own heart, not the expectations of others | I am gentle with myself | I know I will make mistakes and I understand that is a great way to learn. | I love the person that I am and the person I am becoming | I am not less for making mistakes, I am more, and I learn from them |
| I am strong, beautiful, and confident | I deserve good things to come to me | I am loved by others and by myself | I accept and love myself for who I am | I set boundaries and respect them |
| I stand up for myself | I can do anything I put my mind to | My feelings deserve to be expressed | I am doing my best and that is enough | I nourish my body and soul |
| | I make time to take care of myself | I am capable of amazing things | I am free to be who I want to be | I can and will conquer my fears and not allow them to hold me back |

These positive affirmations need to be used on a regular basis for a period of time to realign the internal structure of the self-concept. They are most effective if you make these statements while looking in the mirror. This allows you to process these statements and fully connect with them.

## 2. Model People with a Strong Sense of Self

Model the behaviours of people who you identify as having a healthy sense of self.

The people we associate and surround ourselves with have a major impact on the person we choose to become. We learn much of what we do from modelling, regardless of whether we are observing constructive or destructive behaviour. One of the best ways to begin feeling more confident is to learn how a confident person thinks, behaves, believes and interacts with others. Much wisdom can be gained from persons who have learned to channel their self-worth and potential. Find someone you admire and can connect with and learn from. Ask this person to be a mentor and to guide you as you grow and develop a healthy self-concept.

## 3. Use positive self-talk and avoid negative self-talk

You absolutely must manage your self-talk so that it is aligned with the self-concept you are developing.

If you believe that you are competent but are constantly undermining this with negative self-talk, you are damaging the clarity of your internal self-structure. You need to program your brain to focus your internal chatter so that it aligns with your sense of self and not with negative and unhelpful thoughts. When you have a positive attitude and positive self-talk, you feel more confident, think more clearly and perform better. Using positive self-talk enhances the health of your self-concept. When you catch yourself using self-defeating language, stop this cycle by reframing your thoughts and refocusing on positive things, such as your strengths your achievements or simply being grateful for what you have. Gratitude is a very powerful emotion that shifts the focus from negative emotions to positive ones.

### 4. Create a High Self-esteem Living Space

Ensure that you make your living space a place where you can go to recharge and unwind. For most people, where they live is a really important aspect of their life. If you feel unhappy in your home or the environment causes stress, this can translate into how you feel about yourself. Make your home inspiring and conducive to your building a healthy sense of self. No matter where you live, find ways to keep it clean, uncluttered, attractive and comfortable.

"It's only when you take responsibility for your life, that you discover how powerful you truly are."

Allanah Hunt

# CHAPTER 11

# DEVELOPING YOUR INTERNAL LOCUS OF CONTROL

In developing our resilience, locus of control is the second dimension identified in the research. The construct of locus of control falls squarely within the literature related to individual differences and is closely associated with the discussions of self-concept well-being. Locus of control is one of the most studied constructs in psychology and focuses on individual differences.

In this chapter, we will define the construct of locus of control and give an overview of the evolution of the construct, a review of the research, and definitions of some tools to enhance your resilience by developing and maintaining an internal locus of control.

Let's unpack each in greater detail.

## 11.1 Defining Locus of Control

Rotter (1990) coined the term 'locus of control', which he defined as the extent to which people vary in how they perceive their actions and the level of causality in the outcomes that are experienced. Locus of control does not indicate an actual command of the environment; rather, it indicates a perception of control or command of one's reactions and actions related to external stimuli. It has been defined as 'the assumed internal state that explains why certain people actively, resiliently and willingly try to deal with difficult circumstances, while others succumb to a range of negative emotions' (Lefcourt, 1991, p. 423). Others have described an internal locus of control as the extent to which individuals assess and have control of their reaction to things that affect them (Rotter, 1990).

In defining locus of control, Rotter identifies two very different strategies and responses—an internal locus of control and an external locus of control. Those with an internal locus believe that their actions and behaviours have a direct impact on the external environment and the results they experience. An internal locus of control refers to an individual's perception that external reinforcement and outcomes are contingent on their behaviour and personal capacity. Individuals who have an internal locus of control also believe that their actions have an impact on their life events and outcomes. In a leadership context, this belief allows the individual to take responsibility for their actions and change their responses to achieve different results. This empowers leaders to control their reactions and behaviour and to recognise that both they and their companies benefit from smart choices and swift, strategic action to mitigate challenges in the environment. This aligns with resilience research, as a key aspect of resilience is a belief that personal responses and actions have an impact on outcomes attained (Lachman & Firth, 2004).

Individuals with an external locus believe that the outcomes they experience are largely out of their control and are a result of fate and/or chance. They believe that they are at the mercy of the external world and do not perceive any benefit in changing their actions or reactions to enhance their circumstances or their impact on the external world.

Those who consider that they are at the mercy of the external world will become passive in their responses and will not attempt to take actions that will assist them in bouncing back (Rotter, 1975). This approach will result in what Seligman calls learned helplessness, or, as we know it in the workplace, a 'victim' mentality. No matter how hard they work, how smart they are, or how prepared they try to be, at the end of the day they will simply become victims of circumstance and other people's actions. An approach like this doesn't align with resilience or effective leadership. In fact, it is just the opposite. Those that choose to allow an external locus of control to dominate their internal processing will generally have the attitude that changing their actions or making a decision to take action will have no impact on the end outcome.

Individuals who have developed an external locus of control can sometimes be very aggressive and antagonistic in times of challenge and change. They feel out of control and therefore hit out at the external factors in an attempt to somehow gain some level of control. This external locus of control is likely to be deeply unconscious and, depending on the individual, may permeate specific aspects of their life or all aspects of life. Rotter distinguished between generalised and specific locus of control. In specific situations, an individual's locus of control may be based on reinforcements from the past that have affected the person's expectations in that particular setting. For example, if someone has previously been made redundant and has developed an external locus of control to this circumstance, should their company make an announcement that they are doing a restructure, their reaction will be externally driven and unhealthy.

In the leadership space, transformational leaders are required to ensure that they take measures to enhance their intra-personal leadership. To do so, they cannot have a victim mentality (Bass, 1985). An internal locus of control and the choice to take responsibility for results is a prerequisite for transformational leadership and effective intra-personal leadership (Lefcourt, 1976).

## 11.2 Evolution of the Construct Locus of Control

Research on locus of control dates back to the early 1960s, when researchers showed that cognitive perceptions of personal control played a role in adjustment and well-being (Liverant, 1960; Phares, 1965; Rotter, 1966). The reason for the continued interest in this topic is that it has been shown to have a significant impact on health, well-being and effectiveness in a variety of domains. As we focus on our own successes in life and in leadership, we can simultaneously make changes in the world around us. We, as humans, are not subject to the roller coaster of an uncontrolled life unless we choose to be (Lillevoll, Kroger & Martinussen, 2013; Ng, Sorensen & Eby, 2006). Rather, we get to choose the direction in which we travel. However, in making the choice of direction, we have to accept that the outcomes that we get are the results of our choices. For example, if we choose not to put any effort into a project, then expecting it to be successful is unrealistic. If we choose to procrastinate on an issue, then we should not be surprised when we are unable to keep up with our workload.

The three originators of the concept of locus of control, Shepherd Liverant, Jerry Phares, and Julian Rotter, were clinical personality psychologists with a social learning focus. Their conceptualisation of the construct evolved out of social learning theory and involved the integration of stimulus-response theories and cognitive theories (Robinson et al., 1991). Liverant, Phares, and Rotter predicted that behaviour is a result of expectations and values that lead to an assessment of how much control an individual perceives themselves to have over their personal outcomes. Today, we believe this is predominantly true. That is why leaders should regularly focus on self-improvement, development and evolving their skillset to become better leaders.

The early work of behaviourists gave indications of the impact of assessed control from the perspective of learned helplessness (Overmier & Seligman, 1967). They showed that animals placed in perceived helpless conditions demonstrated withdrawal behaviours and an acceptance of the condition, which resulted in inaction (Maier & Seligman, 1976). This early behavioural research provided evidence of the impact of perceived control on outcomes and well-being (Overmier & Seligman, 1967). Maier and Seligman's study on animals supports Rotter's research into the assignment of causality. Rotter's research showed that some people are unable to see the relationship between their actions and the consequences, while others are able to positively identify the impact of their behaviours on the results they experienced. These two findings have very diverse implications for well-being. As you can imagine, those who can see the benefit of making positive choices to take action will experience higher levels of resilience than those who choose to become victims of the environment.

## 11.3 Locus of Control: Dispositional Attribute or Trait?

This leads to an important question—one we have asked in terms of each of the constructs. Is locus of control a stable trait, consistent over time, or is it a dispositional attribute with the capacity to change over time? (Bledsoe & Baber, 1978; Lefcourt, 1992). That question has been the subject of great debate over the years. Bledsoe and Baber conceptualised locus of control as a stable, underlying personality construct, arguing that it was a trait. However, Lefcourt (1992) described locus of control as a dispositional attribute, noting that it can change and adapt to time and situations. Levenson (1973) also conceptualised locus of control as adaptable and changeable. A substantial body of research indicates that locus of control is largely learned and can be enhanced with interventions designed to develop an individual's internal locus of control (Bledsoe & Baber, 1978; Lefcourt, 1992). The origins of locus of control in social learning theories indicate that it is a dispositional attribute. If locus of control is part of our social learning, then it can definitely be learned or unlearned.

Locus of control is therefore a dispositional attribute with the capacity to change and develop over time. Those who choose to can develop an internal locus of control, and if they make a decision to take responsibility for their actions, they can shape their outcomes and results. Thus, it is an empowering phenomenon in the leadership arena, as leaders must be able to make adjustments and change their results and outcomes.

A leader who has fallen into the trap of being a victim of their situation or of the people around them will inevitably fail. By contrast, a leader who takes responsibility for the situation and for the people around them has the power to be transformational.

## 11.4 Locus of Control Research

Research has clearly shown that locus of control has a range of positive outcomes for health and well-being (Bandura, 1997; Ong, Bergeman & Bisconti, 2005). An association has been shown between internal locus of control and better physical and mental health, enhanced psychological well-being, lower levels of reactivity to daily life and coping with ageing (Bandura, 1997; Neupert, Almeida & Charles, 2007; Shamir et al., 1993). Internal locus of control has also been found to be predictive of social action, information seeking, and the ability to cope with stress (Hahn, 2000; Kobasa, 1979; Lefcourt, 1992; Levenson, 1974). Research shows that those who develop an internal locus of control and actively seek to own their own actions and results will be more adept at dealing with a broad range of challenges.

A number of studies have shown a direct correlation between locus of control and resilience (Chorpita & Barlow, 1998; Hart, Hofmann, Edelstein & Keller, 1997). Internal locus of control has been shown to correlate with high levels of long-term resilience, enhanced levels of personal confidence in taking action and the ability to cope with change (Glass & Singer, 1972; Gore & Rotter, 1963; Seeman, 1963). For example, Leontopoulou found that locus of control was a significant factor in coping strategies and the ability to remain resilient in challenging situations. Lefcourt and Davidson-Katz (1990) also found that an internal locus of control supports resilience in stressful situations and that it acts as a stress moderator. They concluded that an external locus of control can be used to predict the onset of illness in individuals under pressure.

Leaders who take responsibility for their actions and results are more likely to take action in high-pressure environments and readjust their decisions should the situation call for this. They don't settle for things being done to them, nor do they become victims of their circumstances. They know it is their actions, their decisions and their focus on improving outcomes that leads to success. They also know that if the decision they make does not deliver the results they want, then they can change that decision and shift the results. For years, we have tried to turn leadership into a systematic, step-by-step process, so that if we do certain things, then we are leading effectively. This really does not work in today's world. We live in an ever-changing environment where what works today won't necessarily work tomorrow. In this context, an internal locus of control is imperative. An effective leader must be constantly making decisions, evaluating the impact and, where necessary, readjusting to meet the needs of the changing environment.

The locus of control has many links to other dispositional attributes (Chorpita & Barlow, 1998). Today, researchers continue to look at the impact of locus of control on various characteristics and the resultant implications for health and well-being (Hart et al., 1997). Research in this field has linked locus of control to two constructs closely aligned with resilience—identity and optimism (Lefcourt, 1976; Seligman, 1998). Seligman showed that an internal locus of control is associated with an optimistic outlook that enhances an individual's ability to bounce back. Why wouldn't it? We control our outcomes by taking action, not by passive acceptance of our circumstances. An internal locus of control enhances an individual's level of optimism, sense of identity, well-being and healthy psychological functioning.

## 11.4.1 Locus of Control and Organisational Research

In terms of organisational research, locus of control is one of the more broadly researched dispositional attributes. A growing body of research is now looking at locus of control and its impact on a range of areas in an organisational setting. An internal locus of control has been positively associated with health and well-being outcomes in a business setting (Bartholomew & Horowitz, 1990; Judge & Bono, 2001). Spector's (1997) review found a correlation between an internal locus and higher levels of motivation, enhanced job performance and higher levels of success in organisations. Chen and Silverthorne (2008) showed that an internal locus of control positively moderated levels of job stress while enhancing individuals' experience at work, levels of job performance and motivation. Story and Barbuto (2011) showed significant positive relationships between locus of control, self-concept and levels of motivation in an organisational setting. Judge and Bono's (2001) meta-analysis of research on this topic showed a positive association between an internal locus of control and work outcomes, such as achievement of tasks, higher levels of motivation and enhanced social experiences at work. Flytzani and Nijkamp (2008) found that an internal locus of control was associated with the enhanced ability needed by expatriate managers to adjust to international assignments and the complexity involved in relocating to a different country.

Research has established a strong positive link between our internal locus of control, leadership and the outcomes of leadership (Bass, 1985). Lefcourt (1992) reported a positive correlation between an internal locus of control and healthy outcomes of leadership. Collins's (2001) popular book, *Good to great*, described the results of a five-year study of over 1,400 companies. Collins observed that great organisations are led by individuals who display what is described as 'level five leadership'. This leadership level incorporates an assessment of personal control as a key attribute. Research has positively linked an internal locus of control to several leadership behaviours, such as servant leadership, goal setting, business performance and leadership effectiveness (Bartholomew & Horowitz, 1990; Howell & Avolio, 1993; Noble, 2001). An internal locus of control has also been identified as an essential underlying requirement for leaders to maintain a transformational leadership style (Bass & Riggio, 2006).

Transformational leadership requires that individuals maintain their resilience and take responsibility for their actions and decisions and that an internal locus of control is essential in the maintenance of this. Runyon (1973) found that individuals with an internal locus of control preferred to utilise a participative management style, while those with an external locus of control preferred a more directive style. Howell and Avolio (1993) reiterated this by showing that an internal locus of control was positively related to a preference for a participative management style and increased levels of intellectual stimulation in followers. In an organisational context, strong links are evident between an internal locus of control, the use of healthy leadership styles and the delivery of positive organisational outcomes (Howell & Avolio, 1993).

## 11.5 Locus of Control Simplified

The research on locus of control is well established; however, we need to understand in simple terms what it means to have an internal or external locus of control. Specifically, what does this mean for leaders as they seek to enhance their resilience? Some observable behaviours related to a person's locus of control can help us to understand what this means in simpler terms. These easily observable behaviours can be monitored and observed in ourselves and in the world around us.

- If someone has an **internal locus of control:**

  They will take action to resolve issues and find ways around challenges. They will seek to constructively work with others to achieve outcomes. They will openly talk about their belief that their actions will improve results. Their emotions will be well managed, even under pressure, and they will show realistic reactions to the situation.

- If a person has an **external locus of control:**

  They will regularly seek to blame others for their situation or any mistakes, but they will be happy to take the praise when things go well. If challenges arise, they will back out and not be prepared to take any responsibility for outcomes. They will generate conflict and become divisive by externalising blame and responsibility for outcomes that they don't like or don't agree with. They will become emotionally charged (could show up as aggression, withdrawal, depression, anxiety or emotional overwhelm) and will demonstrate unconsciously driven, emotive reactions.

The world of social media, online influencers and reality television is replete with evidence of the external locus of control described above. While it may look like these individuals have internal strength, we can very easily observe the external locus of control in their actions and behaviours. In these contexts, if individuals have an external locus of control, they will constantly be seeking validation from the external world. If they don't get this validation, then they will seek to blame someone or something else for their circumstances. They will not be able to accept criticism without resorting to external blame, which will turn into very negative reactions and actions.

In simple terms, here is a summary of the external and internal locus of control.

**People who have an external locus of control:**

o   Believe that outcomes are under the control of other people, fate or luck;

o   Are defensive when challenges arise;

o   Blame external factors or people for their circumstances;

o   Believe they are victims of the situation and nothing they do can make a difference;

o   Don't see any point in taking action or they apportion blame to others;

o   Require lots of external validation;

o   Are naturally pessimistic.

**People who have an internal locus of control:**

o   Believe that one's own behaviour makes a difference to the outcomes achieved;

o   Take ownership when things go wrong;

o   Feel responsible for outcomes;

o   Are able to validate themselves and don't require positive validation to stay optimistic;

o  Are naturally optimistic;

o  Make adjustments to situations to improve results;

o  Don't blame others, but seek to work with others to change the outcomes;

When a person is under pressure, the impact of locus of control is very observable. The differences are defined below.

| INTERNAL LOCUS OF CONTROL | EXTERNAL LOCUS OF CONTROL |
|---|---|
| • Looks for ways to remain positive<br>• Recognises that everyone is doing their best<br>• Finds solutions to issues that arise<br>• Looks for opportunities to help others and contribute for the greater good<br>• Lives life to its fullest, even when circumstances are not ideal<br>• Appreciative and grateful | • Looks for someone to blame<br>• Does not take action to do things differently<br>• Easily irritable and agressive<br>• Critical of everyone<br>• Talks about and listens to things that are negative<br>• Constantly moans and complains |

TABLE 5: INTERNAL AND EXTERNAL LOCUS OF CONTROL

## 11.6 Improving Your Locus of Control

Decades of research outline a strong correlation between an internal locus of control and resilience. If you truly intend to be a transformational leader and want to build your resilience, then you will need to ensure you maintain an internal locus of control in leading your team and your organisation. To shift from external to internal requires a significant realignment of your views about control.

Three key areas require focus when developing an internal locus of control:

1. Accepting that you do not have control over the world around you or the actions of others;

2. Learning to choose your reaction regardless of the challenges you face;

3. Developing strategies to maintain a belief that you are responsible for your outcomes and your actions.

The tools outlined below are by no means comprehensive, but they offer a range of options to develop an internal locus of control.

## 1. JOURNALLING

As noted in the section on self-concept well-being, journalling is a powerful tool to unpick your internal reactions.

## 2. FEEDBACK

Feedback is key to shifting your unconscious behaviours and reactions. You are unlikely to be able to always objectively assess your own behaviours and actions; therefore, seeking feedback from others, reflecting on it, processing it and taking appropriate actions are critical. The best choice is to have someone close to you who will honestly tell you when you are becoming a victim and demonstrating an external locus of control. Spotting people who have shifted over to an external locus is very easy, as the change is evident in their language and what they talk about. If you are constantly complaining about other people's actions or reactions, situations you don't like or want or things that are impacting you that you don't like, then you are very likely en route to becoming the victim. Having someone who can help to point this out for you is advantageous. Everyone moves to an external locus of control at some point: the challenge is to see when you have and move back to an internal locus. Feedback is key to this.

## 3. OBSERVE YOUR LOCUS OF CONTROL—INTERNAL VS EXTERNAL

One of the first things you will need to learn to do is to notice when you are becoming reactive to issues and using an external locus of control. To do this, you will need to step back from the issue that is causing you to become externally driven. This will allow you to give yourself the space to reflect on why you are being reactive and will provide the opportunity to adjust your reaction. Stephen Covey talks about the essence of this in Habit 1 – Be proactive. He describes it as being able to put a gap between an external stimulus and the response that we choose. In that gap is the capacity to select an internal locus of control. Without this, we simply become reactionary to the world around us.

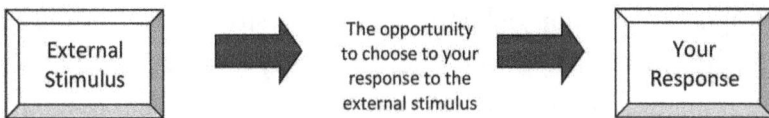

*Figure 18: Be Proactive (Covey)*

The key to developing an internal locus of control is the ability to recognise that we all have the potential to be reactive to a stimulus. Actively putting a gap between stimulus and response will enable us to choose our responses rather than becoming reactive. If we are reactive, we are simply allowing the stimulus to define our response and we become a victim of the circumstances. To change this, we need to observe ourselves becoming reactive and make the choice to reassess and select a reaction that is not driven by an external locus of control.

The simplest way to explain this is to use a common experience. We all experience traffic at some point. You have a choice in how you respond:

- You can become reactionary, get angry and stressed and allow yourself to become externally controlled, or

- You can make a choice to put a gap between the stimulus, not react to the traffic and choose a response that will allow you to enjoy the journey.

It is our choice to be reactionary or to put a gap between us and our response. The choice to have a gap between the stimulus and response allows us to take ownership of our actions and reactions and the outcomes we experience. Fundamentally, until we are able to step back from our reactive responses, we are trapped by an external locus of control and will fall into a victim mentality. Whether we are responding reactively to a child's bad behaviour, the behaviour of a colleague, or a major global disaster, it doesn't matter. They are all reducing our resilience over time. This is key in today's world, as we have numerous things that are traps for an external locus of control, such as social media and the reactivity associated with it, conspiracy theories that externalise responsibility for situations and much of our television (reality shows, in particular) that demonstrate an external locus of control.

## 4. BREATHING

Learning to bring your breathing into consciousness will support you in putting a gap between the stimulus and the response. Developing the capacity to notice your breathing and to breathe deeply is very useful when you are pressurised. Simply observing your breath, slowing down your breathing and managing your heart rate will enable you to more effectively put a gap between the stimulus and your response. The Alexander Technique is one of the more well-known strategies in this arena. Most martial arts also have some sort of breathing control technique. It is also possible to observe your breathing.

## 5. MINDFULNESS AND GROUNDING ACTIVITIES

MINDFULNESS ACTIVITIES are useful in situations with any level of pressure. They support you to settle yourself and ensure you don't become reactive. Many mindfulness activities are available that take just a few minutes and will support you in putting a gap between a stimulus and your response. If you find yourself under pressure, you may sometimes need to step away from the situation and centre yourself in order to be able to put a gap between the stimulus and your response.

GROUNDING ACTIVITIES allow you to bring balance and to manage your reactions more effectively. Many martial arts have grounding strategies. However, simple ways are available for grounding ourselves when under pressure: going for a walk and connecting with nature, taking a break to get a coffee or water, giving ourselves a moment to connect with our bodies and get out of our heads, running water over our hands and noticing how this feels and so on.

## 6. SHIFT YOUR PERSPECTIVE

Once you have put a gap between the stimulus and your response, you now need to shift your perspective on the presenting issue. You have probably noticed colleagues that are in victim mode in relation to a specific event or situation. They demonstrate that they have given up on taking action and are blaming the event or situation. These people rarely recognise they have any level of control over what they are experiencing. The same applies to you, if you are in victim mode over a situation, person or event. You will need to shift your perspective on the situation. In place of a victim mentality, you will need to develop the perspective that your decisions and actions do impact on your outcomes in the particular situation.

This change in perspective can be changed:

- Instantly by a shift in mindset,
- By using a journal to process a shift in perspective, or
- By assistance from a counsellor, mentor or coach if you have a more deeply embedded perspective.

Neurolinguistics provides three key strategies to bring about the shift:

- **Disassociation**—mentally remove yourself from the situation, then visualise yourself talking to a mentor and accepting advice and guidance on how to deal with the situation.

- **Content reframing**—if you are constantly anticipating that bad things will happen, then, when the thought comes up, you choose constructive thoughts. For example, if you worry about your partner having an affair, you are likely to become needy and this may cause them to do exactly what you fear. To change this, you must reframe the content and think about all the great things you want to do together.

- **Anchoring**—when you experience negative emotions, focus on something that you know brings positive emotions. For example, if you are fearful of presentations, before you start your presentation, focus on something that makes you feel calm.

## 7. SYSTEMATICALLY ASSESS ALL ASPECTS OF YOUR LIFE— REVIEW FOR INTERNAL/EXTERNAL LOCUS OF CONTROL

Once you have shifted perspective on one situation, the time has come to clean up any other areas of life where you have developed an external locus of control. Recognising that you have control over your outcomes in one situation is not sufficient. Rather, part of owning your resilience is doing all you can to evolve in all aspects. This requires focus. With focus, you can shift your attitude about all aspects of your work environment in which you have become externally driven.

From a leadership perspective, developing your team's internal locus of control is also important, as is supporting them to take responsibility for their actions and their outcomes. Transformational leaders grounded in an internal locus of control will naturally lead their teams in the same direction. You cannot have one without the other. This starts with hiring people who share an internal locus of control; if they don't, then support them to build one.

Locus of control, the second dimension of resilient, transformational leadership, is imperative to your overall development and success as a leader. It is a self-fulfilling prophecy in many ways and is grounded in self-responsibility and the notion that you are responsible for your own outcomes.

"If you want to get positive results you have to refuse to think negative thoughts by substituting them with positive constructive ones. When you develop a positive attitude towards life, your life will start having a positive result."

Roy Bennett

# CHAPTER 12

# DEVELOPING YOUR CONSTRUCTIVE THINKING

Constructive thinking is the third dimension in the model of leader resilience (Folan, 2019). From a research perspective, a long-term interest has been expressed in the impact of cognitive processing on human capacity and individual difference. The cognitive processing capacity of an individual has been shown to differentiate between people in a range of contexts, and much evidence indicates that this plays a key part in our ability to function in our world. We are made very aware of these differences in our journey though the education system in schools and universities. Some people achieve high scores in this setting, while others experience challenges in achieving a pass. For a significant period, the early research into individual differences and cognitive processing focused on developing measures that would allow us to understand the differences in levels of intelligence. Intelligence Quotients (IQ) were used extensively to measure intelligence and to identify the link between IQ and individual success in a range of domains.

Differences in academic attainment have definitely been linked to our IQ levels. Attempts have also been made to link IQ to success in a range of settings. While a link has been shown between IQ and academic attainment, the links between IQ and the success of individuals in other domains are more tenuous. Issues have also been identified with the assumption of a direct link between IQ and success in the broader life context. Not all high-IQ individuals succeed in an academic environment, nor does a high IQ necessarily result in success in broader life. If I asked you to identify someone with very high IQ who has not been successful or who has not achieved their 'potential', you would likely be able to identify someone. In all likelihood, you could also identify someone who is academically average (only scraped through in the school system) but has been incredibly successful and achieved well past the potential that was attributed to them based on their IQ scores. Therefore, the differences in success in both an academic environment and in life in general can't be simplistically attributed to IQ alone. More recent research has shown that attainment of any type requires the effective functioning of the brain as a whole and not just the aspects that are measured by IQ testing.

The ability to effectively utilise the broader functioning of our brain and process information from the external world in a constructive manner is an essential component of a leader's ability to achieve personal, team and organisation success. The following sections outline the definition and evolution of constructive thinking and the research that supports its importance in effective functioning and in achieving success.

## 12.1 Defining Constructive Thinking

For many years, research focused almost exclusively on the study of intelligence, as measured by IQ scores, to assist us in understanding the link between mental processing and individual difference. Early studies in this area focused on overall intelligence and measured this using intelligence quotients (IQ). While interest continues in how IQ influences leadership and organisational outcomes, the research has broadened to look at other aspects of the brain's operation that have an impact on achievement. IQ research has produced mixed results, and IQ evidently does not offer a comprehensive understanding of the depth and complexity of the mental processing required for success. This is particularly the case in relation to leadership and successful outcomes in an organisational setting (Bergman, Corovic, Ferrer-Wreder & Modig, 2014). In fact, most of us could name at least one super smart, high-IQ person who is totally incompetent at leading themselves and others.

Constructive thinking has broadened the focus of research to look not only at IQ and the ability of the brain to process information, but also at the impact of the other aspects of mental processing. Aspects such as the unconscious or emotional processing that occur in the brain may impede or enhance the ability to process information (Bertua, Anderson & Salgado, 2005; Epstein, 2014). Your ability to process your emotions, reactions and biases has significant implications for your ability to effectively access the full capacity of your brain, and serious implications for your ability to maintain resilience during tough times. Much of this processing is unconscious, which makes it more complex and difficult to measure. In addition, it has a significant impact on the ability to effectively lead others.

**Constructive thinking** is the capacity to process and interpret external stimuli, events or circumstances in a way that reduces re-activity and allows you to select responses that support personal effectiveness and maintain personal resilience (Epstein, 2014). In outlining a definition of constructive thinking, Epstein described the operation of two separate minds—the **rational** and the **experiential** mind.

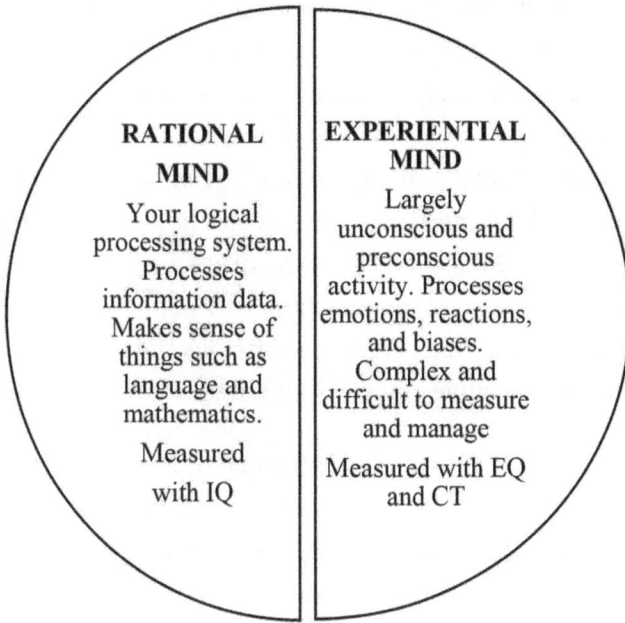

RATIONAL MIND

Your logical processing system. Processes information data. Makes sense of things such as language and mathematics.

Measured with IQ

EXPERIENTIAL MIND

Largely unconscious and preconscious activity. Processes emotions, reactions, and biases. Complex and difficult to measure and manage

Measured with EQ and CT

*Figure 19: The rational and experiential mind (Epstein 2014)*

The **rational** mind houses the capacity to reason and solve mathematical and abstract problems. The ability of this mind is to cognitively process factual and precise data and develop sound thought processes. Unconscious and preconscious activity have limited direct impact on this aspect of the mind. The rational mind makes sense of things such as language, mathematics and data. It is the logical, rational processing system of the brain. When we measure IQ, we are focused on assessing this aspect of the processing system. In many ways, this is how we as a society have traditionally defined intelligence.

The **experiential** mind is a separate aspect of the mind. This aspect is driven by unconscious and preconscious thoughts and is connected to emotions and experiences. This processing is much more challenging to understand and control, as many of the stimuli we experience are unconscious and emotionally driven. This aspect of the mind also influences the operation of the rational mind when it is unconsciously activated. Destructive sequences in the experiential mind can disrupt or interfere with the activity of the rational mind, thereby destabilising an individual and impacting outcomes. For example, a car might cut in front of a driver and trigger an unconscious emotional reaction that overrides the logical mind, so the driver gets out of the car and punches the other driver (road rage). The experiential mind must make sense of unconscious and preconscious thought. If it does not, it will stimulate negative emotions and destructive reactions.

In Epstein's view, the combined influence of the two minds is what defines our behaviour. The experiential mind has a stronger impact on emotions, responses and actions related to well-being and psychological adjustment. By contrast, the rational mind manages the logical aspects of functioning. Epstein (2014, p.21) defined constructive thinking as 'the degree to which a person's automatic thinking—the thinking that occurs without deliberate intention—facilitates solving problems in everyday life at a minimum cost in stress.' Constructive thinking is the filter through which we interpret our world and make negative or positive interpretations of events and experiences.

Our ability to manage this automatic thinking in our experiential mind has a strong correlation with our levels of resilience. To process the environment and surrounding stimuli, we must construct explicit models of our experiences that are formed by our dual cognitive processing system. We filter our daily experiences through this dual-processing system of the rational and experiential mind. This allows us to define our cognitions as either constructive or destructive. Healthy, constructive thinking patterns require that the experiential mind consciously manages the impact of unconscious and preconscious thoughts to deliver healthy responses to the external world. Importantly, the internal constructions must be actively selected rather than unconsciously or emotionally driven. In essence, we need to learn how to consciously manage the unconscious and preconscious aspects of the experiential mind if we are going to be effective in our processing and respond healthily to situations. If we manage this, we are in control; if we don't, then our unconscious and preconscious are in control. Take, for example, the reactions of people to lockdowns during COVID. The purchase of toilet paper was an experiential mind reaction: no matter how logical the advice was regarding no need to panic buy, it still happened. If people were able to logically process the information with their rational mind, they would have been able to make a decision based on the information provided and they would not need to buy excessive quantities of toilet paper. The reactions were driven by the unconscious and preconscious reactions of the experiential mind. The processing in the experiential mind was driven by an unconscious fear reaction to the unknown threat of COVID. No matter how much the politicians and others implored people not to panic buy, it still continued. This panic buying is an example of the experiential mind in action and shows very clearly how this can take over the rational mind's operation.

Constructive thinking is the process whereby the experiential mind aligns with healthy interpretations of events and circumstances and chooses reactions and actions that are constructive. It exposes interpretations that are not useful and that are influenced by unconscious and preconscious thought, thereby ensuring a consistent review before we take action or react to a situation. If done right, we are able to constructively process information and enhance our well-being and resilience.

## 12.2 Evolution of Constructive Thinking

Effective leadership in today's world calls for cognitive and emotional processing of a vast range of internal and external information by individuals, who are required to assess and review situations to deliver balanced decisions and healthy responses (Draghici & Draghici, 2007). In particular, balanced decision-making is an essential aspect of leadership and is imperative for the development of healthy interpersonal relationships and for the delivery of a transformational leadership style.

Constructive thinking is a new and evolving area of organisational psychology which has developed from a long history of research looking at the impact of the mind and its operation on individual differences and leadership. Three key areas of research have significantly influenced constructive thinking models. These are:

1) general intelligence research, which predates constructive thinking research and has a long history in relation to our understanding of individual difference within the field of psychology (Galton, 1869);

2) executive function and modes of thinking within the area of neuropsychology and experimental psychology (Parkin & Java, 1999; Kahneman, 2011); and

3) emotional intelligence (EI) within the field of organisational psychology (Goleman, 1995; Salovey & Mayer, 1990).

## 12.2.1 General Intelligence Research (IQ)

IQ research and the measurement of IQ as a dimension of leadership and success in a work context has a long history in organisational psychology (Bergman et al., 2014; Bertua et al., 2005; Binet & Simon, 1916; Terman & Oden, 1947). The various measures of IQ were among the very earliest areas of research investigating individual differences within the field of psychology (Binet & Simon, 1916; Galton, 1869). The investigation into IQ and its implications for success in a range of domains has remained a consistent area of interest in the search for an enhanced understanding of individual differences (Bergman et al., 2014; Binet & Simon, 1916; Galton, 1869). Research on IQ has demonstrated its importance in accounting for positive outcomes and enhanced levels of success in organisational and academic settings (Bertua et al., 2005; Terman & Oden, 1947). IQ has been associated with success in life, achievement in the work context, academic achievement and leadership ability (Bertua et al., 2005; Chmiel et al., 2012).

IQ undeniably has some positive impact on success in various domains, including leadership effectiveness (Gottfredson, 1997; Terman & Oden, 1947). Research in the organisational context has shown that IQ is positively linked to the ability to deliver a positive leadership style. For example, Nguyen (2002) showed the importance of an individual's IQ in supporting leaders in effective management of themselves and in leading others. However, more recent evidence suggests that other factors are involved in success and academic attainment (Bergman et al., 2014). For example, a longitudinal study by Bergman et al. (2014) showed that although high-IQ individuals are 10 times more likely to obtain a master's degree than those with an average IQ, a proportion of high-IQ people never achieve even a graduate qualification. Epstein and Meier (1989, p. 332) also noted that the results of IQ in a work setting have been mixed, and 'several studies have failed to find significant correlations between IQ and work performance.' In their meta-analysis, DeNeve and Cooper (1998) concluded that other factors aside from IQ have an influence on positive outcomes in a work environment, with factors such as emotional stability, locus of control, hardiness and positive affectivity more likely than IQ to predict subjective well-being and success at work. These findings indicate that while IQ provides some insight into success in a work setting, it does not on its own offer a broad enough understanding of the processing that underpins differences in capability, particularly the capacity to lead others (DeNeve &

Cooper, 1998). For example, de Haro and Costa (2014) found that, after controlling for IQ as measured by general mental ability, emotional intelligence is a more valid predictor of career and leadership success. These findings indicate that although IQ is an important factor in positive outcomes for individuals, other aspects of mental processing play a part in individual achievement and success in an organisational setting.

Constructive thinking is a new and evolving area of research, but it offers a significant and important understanding of cognitive processing, including IQ, as well as an approach for exploring other aspects of mental processing. This broader conceptualisation has a high level of relevance to our understanding of resilience and its impact on leadership in today's world. Constructive thinking broadens the focus on mental processing to include the subjective interpretation of events and experiences that are not only cognitive but have implications for the maintenance of well-being and resilience (Epstein, 2014).

### 12.2.2 Executive Function

The second area of research that has links to constructive thinking research is the executive function and modes of thinking (Baddeley, 1996; Kahneman, 2011). The executive function has been studied for many years within the field of neuropsychology (Baddeley, 1996; Santos-Ruiz et al., 2012), with studies describing the operation of the brain on memory, processing and decision-making. This research provides a neurological understanding of the aspects of the brain that support successful processing and enable leaders to constructively process their experiences to enhance outcomes (Baddeley, 1996).

Executive function has been described as consisting of an integrated set of neurological systems that play a part in memory, mental functioning, flexibility and accuracy of decision-making (Santos-

Ruiz et al., 2012). Research on executive function shows that the operation of the mind is significantly impacted by conscious and unconscious processes and that this has a direct link to well-being and adaptive functioning (Baddeley, 1996). This conceptualisation of executive function is closely aligned with Epstein's (1998) description of the dual-processing system of the rational and the experiential mind. From a leadership perspective, this has significant implications for a leader's ability to effectively manage the large volumes of data that they are exposed to and the emotional impact of working with people (Epstein, 2014).

A variety of conceptualisations have been put forward for the executive function, with some researchers postulating it as a single entity. Conversely, others argue that it is a dual-processing system responsible for the processing and organisation of emotions, thoughts, memories and decision-making and that this entity results in a broad range of human reactions and behaviours (Parkin & Java, 1999; Santos-Ruiz et al., 2012). Kahneman's (2011) definition of two processing systems is very closely aligned with Epstein's (1998) constructive thinking. The theory defines two systems of thinking: system 1, the intuitive thinking system, which is instinctive and emotional, and system 2, the deliberate, analytic system where reason dominates. System 1 has the capacity to impact the effectiveness of system 2 and undermine logical processing. This aligns closely with Epstein's (1998) two minds that together perform the function of mediating, integrating and processing.

These processing systems play an important part in the development and maintenance of resilience and well-being, with direct implications for the ability of leaders to deliver a consistent and positive style (Baddeley, 1996; Epstein, 2014). Cerni, Curtis and Colmar (2010, 2014) showed a positive correlation between global constructive thinking and transformational leadership.

### 12.2.3 Emotional Intelligence

One area of research is closely associated with constructive thinking and has high relevance to the discussions on resilience in a work and leadership frame; this is emotional intelligence (EI). EI has played an important role in the evolution of the theories of leadership and constructive thinking (Salovey & Mayer, 1990). It is also a highly debated topic in popularist leadership literature. It has generated an ongoing volume of research over the last two decades in the field of organisational psychology (Goleman, 1995; Salovey & Mayer, 1990). The research on EI broadens the discussion on individual differences by challenging traditional thinking around what is required for success and opening up the discussion of multiple intelligences.

The concept of multiple intelligences started the debate and assisted us in moving away from the idea of individual differences that focused almost exclusively on IQ. A number of descriptions of other types of intelligence have been presented over the years, including visual, spatial, musical, kinaesthetic, social, linguistic and emotional (Hernández-Torrano et al., 2014). However, outside of IQ, EI is the only one that has gained significant momentum in the organisational psychology domain.

For the last 20 years, the topic of EI and its implications for work and leadership success have had a strong focus. EI is the ability to monitor and manage feelings and emotions in oneself and others and to make use of this to define appropriate actions and reactions. Goleman popularised the construct of EI with his bestselling book Emotional intelligence (1996). We have seen a continued growth and interest in EI in the work setting and particularly in relation to leadership.

Research has shown that higher levels of EI result in enhanced levels of resilience and positive life outcomes (Maulding, Peters, Roberts,

Leonard & Sparkman, 2012; Schneider, Lyons & Khazon, 2013). For example, Di Fabio and Saklofske (2014) have shown that higher levels of EI promote enhanced personal resources and are thus associated with higher levels of resilience. Research in this area has been extended into the leadership domain to show that EI enhances resilience and leads to higher levels of leadership capability (Maulding et al., 2012). Research has also found a positive correlation between higher levels of EI and the ability to deliver a transformational leadership style.

Constructive thinking appears to offer an even broader perspective on this aspect of human difference by integrating aspects of both IQ and EQ in its conceptualisation. A clear link exists between the concept of EQ and the experiential mind, whereas IQ is associated with the functioning of the rational mind. Both minds have implications for effective human functioning and individual resilience.

EI is the ability to develop an awareness of emotional reactions and to manage these in an appropriate way. From the perspective of constructive thinking, the starting point of emotional responses is the healthy or unhealthy processing of information in the dual minds: experiential and rational. The cognitive construction that is created from this processing results in either a constructive or destructive sequence that then triggers an emotional reaction (either positive or negative). This view of emotional management asserts that if the cognitive processing is constructive, then a healthy emotional response will be elicited and no management of the emotion will be required (Epstein, 2014; Goleman, 1995).

Epstein showed that if we can actively process and manage our pre-conscious and unconscious thoughts, then we have the capacity to define an incident as constructive before it affects our brain in a way that provokes a negative emotional reaction. Constructive thinking is therefore the cognitive ability to process external stimuli in a healthy way through the experiential mind to ensure maintenance of positive emotions which result in well-being. This ability for constructive processing creates elevated levels of resilience and the ability to bounce back from challenge and adversity.

## 12.3 Constructive Thinking: Dispositional Attribute or Trait

Now that we have explored each of the three dimensions of resilience, we need to consider whether constructive thinking is a dispositional attribute or a trait. We have already positioned self-concept well-being and locus of control as dispositional attributes. The same debate exists in the research on constructive thinking. Therefore, reviewing the issue is important to decide whether constructive thinking falls within the trait or dispositional attribute conceptualisation.

We define rational thinking, one aspect of constructive thinking, as an individual difference in the tendency to think logically, consciously and rationally. If separated out from the activity of the experiential mind, this ability is found consistently over time. Therefore, rational thinking, as measured by IQ, is more closely linked to trait research. Conversely, the operation of the experiential mind is more volatile and adaptable and may change over time and circumstances, depending on the impact of unconscious and preconscious constructions. The changeability of the experiential mind places it firmly within the arena of a dispositional attribute.

Epstein has shown that we can develop the experiential mind to enhance our ability to process unconscious and preconscious thoughts, thereby increasing the capacity to cope, adapt and maintain well-being. We see this all the time, as individuals change their perception of an incident and are then able to change their reactions and respond positively to something that was previously generating a negative response. The more we can ensure that our processing of events is constructive, the better we are able to manage our emotions.

Remember, constructive thinking is linked to the processing strategy of the experiential mind that has the capacity to adapt and change. The experiential mind directly influences the rational mind's ability to process and make decisions. Therefore, constructive thinking aligns as a dispositional attribute with the previous two dimensions: self-concept well-being and internal locus of control.

## 12.3.1 Constructive Thinking Research

This is a new area of study in psychology, with a limited number of studies and even fewer studies in the organisational arena (Epstein & Meier, 1989). Most of Epstein's (1998) early research on constructive thinking focused on the development and validation of the construct and the Constructive Thinking Inventory. Erez and Judge (2001) conducted further research to validate the inventory and showed a strong correlation between constructive thinking and emotional coping. They also found strong links between constructive thinking and locus of control, self-efficacy, self-esteem, and emotional stability (Erez & Judge, 2001).

From a well-being perspective, research has found that constructive thinking is positively correlated with psychological adjustment and well-being (Bostic, 2003). Research has shown that high levels of constructive thinking result in greater vitality, improved mental health and fewer unhealthy physical symptoms (Bostic, 2003). Constructive thinking also predicts enhanced levels of well-being, positive affect and happiness over time (Harris & Lightsey, 2005). Destructive thinking patterns, such as perfectionism and overgeneralisation, will lead to lower levels of well-being and reduced positive affect. Research in this area has also demonstrated that high levels of constructive thinking contribute significantly to reducing stress, promoting efficiency and enhancing the ability to interpret pressure in a positive way, while allowing individuals to process real threats more effectively (Epstein, 1998; Evers et al., 2004).

From a resilience perspective, constructive thinking contributes to the ability to bounce back and deal with challenges and setbacks. It contributes to resilience, satisfaction in life, coping and a sense of personal coherence. The sound and healthy processing of cognitive reactions results in balanced and sustainable decision-making and reactions in a business setting (Curtis, King & Russ, 2017).

From a leadership perspective, constructive thinking has a significant impact on positive ratings for transformational leadership (Atwater & Yammarino, 1993; Cerni, Curtis & Colmar, 2008). Based on the research to date, constructive thinking has important implications for our understanding of differences in leadership capability. It is a key dimension of resilience that supports the ability of individuals to deliver a transformational leadership style (Epstein, 2014; Erez & Judge, 2001).

As the third dimension of resilient leadership, constructive thinking allows leaders to quickly and efficiently process otherwise challenging obstacles and make important decisions. In the fast-moving world of business, leaders often have only a split second to decide on the direction they should take. Constructive thinking empowers a quick evaluation of the facts and then identification of the stressors and touch points.

As you enhance the management of your internal processing system, you will notice that it produces remarkable results for you in managing adversity and coping with tough times. You will no longer be driven by unconscious and preconscious reactions that are outside your control; you will be able to select your reactions effectively. As a leader, you must have the capacity for healthy processing and responding to issues even when you are under pressure. In simple terms, no matter how smart you are or what your IQ is, if you don't manage your experiential mind, your ability to make good decisions and effectively lead others is compromised.

When our mental processing isn't helpful, we call it destructive, and this can result in cognitive distortions and mental processing challenges (Epstein, 2014). If these distortions remain unchallenged, they become part of the automatic processing that occurs in our minds. When we are stressed, anxious or under pressure, these distortions will dominate our thinking. Unmanaged, these become habitual thinking styles that do not serve us well and are likely to stimulate negative emotions. This processing is largely unconscious and occurs so rapidly that we hardly notice it and are unlikely to be able to stop to question this thinking. The only way to make a change is to bring the distortions to the conscious mind and then to make a decision to shift this destructive thinking. These cognitive distortions can profoundly affect our ability to think and act in a calm, rational and effective manner.

Here are some common **cognitive distortions** that can occur:

- **Irritation fixation:** we only focus on what's wrong or irritating. This narrows our view of the world and ignores other positive or neutral aspects.

- **Mind-reading:** we assume we know what others are thinking without confirming. This can result in very serious misconceptions that have no basis in reality.

- **Fortune-telling:** we assume, and pessimistically predict, a negative outcome without testing the evidence. This stops us from predicting or imagining potential positive outcomes.

- **Catastrophised thinking:** we make things out to be much worse than they actually are. We assume that something is so awful or horrid that it will affect all aspects. We seek external validation of this from others who share the same views.

- **Perfectionistic thinking:** we demand perfection in a world that is not perfect. This thinking is pervasive, impacting both ourselves and others. It places unrealistic expectations that can't be attained.

- **All-or-nothing thinking:** we think in extremes and are unable to open ourselves to the possibility that it may be some, rather than all or nothing. This creates arousal, reduces self-esteem or colours one's opinions of others. There is no middle ground in this thinking.

- **Tyranny of the shoulds/musts/oughts:** these are rigid demands and unrealistic expectations we make of ourselves, others or the world. The underlying and unspoken assumption is that consequences will be dire if these demands aren't met; for example, 'I must be right', 'Why can't you see things my way?'

- **Overgeneralising:** deciding that our negative experience applies to all situations. Words such as always, never, everyone, nobody, all or none indicate overgeneralisations.

- **Abusive labelling:** we give ourselves or others a label, as though a single word could describe a complex person completely. For example, 'I'm lousy', 'I'm stupid'. Over time, we become what we are thinking or we treat others in the way we have defined them.

- **Judgemental thinking:** we judge others and ourselves against unrealistic expectations.

- **Blame thinking:** this is a learned thinking style that forces us to find someone to blame when things go wrong. It is a protection mechanism to stop us from feeling bad about mistakes in the short term, but it has long-term implications for stress.

- **Deletion:** we simply delete information and data that are not aligned with our thinking or we choose not to hear that someone else may have a point of view or an opinion.

- **Distorted thinking:** we distort what we hear and fit our perception into our own distorted picture of the world. We are unable to view things accurately.

- **Flatlining:** we have taught ourselves not to react to anything that may stimulate an emotional reaction. This stops you from feeling pain, but it also stops you from feeling pleasure and happiness. This emotionless reaction to life causes others to see you as cold and aloof.

Identifying negative destructive thinking isn't always easy. In many ways, it is like a computer program operating in the background. You aren't even aware it is impacting your thinking, your ability to manage pressure and your life. Rest assured, if you do not make this thinking conscious, it can and will derail your ability to develop your resilience and evolve into a transformational leader. To that end, what is the cure for destructive thinking? The answer to that question rests in our choice to make our thinking conscious and then to make changes to this thinking where required. Before we move on to strategies though, let's explore constructive thinking from a pragmatic perspective.

## 12.4 Constructive Thinking Simplified

The research on constructive thinking, while new, is having a significant impact in bringing about change in resilience levels. We have discussed the research and the development of this construct, but what does it mean in simple terms? According to Epstein, once we have constructed events in a destructive way, our behaviour is harder to moderate. If we can first change the way we interpret and construe the situation in our brain, then our emotions and behaviour will follow.

How the brain works to support constructive and destructive thinking.

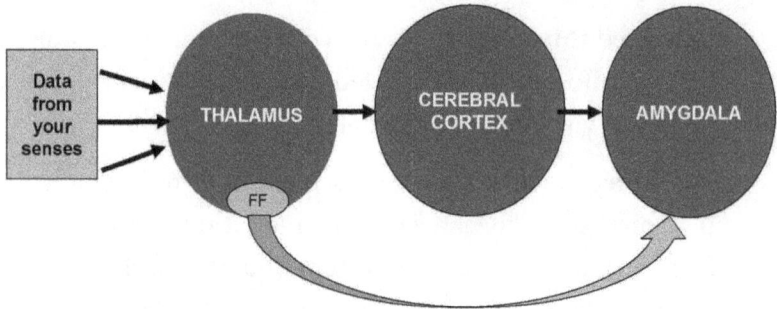

*Figure 20: Constructive thinking and the brain*

Data from the world around you enters your brain via your thalamus, a small receptor organ in the brain. This information is then passed through the cerebral cortex, which is your central processing system. Your cerebral cortex is a bit like the hard drive of your computer. Just as the hard drive of your computer has all your information, the cerebral cortex houses all your information about you. This includes your values, beliefs, experiences, personality, language, upbringing, family culture and all other the data that you have collected over a lifetime. Information and data from the external world are sifted through the cerebral cortex. This is an unconscious process and happens almost instantly in most cases. Once you have processed your experience through your cerebral cortex, you then stimulate an emotional reaction in your amygdala. In essence, your choice of emotions is driven by your cerebral cortex evaluation of the situation and not the situation itself.

If we are going to enhance our internal processing, we must first clean up unhelpful data in our cerebral cortex and become more conscious of the health of our processing. This will enable us to respond more positively and shift our thinking when required. Once the cerebral cortex has processed the data, it then stimulates the emotional response in the amygdala. If we are going to enhance our resilience, we need to ensure that our cerebral cortex is not running viruses or distortions that will affect information processing and cause an unnecessary negative emotion. In practical terms, the processing of external situations in our heads can often have only a limited correlation with the actual situation.

To define how this works, we will use a very simple event that most of us have experienced or seen happen: Mary, one of the team members, has walked into the office and not said hello. We will start by looking at how a constructive sequence can be formed in the amygdala and then how a destructive sequence can be formed. An important point to understand is that the sequence is not defined by Mary's behaviour but by our processing of this behaviour in our cerebral cortex.

*Constructive Sequence*

The internal processing of the event in this sequence is positive and has a positive impact on the relationship with Mary.

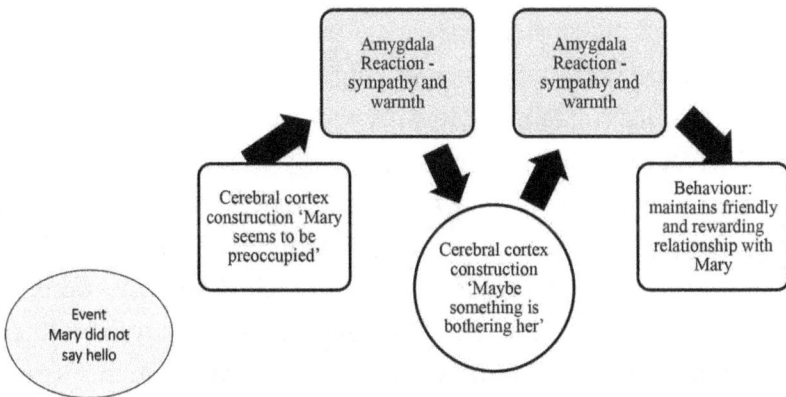

*Figure 21: Constructive sequence*

*Destructive Sequence*

This sequence has nothing to do with Mary; it is an internal construction that you define in your brain and this destructive processing will damage your resilience and your relationship with Mary.

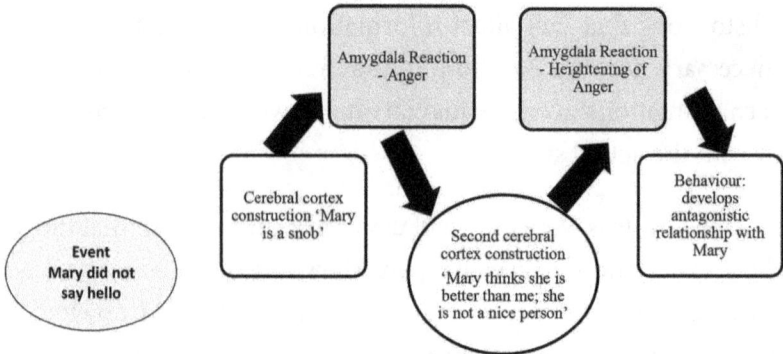

*Figure 22: Destructive sequence*

## 12.5 Shifting Destructive Thinking to Constructive Thinking

This is a relatively new area of research, and we are still developing our understanding and strategies that support us to remain constructive. Unfortunately, our world is being widely influenced by destructive thinking, creating greater challenges for people to remain constructive. The impact of destructive thinking is evident in a range of technology platforms, gaming platforms and social media platforms. In the past, destructive thinking was generally contained in our brains or in our direct interactions with other people. In today's world, the range of technology, gaming and social media platforms has provided the opportunity for people to externalise their destructive thinking without being responsible for its impact. As a society, we absolutely must shift our thinking to more constructive pathways so that we can manage our resilience.

We need to do two essential things to develop effective constructive thinking:

1.  **We need to clean up and continue to clean up our cerebral cortexes.**

    This requires that we clean up cognitive distortions, limiting beliefs, damaging values-based assumptions, destructive attitudes and residuals from unmanaged negative emotional reactions.

2.  **When destructive thinking happens, we need to become conscious of it and change our thinking to constructive as quickly as possible.**

    This sounds simple, but most of us do our destructive thinking totally unconsciously, and a significant level of awareness is required to become conscious of instances when we are being destructive. The best place to start with developing awareness is to notice when our moods and emotions are becoming negative. This is a clear indicator that our mental processing has become destructive. The second stage is to reframe the destructive thinking into something more constructive.

## 12.6 Tools for Enhancing Constructive Thinking

The tools outlined below are by no means comprehensive, but they provide you with an opportunity to work on your constructive thinking.

### 1. Become the observer of your thoughts

Becoming aware of your thoughts and the discussions that you have in your head is a starting point for enhancing your thinking. A large percentage of your thoughts are unconscious, so until you bring them to your conscious attention, you will not change your thinking strategies. Once they are conscious, you can then begin to identify when your thinking has become negative or destructive.

## 2. Journalling—capturing your thinking

This is a powerful strategy for developing your resilience in general, and it has particular relevance for enhancing your mental processing. A large percentage of our thinking is unconscious, so it is hugely helpful to bring it to consciousness by documenting your thinking.

## 3. Mentor or coach

Work with a mentor or coach who has the expertise to support you in identifying when your thinking has become destructive. Unfortunately, most of your friends simply support your negative thinking by sympathising with your frustrations. Therefore, having people who can provide you with honest feedback is important when you have become negative in your thinking, as these people can support you in uncovering destructive sequencing.

## 4. Constructive statements to counteract your destructive thinking

Develop a set of constructive statements that are designed to counteract any repetitive negative thinking patterns. For example:

o  If you regularly make statements to yourself that you are not good enough, then a statement to counteract this would be: 'I am good enough and value the amazing things that I achieve.'

o  If you regularly limit yourself and underestimate what you can achieve, then a statement to counteract this would be: 'I know I can accomplish anything I set my mind to.'

o  If you regularly beat yourself up for not getting things right or not being perfect, then a statement to counteract this would be: 'I forgive myself for not being perfect because I know I'm human.'

n terms of statements to counteract repeated negative thinking patterns, one useful strategy is to have a statement that openly counteracts thoughts that you don't want to be hooked by. For example, 'that is just a thought, it is not me, and I am not going to react to it or get captured by it.'

## 5. Meditation (moving and silent) and mindfulness activities

A large body of research now shows that meditation and mindfulness support healthy mental processing and have a positive effect on mental health issues. Mindfulness calms the mind and relaxes the body, thereby bringing cognitive, emotional and physical benefits. Some cognitive benefits include improved concentration, attention, focus, cognitive flexibility and clarity and reduced rumination.

The actual technique or style of mediation or mindfulness is very much up to the individual. Some people prefer a moving meditation, such as yoga or Tai Chi; other people prefer a seated practice, such as transcendental meditation, breath meditations or Buddhist meditation. The best plan is to explore a range of options and find the technique that works for you. If you want to enhance your mental processing, having some form of regular meditation practice and mindfulness activities is essential.

## 6. Build an optimistic mindset

When things don't go as planned, how do you handle it? Do you accept your plight and give up, or do you have faith that things will turn around? You will have times when you fail and run into unforeseen circumstances; therefore, being able to view the future as bright in these challenging times is crucial. Having an optimistic outlook provides the key to staying more positive, resilient and confident and is a very effective way to adapt to your environment. An optimistic outlook will aid in solving problems and staying engaged with your goals and aspirations. The way you feel and think about yourself will translate into every situation and encounter you have. Being able to make a favourable impression by having a positive attitude will be a deciding factor in your professional and personal success. You must become okay with who you are as a person before you can influence and inspire others. Knowing you are worthy, capable and courageous, despite your current conditions, is what self-esteem is all about.

Some key strategies to use to develop optimism are to use

- **Positive affirmations**—these were used extensively in the 1980s and have become less popular; however, if we are going to actively take on an optimistic attitude to life, positive affirmations are a helpful strategy.

- **Gratitude activities**—this is a simple and healthy practice to assist you in focusing on the positive and ensuring optimism.

- **Choose to be a glass half-full person**—if you know you are a glass half-empty person, then this is a key area to focus on. It is damaging your resilience and well-being to maintain this view of the world and will take discipline and work to make the shift.

- **Be selective on who and what you give your time and energy to**—if you want to develop optimism, surrounding yourself with people that are optimistic is important, as is exposing yourself to environments that support optimism.

### 7. Adjust your unhealthy beliefs

'A belief is nothing more than a feeling of certainty.' Robins (2018)

'Your personal beliefs determine your peak of performance.'
O'Connor & Prior (2001)

Our beliefs are the convictions that we trust, and they form around our deeply held values. For example, if you have a strongly held value of integrity, you may hold a belief that 'someone who lies is purposefully attempting to damage you.' The value at its deeper level is not judgemental and does not seek to find fault in oneself or in others; however, when it starts to impact our beliefs, it can develop an edge that is unhealthy. If we are running unhealthy beliefs, these need to be addressed and shifted.

Our internal processing is affected by the assumptions, attitudes and beliefs that we hold about ourselves, others and our world around us. Negative beliefs are typically key messages that we have been conditioned to believe in early life. To develop a wider repertoire of skills, we need to come to terms with the negative beliefs or blocks, to understand them and to challenge their relevance to the here and now.

We will take a common negative belief and unpick the impact of this on our behaviour:

The belief is – 'If I state what I want in a very direct way, my demands will be rejected.' This belief is likely to have been conditioned in early life by parents, teachers or other significant adults. The result of this is that typically the person will avoid clearly stating what they want and will therefore find assertive behaviour very difficult to deliver. When they attempt to be assertive, a 'tape' switches on inside their head which says, 'this feels wrong,' and they will either avoid being assertive or come across in such a wishy-washy way that no one takes them seriously. Their ability to learn this behaviour has been thwarted by a vicious cycle of self-perpetuating thoughts, as shown in Figure 19.

*Negative Belief Cycle*

Counteracting negative beliefs that are getting in the way requires discipline. We must repeatedly shift the negative belief with logical arguments that counteract it. If we can change the way we think about a situation, we can change the way we feel about it and thus reduce our stress. We can also start looking for positive clues in situations rather than negative ones. We can decide and interpret the ambiguous ones as positive rather than negative. We can also give our internal feelings a positive interpretation rather than a negative one. So, to counteract our negative belief, we must choose a positive one and then actively manage it in situations where we need to state our expectations clearly in an influential way.

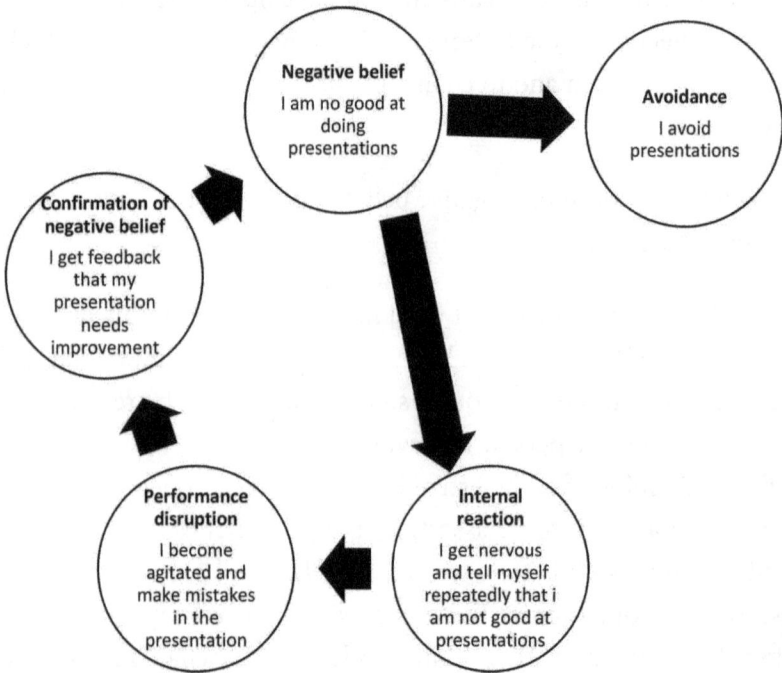

*Figure 23: Negative belief cycle*

*Positive Belief Cycle*

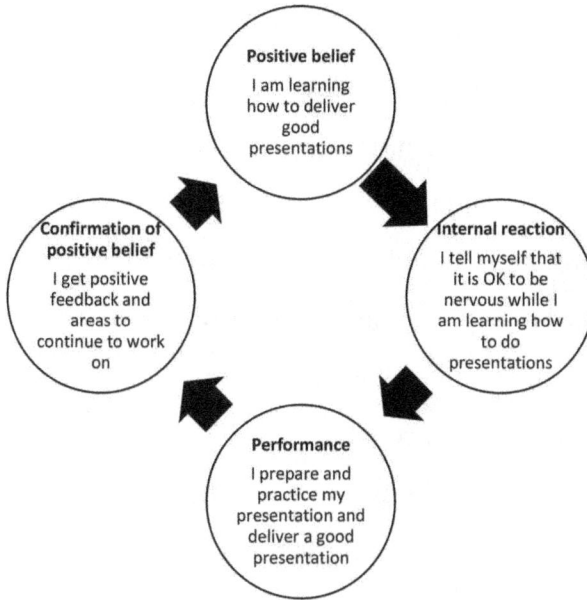

*Figure 24: Positive belief cycle*

Another example is fear of presentations. Very often, people put a negative belief on the emotions at the commencement of a presentation. To change this, we can build the belief that high adrenalin at the start of a presentation indicates enthusiasm and excitement rather than fear. Or we can watch others perform the skill, observe exactly what they do, and try it ourselves. This is a method that must be used in a safe environment where the risk is very low. Each small improvement should be backed up by positive feedback that will reduce the impact of the negative belief. We need to 'wipe the tape clean' and build and retain a new positive belief.

Some typical beliefs that get in the way of effectiveness and should be wiped clean and replaced with a new belief are the following:

- I need to get things perfect
- I am not important
- I must always appear to be totally competent
- I must never appear to lose
- I am better than everyone
- I am always right
- I must have control of everyone around me
- I need to oppose others' ideas to gain respect
- I must duck difficult issues
- I don't like conflict
- I must not oppose anyone else's ideas
- If I expect too much, I won't get it
- I don't come across well in presentations
- If I participate actively in meetings, my ideas will be rejected
- I must always please other people
- I want to be liked
- I need to hurry up
- I must always appear to be strong
- I must not show weakness
- My ideas won't be accepted unless I push hard
- If I listen actively, others will think I agree with their position
- If I disclose my uncertainty, others will not respect me

The most helpful process for working through any negative beliefs is to work with a friend or colleague to process your thinking and realign the belief to support your success rather than undermining it.

### 8. Restructuring your thinking—constructive sequencing

When we process events, we have a choice to develop a constructive sequence or a destructive sequence. This has significant implications for our ability to maintain healthy mental processing and enhance our resilience and our ability to lead others effectively. First, we need to observe our thinking patterns and identify when we have moved into destructive sequencing. This awareness is the first step in bringing about a change in our internal processing. Once we are aware, then we need to change the destructive frames that we have created or simply stop thinking the destructive thoughts.

### 9. Clean up your brain

If you are going to systemically shift your destructive thinking, you need to be consistently cleaning up your brain. Clean up and release redundant or irrelevant emotional reactions from the past. Readjust all aspects of your mind that get in the way of you being all that you can be. This takes discipline and focus and will require support from a professional coach or qualified therapist.

## 12.7 The Challenge—Build Your Resilience and Reach Your Full Potential

Each of the strategies articulated in the last three chapters has the capacity to enhance your resilience and ensure that you have the capacity to bounce back from challenge and adversity to deliver a transformational leadership style. The choice is yours: if you want to build your resilience and transform your leadership, you have a range of strategies to pick from to get started. The beauty of building your resilience is that it has a personal and professional impact. While building your resilience will require focus and discipline, the investment will pay dividends that far outweigh the effort required.

We have taken time to explore the importance of resilience in building a transformational leadership style, and before we close our discussions, we will take a brief look at the key aspects required to build a resilient organisation. If you can be a part of a team that has the opportunity to build a resilient organisation and that supports resilient leaders to be their best, you will be amazed at the things you can achieve. I have personally been lucky enough to work in two organisations that fully embraced the seven habits of organisational resilience described in chapter 7. They were both amazing organisations to be a part of and, as a leader, I was offered the opportunity to thrive and to evolve my resilience. If you build your resilience first, you will have the opportunity to contribute to building a resilient organisation.

In conclusion, my hope after you have read this book is that you will take up the challenge to transform your resilience and reach your full potential as a leader. Having supported leaders across the globe to transform their resilience, positively evolve their teams and revolutionise their businesses, I know that if you take up the challenge and build your resilience, you will experience a transformation.

I can offer no shortcuts or quick fixes; however, if you consistently build all aspects of your resilience on an ongoing basis, you will find that when you face challenges or adversity you will be able to bounce back and maintain the capacity to be a transformational leader.

# REFERENCES

Abbott, R. A., Ploubidis, G. B., Huppert, F. A., Kuh, D., Wadsworth, M. E. & Croudace, T. J. (2006). Psychometric evaluation and predictive validity of Ryff's psychological well-being items in a UK birth cohort sample of women. *Health and Quality of Life Outcomes, 4,* 76.

Abouserie, R. (1994). Sources and levels of stress in relation to locus of control and self esteem in university students. *Educational Psychology, 14*(3), 323–330.

Abramson, L. Y., Seligman, M. E. & Teasdale, J. D. (1978). Learned helplessness in humans: Critique and reformulation. *Journal of Abnormal Psychology, 87*(1), 49–74.

Adler, A. (1979). *Superiority and social interest: A collection of later writings* (rev. ed.). New York, NY: Norton.

Adler, A. B., Williams, J., McGurk, D., Moss, A. & Bliese, P. D. (2015). Resilience training with soldiers during basic combat training: Randomisation by platoon. *Applied Psychology: Health and Well-Being, 7*(1), 85–107.

Allinson, C. W., Armstrong, S. J. & Hayes, J. (2001). The effects of cognitive style on leader-member exchange: A study of manager-subordinate dyads. *Journal of Occupational and Organisational Psychology, 74*(2), 201–220.

Anazonwu, C. O. (1995). Locus of control, academic self-concept, and attribution of responsibility for performance in statistics. *Psychological Reports, 77*(2), 367–370.

Anthony, E. J. (1987). Risk, vulnerability, and resilience: An overview. In E. J. Collins & B. J. Choler (Eds.), *The invulnerable child* (pp. 3–48). New York, NY: Guilford Press.

Antonakis, J. (2001). *The validity of the transformational, transactional, and laissez-faire leadership model as measured by the Multifactor Leadership Questionnaire (MLQ 5X).* Retrieved from ProQuest Digital Dissertations (Order No.AAI3000380).

Antonakis, J., Avolio, B. J. & Sivasubramaniam, N. (2003). Context and leadership: An examination of the nine-factor Full-Range Leadership Theory using the Multifactor Leadership Questionnaire. *The Leadership Quarterly, 14*, 261–295.

Argyris, C. & Schön, D. (1996). *Organisational learning II: A theory of action perspective.* Reading, MA: Addison-Wesley.

Arnetz, B. B., Nevedal, D. C., Lumley, M. A., Backman, L. & Lublin, A. (2009). Trauma resilience training for police: Psychophysiological and performance effects. *Journal of Police and Criminal Psychology, 24*(1), 1–9.

Ashford, S. & DeRue, S. (2010). *Five steps to addressing the leadership talent shortage* [Web log]. Retrieved from https://hbr.org/2010/06/5-steps-to-addressing-the-lead/

Atwater, L. E. & Yammarino, F. J. (1993). Personal attributes as predictors of superiors' and subordinates' perceptions of military academy leadership. *Human Relations, 46*(5), 645–668.

Avolio, B. J. & Bass, B. M. (1995). Individual consideration viewed at multiple levels of analysis: A multi-level framework for examining the diffusion of transformational leadership. *The Leadership Quarterly, 6*(2), 199–218.

Avolio, B. J., Bass, B. M. & Jung, D. I. (1999). Re-examining the components of transformational and transactional leadership using the multifactor leadership questionnaire. *Journal of Occupational and Organisational Psychology, 72*(4), 441–511.

Avolio, B. J. & Hannah, S. T. (2008). Developmental readiness: Accelerating leader development. *Consulting Psychology Journal: Practice and Research, 60*(4), 331–347.

Avolio, B. J., Sosik, J. J. & Berson, Y. (2013). *Leadership models, methods, and applications: Progress and remaining blind spots.* Hoboken, NJ: John Wiley & Sons.

Ballou, R., Bowers, D., Boyatzis, R. E. & Kolb, D. A. (1999). Fellowship in lifelong learning: An executive development program for advanced professionals. *Journal of Management Education, 23*(4), 338–354.

Baddeley, A. D. (1986). *Working memory.* Oxford: Oxford University Press.

Baddeley, A. D. (1996) Exploring the central executive. *Quarterly Journal of Experimental Psychology Section A: Human Experimental Psychology, 49A*, 5–28.

Baddeley, A. D. & Hitch, G. (1974). Working memory. In G. H. Bower (Ed.), *The psychology of learning and motivation: Advances in research and theory* (Vol. 8, pp. 47–89). New York: Academic Press.

Bandura, A. (1978). The self system in reciprocal determinism. *American Psychologist, 33*(4), 344–358.

Bandura, A. (1997). *Self-efficacy: The exercise of control.* New York, NY: W. H. Freeman.

Brannick, M, T., Chan, D, Conway, J, M., Lance, C, E. & Spector, P. E. (2010). What is method variance and how can we cope with it? A panel discussion. *Organisational Research Methods, 13*(3), 407–420.

Barling, J., Weber, T. & Kelloway, E. K. (1996). Effects of transformational leadership training on attitudinal and financial outcomes: A field experiment. *Journal of Applied Psychology, 81*(6), 827–832.

Barrett. G. V., Miguel, R. F., Tan, J. A. & Hurd, J. M. (2001, April). *Emotional intelligence: The Madison Avenue approach to professional practice.* Presentation at the 16th Annual Conference of the Society for Industrial and Organisational Psychology, San Diego, CA.

Bartholomew, K. & Horowitz, L. M. (1990). Attachment styles among adults: A test of a four-category model. *Journal of Personality and Social Psychology, 61*(2), 226–244.

Bass, B. M. (1981). *Stogdill's handbook of leadership: A survey of theory and research* (2nd ed.). New York, NY: Free Press.

Bass, B. M. (1985). *Leadership and performance beyond expectations.* New York, NY: Free Press.

Bass, B. M. (1998). *Transformational leadership: Industry, military, and educational impact.* Mahwah, NJ: Erlbaum.

Bass, B. M. & Avolio, B. J. (1990). *Transformational leadership development: Manual for the Multifactor Leadership Questionnaire.* Palo Alto, CA: Consulting Psychologists Press.

Bass, B. M. & Avolio, J. B. (1993). Transformational leadership and organisational culture. *Public Administration Quarterly, 2*(12), 112–121.

Bass, B. M. & Avolio, B. J. (1997). *Full range leadership development: Manual for the multifactor leadership questionnaire.* Palo Alto, CA: Mindgarden.

Bass, B. M. & Avolio, B. J. (2000). *MLQ Multifactor Leadership Questionnaire.* Redwood City: Mind Garden.

Bass, B. M., Avolio, B. J., Jung, D. I. & Berson, Y. (2003). Predicting unit performance by assessing transformational and transactional leadership. *Journal of Applied Psychology, 88*(2), 207–218.

Bass, B. M. & Riggio, R. E. (2006). *Transformational leadership* (2nd ed.). Mahwah, NJ: Lawrence Erlbaum Associates Publishers.

Baumeister, R. F. (Ed.). (1998). *The self in social psychology*. New York, NY: McGraw-Hill.

Baumeister, R. F., Smart, L. & Boden, J. M. (1996). Relation of threatened egotism to violence and aggression: The dark side of high self-esteem. *Psychological Review, 103*(1), 5–33.

Baumeister, R. E, Tice, D. M. & Hutton, D. G. (1989). Self-presentational motivations and personality differences in self-esteem. *Journal of Personality, 57,* 547–579.

Baumgardner, A. H. (1990). To know oneself is to like oneself: Self-certainty and self-affect. *Journal of Personality and Social Psychology, 58*(6), 1062–1072.

Becker, E. (1973). *The denial of death*. New York, NY: Free Press.

Beer, M., Finnstrom, M. & Schrader, D, (2016). Why Leadership Training Fails – and what to do about it. *Harvard Business Review*, 50–57.

Bennis, W. & Nanus, B. (1985). *Leaders: The strategies for taking charge*. New York, NY: Harper and Row.

Benson, P. L. (2006). *All kids are our kids: What communities must do to raise caring and responsible children and adolescents* (2nd ed.). San Francisco, CA: Jossey-Bass.

Bergman, L. R., Corovic, J., Ferrer-Wreder, L. A. & Modig, K. (2014). High IQ in early adolescence and career success in adulthood: Findings from a Swedish longitudinal study. *Research in Human Development, 11*(3), 165–185.

Bertua, C., Anderson, N. & Salgado, J. F. (2005). The predictive validity of cognitive ability tests: A UK meta-analysis. *Journal of Occupational and Organisational Psychology, 78*(3), 387–409.

Bernerth, J. B., Armenakis, A. A., Field, H. S., Giles, W. F. & Walker, H. J. (2007). Leader-member social exchange (LMSX): Development and validation of a scale. *Journal of Organisational Behavior, 28*(8), 979–1003.

Bills, R., Vance, E. & McLean, O. (1951). An index of adjustment and values. *Journal of Consulting Psychology, 15*(3), 257–261.

Binet, A. & Simon, T. (1916). *The development of intelligence in children (the Binet-Simon scale)*. Baltimore: Williams & Wilkins.

Binney, G. (1992). *Making quality work: Lessons from Europe's leading companies*. London, UK: The Economist Intelligence Unit.

Biro, P. & Adriaenssens, B. (2013). Predictability as a personality trait: Consistent differences in intraindividual behavioral variation. *The American Naturalist, 182*(5), 621–629.

Biron, C., Karanika-Murray, M. & Cooper, C. (2012). *Improving organisational interventions for stress and wellbeing: Addressing process and context.* Hove: Routledge.

Blascovich, J. & Tomaka, J. (1991). Measures of self-esteem. In J. P. Robinson, P. R. Shaver & L. S. Wrightsman (Eds.), *Measures of personality and social psychological attitudes* (Vol. I, pp. 115–160). San Diego, CA: Academic Press.

Blau, P. M. (1964). *Exchange and power in social life.* New York, NY: Wiley.

Bledsoe, J. C. & Baber, W. C. (1978) Personality correlates of locus of control among college women. *Psychological Reports, 43*(3), 1129–1130.

Bleidorn, W. & Ködding, C., (2013). The divided self and psychological maladjustment - A meta-analytic review. *Journal of Research in Personality, 47*(5), 547–552.

Bleuler, M. (1978). *The schizophrenic disorders: Long-term patient and family studies.* New Haven, CT: Yale University Press.

Block, J. (1961). Ego identity, role variability, and adjustment. *Journal of Consulting Psychology, 25*(5), 392–397.

Boddy, C. R. (2006). The dark side of management decisions: Organisational psychopaths. *Management Decision, 44*(9/10), 1461–1475.

Boddy, C. R. (2014). Corporate psychopaths, conflict, employee affective well-being and counterproductive work behaviour. *Journal of Business Ethics, 121*(1), 107–121.

Bonanno, G. A. (2004). Loss, trauma, and human resilience: Have we underestimated the human capacity to thrive after extremely aversive events? *American Psychologist, 59*(1), 20–28.

Bono, J. E. & Judge, T. A. (2003). Self-concordance at work: Towards understanding the motivational effects of Transformational leaders. *Academy of Management Journal, 46*(5), 554–571.

Boomsma, A. (1982). Robustness of LISREL against small sample sizes in factor analysis models. In K. G. Joreskog & H. Wold (Eds.), *Systems under indirection observation: Causality, structure, prediction. Part I* (pp. 149–173). Amsterdam, Netherlands: North Holland.

Bossick, B. E. (2008). *An empirical examination of the relationship between posttraumatic growth and the personality traits of hardiness, sense of coherence, locus of control, self-efficacy, resilience, and optimism* (Unpublished doctoral thesis). The University of Akron, Akron, OH.

Bostic, T. J. (2003). Constructive thinking, mental health, and physical health: An explanatory model of correlated constructs in health psychology. *The Sciences and Engineering, 63*(7B), 3465–3487.

Boud, D., Keogh, R. & Walker, D. (1985). Promoting reflection in learning: A model. In D. Boud, R. Keogh & D. Walker (Eds.), *Reflection: Turning experience into learning* (pp. 18–40). London, UK: Kogan Page.

Bowlby, J. (1969). *Attachment and loss. Attachment* (Vol. 1). New York, NY: Basic Books.

Bowling, N. A., Eschelman, K. J., Wang, Q., Kirkendall, C. & Alarcon, G. (2010). A meta-analysis of the predictors and consequences of organisation-based self-esteem. *Journal of Occupational and Organisational Psychology, 83*(3), 601–626.

Bowling, N. A. & Hammond, G. D. (2008). A meta-analytic examination of the construct validity of the Michigan Organisational Assessment Questionnaire Job Satisfaction Subscale. *Journal of Vocational Behavior, 73*(1), 63–77.

Boyatzis, R. E. (2008). Leadership development from a complexity perspective. *Consulting Psychology Journal: Practice and Research, 60*(4), 298–313.

Bradwick, J. M. (2008). *One foot out the door: How to combat the psychological recession that's alienating employees and hurting American business.* New York, NY: AMACOM.

Breverton, P. & Millward, L. (2001). *Organisational research methods: A guide for students and researchers.* London, UK: SAGE Publications.

Brockner, J. (1988). *Self-esteem at work: research, theory, and practice.* Lanham, MD: Lexington Books.

Brockner, J. & Hess, T. (1986). Self-esteem and task performance in quality circles. *Academy of Management Journal, 29*(3), 617–623.

Burke, M. J. & Day, R. R. (1986). A cumulative study of the effectiveness of managerial training. *Journal of Applied Psychology, 71*(2), 232–245.

Burns, J. M. (1978). *Leadership.* New York, NY: Harper & Row.

Button, S. B., Mathieu, J. E. & Zajac, D. M. (1996). Goal orientation in organisational research: A conceptual and empirical foundation. *Organisational Behavior and Human Decision Processes, 67*(1), 26–48.

Butts, M. M., Vandenberg, R. J., DeJoy, D. M., Schaffer, B. S. & Wilson, M. G. (2009). Individual reactions to high involvement work processes: Investigating the role of empowerment and perceived organisational support. *Journal of Occupational Health Psychology, 14*(2), 122–136.

Bycio, P., Hackett, R. D. & Allen, J. S. (1995). Further assessment of Bass's (1995) conceptualization of transactional and transformational leadership. *Journal of Applied Psychology, 80*(4), 468–478.

Byrne, D. (1971). *The attraction paradigm*. New York, NY: Academic Press.

Cacioppe, R. (1998a). An integrated model and approach for the design of effective leadership development programs. *Leadership & Organisation Development Journal, 19*(1), 44–53.

Cacioppe, R. (1998b). Leaders developing leaders: An effective way to enhance leadership development programs. *Leadership & Organisation Development Journal, 19*(4), 194–198.

Cacioppe, R. & Albrecht, P. (2001). Understanding and developing leadership and management using the holon model. In K. Parry (Ed.), *Leadership in the antipodes: Findings, implications, and a leader profile* (pp. 121–142). Melbourne, Australia: Victoria University.

Cacioppe, R. & Edwards, M. (2005). Seeking the holy grail of organisational development: A synthesis of integral theory, spiral dynamics, corporate transformation and action inquiry. *Leadership & Organisation Development Journal, 26*(1), 86–105.

Cacioppe, R. & Lloyd, A. (2005). *A study of integral leadership and management competencies in West Australian public sector managers*. Perth, Australia: University of Western Australia.

Callahan, R. E., Fleenor, C. P. & Knudson, H. R. (1986). *Understanding organisational behavior: A managerial viewpoint*. Columbus, OH: Merrill Publishing.

Calori, R. & Sarnin, P. (1991). Corporate culture and economic performance: A French study. *Organisation Studies, 12*(1), 49–74.

Cameron, J. J., Holmes, J. G. & Vorauer, J. D. (2009). When self-disclosure goes awry: Negative consequences of revealing personal failure for lower self-esteem individuals. *Journal of Experimental Social Psychology, 45*(1), 217–222.

Campbell, J., Dunnette, M. D., Lawler, E. E. & Weick, K. E. (1970). *Managerial behavior, performance and effectiveness*. New York, NY: McGraw-Hill.

Campbell, J. D. (1990). Self-esteem and clarity of the self-concept. *Journal of Personality and Social Psychology, 59*(3), 538–549.

Campbell, J. D., Assanand, S. & Di Paula, A. (2003). The structure of the self-concept and its relation to psychological adjustment. *Journal of Personality, 71*(1), 115–140.

Campbell, J. D. & Lavallee, L. F. (1993). Who am I? The role of self-concept confusion in understanding the behavior of people with low self-esteem. In R. F. Baumeister (Ed.), *Plenum series in social/clinical psychology. Self-esteem: The puzzle of low self-regard* (pp. 3–20). New York, NY: Plenum Press.

Campbell, J. D., Trapnell, P. D., Heine, S. J., Katz, I. M., Lavallee, L. F. & Lehman, D. R. (1996). Self-concept clarity: Measurement, personality correlates, and cultural boundaries. *Journal of Personality and Social Psychology, 70*(1), 141–156.

Cantor, N., Markus, H., Niedenthal, P. & Nurius, P. (1986). On motivation and the self-concept. In R. M. Sorrentino & E. T Higgins (Eds.), *Handbook of motivation and cognition: Foundations of social behavior* (pp. 96–121). New York, NY: Guilford Press.

Cartwright, D. (1959). *Studies in social power.* Oxford, UK: University of Michigan Press.

Cartwright, S. & Whatmore, L. C. (2005). *Stress and individual differences: Implications for stress management.* In A-G. A. Antoniou & C. L. Cooper (Eds.), *Research companion to organisational health psychology* (pp. 163–173). Northampton, MA: Edward Elgar Publishing.

Carver, C. S. & Scheier, M. F. (1998). *On the self-regulation of behavior.* New York: Cambridge University Press.

Caza, B. B. (2007). *Experiences of adversity at work: Toward an identity-based theory of resilience.* Retrieved from ProQuest Digital Dissertations (Order No. AAI3276107).

Cerni, T., Curtis, G. J. & Colmar, S. (2010). Increasing transformational leadership by developing leaders' information-processing systems. *Journal of Leadership Studies, 4*(3), 51–65.

Cerni, T., Curtis, G. J. & Colmar, S. H. (2008). Information processing and leadership styles: Constructive thinking and transformational leadership. *Journal of Leadership Studies, 2*(1), 60–73.

Cerni, T., Curtis, G. J. & Colmar, S. H. (2014). Cognitive-experiential leadership model: How leaders' information-processing systems can influence leadership styles, influencing tactics, conflict management, and organisational outcomes. Journal of *Leadership Studies, 8*(3), 26–39.

Cha, S. H. (2009). *Explaining teachers' job satisfaction, intent to leave, and actual turnover: A structural equation modelling approach.* Retrieved from ProQuest Digital Dissertations (Order No. AAI3321463).

Chmiel, M., Brunner, M., Keller, U., Schalke, D., Wrulich, M. & Martin, R. (2012). Does childhood general cognitive ability at age 12 predict subjective well-being at age 52? *Journal of Research in Personality, 46*(5), 627–631.

Chen, J.-C. & Silverthorne, C. (2008). The impact of locus of control on job stress, job performance and job satisfaction in Taiwan. *Leadership & Organisation Development Journal, 29*(7), 572–582.

Cheng, H. & Furnham, A. (2004). Perceived parental rearing style, self-esteem and self-criticism as predictors of happiness. *Journal of Happiness Studies, 5*(1), 1–21.

Choi, S., Kluemper, D. H. & Sauley, K. S. (2013). Assessing emotional self-efficacy: Evaluating validity and dimensionality with cross-cultural samples. *Applied Psychology: An International Review, 62*(1), 97–123.

Chorpita, B. F. & Barlow, D. H. (1998). The development of anxiety: The role of control in the early environment. *Psychological Bulletin, 124*(1), 3–21.

Cicchetti, D. & Garmezy, N. (1993). Prospects and promises in the study of resilience. *Development and Psychopathology, 5*(4), 497–502.

Ciulla, J. B. (2009). Leadership and the ethics of care. *Journal of Business Ethics, 88*(1), 3–4.

Clements, C. & Washbrush, J. B. (1999). The two faces of leadership: Considering the dark side of leader-follower dynamics. *Journal of Workplace Learning, 11*(5), 170–176.

Cohn, A. & Pakenham, K. (2009). Efficacy of a cognitive-behavioral program to improve psychological adjustment among soldiers in recruit training. *Military Medicine, 173*(12), 1151–1157.

Cole, D. A. & Maxwell, S. E. (2003). Testing meditational models with longitudinal data: Questions and tips in the use of structural equation modeling. *Journal of Abnormal Psychology, 112*, 558–577.

Collican, H. (1994). *Research methods and statistics in psychology* (2nd ed.). London, UK: Hodder and Stoughton Educational.

Collins, J. C. (2001). *Good to great: Why some companies make the leap...and others don't*. New York, NY: Harper Business.

Conger, J. A. (1989). *The charismatic leader: Behind the mystique of exceptional leadership*. San Francisco, CA: Jossey-Bass.

Conner, D. R. (1992). *Managing at the speed of change: How resilient managers succeed and prosper where others fail*. New York, NY: Villard Books.

Conte, J. M. (2005). Review and critique of emotional intelligence measures. *Journal of Organisational Behavior, 26*(4), 433–440.

Conley, J. (1984). The hierarchy of consistency: A review and model of longitudinal findings on adult individual differences in intelligence, personality and self-opinion. *Personality and Individual Differences, 5*(1), 11–25.

Cook, T. D., Campbell, D. T. & Peracchio, L. (1990). Quasi experimentation. In M. D. Dunnette & L. M. Hough (Eds.), *Handbook of industrial and organisational psychology* (pp. 491–576). Palo Alto, CA: Consulting Psychologists Press.

Cooley, C. H. (1902). *Human nature and the social order.* New York, NY: Scribner's.

Cooper, C. & Flint-Taylor, J. & Pearn, M. (2013). Building resilience for success: A resource for managers and organisations. UK: Palgrave Macmillan.

Coopersmith, S. (1967). *The antecedents of self-esteem.* San Francisco, CA: W. H. Freeman.

Cortina, J. M. (1993). What is coefficient alpha? An examination of theory and applications. *Journal of Applied Psychology, 78*(1), 98–104.

Covey, S. R. (1989). *The seven habits of highly effective people.* London, UK: Simon & Schuster.

Covey, S. R. (1991). *Principle-centered leadership.* New York, NY: Summit Books.

Cowdrey, F. A. & Walters, S. L. (2013). Salvatore R. Maddi: Hardiness, turning stressful circumstances into resilient growth. *Applied Research Quality Life, 8*(2), 265–267.

Crandall, V. J., Katkovsky, W. & Crandall, V. C. (1965). Children's belief in their own control of reinforcement in intellectual-academic achievement situations. *Child Development, 36,* 91–109.

Creed, P. A. & Davies, M. (2009). Improving well-being and confidence of senior managerial staff through mental strategies training. *Management Development Forum, 3*(1), 27–29.

Crocker, J., Thompson, L. L., McGraw, K. M. & Ingerman, C. (1987). Downward comparison, prejudice, and evaluations of others: Effects of self-esteem and threat. *Journal of Personality and Social Psychology, 52*(5), 907–916.

Cross, R., Ernst, C., & Pasmore, B. (2013). A bridge too far? How boundary spanning networks drive organisational change and effectiveness. Organisational Dynamics, 42(2), 81-91.

Cunliffe, A. L. & Eriksen, M. (2011). Relational leadership. *Human Relations, 64*(11), 1425–1449.

Curtis, G. J., King, G. & Russ, A. (2017). Reexamining the relationship between thinking styles and transformational leadership: What is the contribution of imagination and emotionality? *Journal of Leadership Studies, 11*(2), 8–21.

Dabholkar, P. A. (2000). Technology in service delivery: Implications for self-service and service support. In T. A. Swartz & D. Iacobucci (Eds.), *Handbook of services marketing and management* (pp. 103–110). Thousand Oaks, CA: SAGE Publications.

Dansereau, F., Cashman, J. & Graen, G. (1973). Instrumentality theory and equity theory as complementary approaches to predicting the relationship of leadership and turnover among managers. *Organisational Behavior and Human Performance, 10*(2), 184–200.

Dansereau, F., Graen, G. & Haga, W. J. (1975). A vertical dyad linkage approach to leadership within formal organisations: A longitudinal investigation of the role making process. *Organisational Behavior and Human Performance, 13*(1), 46–78.

D'Arienzo, J. A. (2010). Hardiness enhancement: A pathway to resilience. In S. S. Fehr (Ed.), *101 interventions in group therapy* (pp. 99–103). New York, NY: Routledge.

Davydov, D. M., Stewart, R., Ritchie, K. & Chaudieu, I. (2010) Resilience and mental health. *Clinical Psychology Review, 30*, 479–495.

Day, D. V. (2001). Leadership development: A review in context. *Leadership Quarterly, 11*(4), 581–613.

Day, D. V. & Lord, R. G. (1988). Executive leadership and organisational performance: Suggestions for a new theory and methodology. *Journal of Management, 14*(3), 453–464.

Day, D. V., Harrison, M. M. & Halpin, S. M. (2009). *An integrative approach to leader development: Connecting adult development, identity, and expertise.* New York, NY: Routledge.

Day, D. V. & Sin, H. P. (2009). Leader development, identity and goal orientation: A study of personal change trajectories. In *Academy of Management Proceedings* (Vol. 2009, No. 1, pp. 1–6). Birmingham, AL: Academy of Management.

Day, D., Harrison, M. M. & Halpin, S. M. (2009). *An integrative approach to leader development: Connecting adult development, identity, and expertise* (1st ed.). New York, NY: Taylor & Francis.

Deluga, R. J. (1991). The relationship of leader and subordinate influencing activity in naval environments. *Military Psychology, 3*(1), 25–39.

Deluga, R. J. (1994). Supervisory trust building, leader-member exchange and organisational citizenship behavior. *Journal of Occupational and Organisational Psychology, 67*(4), 315–326.

Deluga, R. J. (1998). Leader-member exchange quality and effectiveness ratings: The role of subordinate-supervisor conscientiousness similarity. *Group & Organisation Management, 23*(2), 189–216.

Deluga, R. J. & Perry, J. T. (1994). The role of subordinate performance and ingratiation in leader-member exchanges. *Group & Organisation Management, 19*(1), 618–686.

Demo, D. H. (1985). Measurement of self-esteem: Refining our methods. *The Journal of Personality and Social Psychology, 48*(6), 1490–1502.

DeNeve, K. M. & Cooper, H. (1998). The happy personality: A meta-analysis of 137 personality traits and subjective well-being. *Psychological Bulletin, 124*(2), 197–229.

de Haro Garcia, J. M. & Costa, J. L. C. (2014). Does trait emotional intelligence predict unique variance in early career success beyond IQ and personality? *Journal of Career Assessment, 22*(4), 715–725.

den Hartog, D. N. & Koopman, P. L. (2001). Leadership in organisations. In N. Anderson, D. S. Ones, H. Kepir Sinangil & C. Viswesvaran (Eds.), *Handbook of industrial, work & organisational psychology* (pp. 166–187). London: SAGE Publications.

den Hartog, D. N., van Muijen, J. J. & Koopman, P. L. (1997). Transactional versus transformational leadership: An analysis of the MLQ. *Journal of Occupational and Organisational Psychology, 70*(1), 19–34.

DeNisi, A. & Kluger, A. (2000). Feedback effectiveness: Can 360° appraisal feedback be improved? *The Academy of Management Executive, 14*(1), 129–139.

Denison, D. R. (1990). *Corporate culture and organisational effectiveness.* New York: Wiley.

Denison, D. R. & Mishra, A. K. (1995). Toward a theory of organisational culture and effectiveness. *Organisation Science, 6*(2), 204–223.

DeRue, D. S. & Wellman, N. (2009). Developing leaders via experience: The role of developmental challenge, learning orientation, and feedback availability. *Journal of Applied Psychology, 94*(4), 859–875.

Dewey, J. (1938). *Experience and education.* New York, NY: Macmillan.

Di Fabio, A. & Saklofske, D. H. (2014). Comparing ability and self-report trait emotional intelligence, fluid intelligence and personality traits in career decision. *Personality and Individual Differences, 64*, 174–178.

Di Sipio, A., Falco, A. & De Carlo, N. A. (2012). Positive personal resources and organisational well-being: Resilience, hope, optimism, and self-efficacy in an Italian health care setting. *TPM: Testing, Psychometrics, Methodology in Applied Psychology, 19*(2), 81–95.

Diehl, M. & Hay, E. L. (2010). Risk and resilience factors in coping with daily stress in adulthood: The role of age, self-concept incoherence, and personal control. *Developmental Psychology, 46*(5), 1132–1146.

Diehl, M., Hastings, C. T. & Stanton, J. M. (2001). Self-concept differentiation across the adult life span. *Psychology and Aging, 16*(4), 643–654.

Diener, E. & Diener, M. (1995). Cross-cultural correlates of life satisfaction and self-esteem. *Journal of Personality and Social Psychology, 68*(4), 653–663.

Dienesch, R. M. & Liden, R. C. (1986). Leader-member exchange model of leadership: A critique and further developments. *Academy of Management Review, 11*(3), 618–634.

Dinh, J. E., Lord, R. G., Gardner, W. L., Meuser, J. D., Liden, R. C. & Hu, J. (2014). Leadership theory and research in the new millennium: Current theoretical trends and changing perspectives. *The Leadership Quarterly, 25*, 36–62.

Dixon, T. M. & Baumeister, R. F. (1991). Escaping the self: The moderating effect of self-complexity. *Personality and Social Psychology Bulletin, 17*, 363–368.

Doerfel, M. L., Chewning, L. V. & Lai, C. (2013). The evolution of networks and the resilience of interorganisational relationships after disaster. *Communication Monographs, 80*(4), 533–559.

Domeck, C. E. (2008). *An investigation to determine the perceptions of resilience in educational and business leadership personnel in central Florida*. Retrieved from ProQuest Digital Dissertations (Order No. AAI3335339).

Donahue, E. M., Robins, R. W., Roberts, B. W. & John, O. P. (1993). The divided self: Concurrent and longitudinal effects of psychological adjustment and social roles on self-concept differentiation. *Journal of Personality and Social Psychology, 64*(5), 834–846.

Dozier, M. L. & Lee, S. W. (1995). Discrepancies between self and other reports of psychiatric symptomatology: Effects of dismissing attachment strategies. *Development and Psychopathology, 7*(1), 217–226.

Draghici, A. & Draghici, G. (2007). New business requirements in the knowledge-based society. In M. M. Cunha, B. C. Cortes & G. D. Putnik (Eds.), *Technologies and business integration: Social, managerial and organisational dimensions* (pp. 211–243). Hershey, PA: Idea Group.

Drucker, P. (1999). *Management challenges for the 21$^{st}$ century*. New York, NY: Harper Collins.

Dunn, D. L. (1995). *Resilient reintegration of married women with dependent children: Employed and unemployed*. Retrieved from ProQuest Digital Dissertations (Order No. AAM9507504).

Dunn, J. R. (2008). *Housing as a determinant of mental capital. State-of-science review: SR-E27.* Foresight Mental Capital and Wellbeing Project. London, UK: Government Office for Science.

Dunnette, M. D. (1976). *Handbook of industrial and organisational psychology* (2nd ed.). Chicago: Rand McNally.

Dunning, D., Johnson, K., Ehrlinger, J. & Kruger, J. (2003). Why people fail to recognize their own incompetence. *Current Directions in Psychological Science, 12*(3), 83–87.

Eich, D. A. (2008). A grounded theory of high-quality leadership programs: Perspective from student leadership development programs in higher education. *Journal of Leadership & Organisational Studies, 15*(2), 176–187.

Eizenman, D. R., Nesselroade, J. R., Featherman, D. L. & Rowe, J. W. (1997). Intraindividual variability in perceived control in an older sample: The MacArthur successful aging studies. *Psychology and Aging, 12*(3), 489–502.

Elsass, P. (1992). Strategies for survival: *The psychology of cultural resilience in ethnic minorities.* New York, NY: New York University Press.

Epstein, S. (1992a). *Constructive thinking and mental and physical well-being. Life crises and experiences of loss in adulthood.* Hillsdale, NJ: Lawrence Erlbaum Associates, Inc.

Epstein, S. (1992b). Coping ability, negative self-evaluation, and overgeneralization: Experiment and theory. *Journal of Personality and Social Psychology, 62*(5), 826–836.

Epstein, S. (1998). Constructive thinking: *The key to emotional intelligence.* Westport, CT: Praeger Publishers/Greenwood Publishing Group.

Epstein, S. (2001). *CTI: Constructive Thinking Inventory.* Lutz, Fla: Psychological Assessment Resources.

Epstein, S. (2014). Cognitive-experiential theory: An integrative theory of personality. New York, NY: Oxford University Press.

Epstein, S. & Meier, P. (1989). Constructive thinking: A broad coping variable with specific components. *Journal of Personality and Social Psychology, 57,* 332–350.

Epstein, S. & Katz, L. (1992). Coping ability, stress, productive load, and symptoms. *Journal of Personality and Social Psychology, 62*(5), 813–825.

Epstein, S., Pacini, R., Denes-Raj, V. & Heier, H. (1996). Individual differences in intuitive-experiential and analytical- rational thinking styles. *Journal of Personality and Social Psychology, 71,* 390–405.

Erez, A. & Judge, T. A. (2001). Relationship of core self-evaluations to goal setting, motivation, and performance. *Journal of Applied Psychology, 86,* 1270–1279.

Erikson, E. H. (1950). *Childhood and society.* New York, NY: WW Norton & Co.

Erikson, E. H. (1968). *Identity: Youth and crisis.* New York, NY: WW Norton & Co.

Erikson, E. H. (1980). *Identity and the life cycle.* New York, NY: WW Norton & Co.

Evers, W. J. G., Tomic, W. & Brouwers, A. A. (2004). Constructive thinking and burnout among secondary school teachers. *School Psychology International, 25*(2), 131–148.

Fairhurst, G. T. & Uhl-Bien, M. (2012). Organisational discourse analysis (ODA): Examining leadership as a relational process. *The Leadership Quarterly, 23*(6), 1043–1062.

Falkenberg, J. & Ashurst, C. (2010). Guest editorial: The new normal— Implications for change. *Journal of Change Management, 10*(2), 131–133.

Feather, N. T. & Rauter, K. A. (2004). Organisational citizenship behaviors in relation to job status, job insecurity, organisational commitment and identification, job satisfaction and work values. *Journal of Occupational and Organisational Psychology, 77*(1), 81–94.

Fehring, H. & Herring, H. (2012). The Working Lives project: A window into Australian education and workforce participation. *Journal of Education and Work, 26*(5), 494–513.

Feinberg, B. J., Ostroff, C. & Burke, W. W. (2005). The role of within group agreement in understanding transformational leadership. *Journal of Occupational and Organisational Psychology, 78*(3), 471–488.

Fiedler, F. E. (1967). *A theory of leadership effectiveness.* New York, NY: McGraw Hill.

Fleishman, E. A. & Harris, E. F. (1962). Patterns of leadership behavior related to employee grievance and turnover. *Personnel Psychology, 15*(1), 43–56.

Flemming, J. S. & Courtney, B. E. (1984). The dimensionality of self-esteem: Hierarchical facet model for revised measurement scales. *Journal of Personality and Social Psychology, 46*(2), 404–421.

Flytzani, S. & Nijkamp, P. (2008). Locus of control and cross-cultural adjustment of expatriate managers. *International Journal of Foresight and Innovation Policy, 4*(1–2), 146–159.

Folkman, S. (1984). Personal control and stress and coping processes: A theoretical analysis. *Journal of Personality and Social Psychology, 46*(4), 839–852.

Forrest-Bank, S., Nicotera, N., Anthony, E. K., Gonzales, B. & Jenson, J. M. (2014). Risk, protection, and resilience among youth residing in public housing neighborhoods. *Child and Adolescent Social Work Journal, 31*(4), 295–314.

Forgeard, M. J. C. & Seligman, M. E. P. (2012). Seeing the glass half full: A review of the causes and consequences of optimism. *Pratiques Psychologiques, 18*(2), 107–120.

Forman, C., King, J. L. & Lyytinen, K. (2014). Information, technology, and the changing nature of work. *Information Systems Research, 25*(4), 789–795.

Frankl, V. E. (1963). *Man's search for meaning: An introduction to logotherapy.* Oxford, UK: Washington Square Press.

Frankl, V. E. (1972). The feeling of meaninglessness: A challenge to psychotherapy. *The American Journal of Psychoanalysis, 32*(1), 85–89.

French, J. R. P., Jr. & Raven, B. (1959). *The bases of social power.* Ann Arbor, MI: University of Michigan Press.

Fugate, M., Kinicki, A. J. & Prussia, G. E. (2008). Employee coping with organisational change: An examination of alternative theoretical perspectives and models. *Personnel Psychology, 61*(1), 1–36.

Fuller, J. B., Patterson, C. E. P., Hester, K. & Stringer, D. Y. (1996). A quantitative review of research on charismatic leadership. *Psychological Reports, 78*(1), 271–287.

Fulmer, R. M. & Goldsmith, M. (2000). *The leadership investment: How the world's best organisations gain strategic advantage through leadership development.* New York, NY: American Management Association.

Galton, F. (1869). *Hereditary genius: An inquiry into its laws and consequences.* London: Macmillan.

Garbowski, M. A. (2010). *Transformational leadership and the dispositional effects of hope, optimism, and resilience on governmental leaders* (Unpublished doctoral thesis). Retrieved from ProQuest Digital Dissertations (Order No. AAI3425737).

Gardner, D. G. & Pierce, J. L. (1998). Self-esteem and self-efficacy within the organisational context. *Group & Organisation Management, 23*(1), 48–70.

Gardner, H. (1993). *Multiple intelligences: The theory in practice.* New York, NY: Basic Books.

Gardner, W. L., Avolio, B. J. & Luthans, F. (2005). 'Can you see the real me?' A self-based model of authentic leader and follower development. *Leadership Quarterly, 16*(3), 343–372.

Gardulf, A., Orton, M. L., Eriksson, L. E., Unden, M., Arnetz, B., Kajermo, K. N. & Nordstrom, G. (2008). Factors of importance for work satisfaction among nurses in a university hospital in Sweden. *Scandinavian Journal of Caring Science, 22*(2), 151–160.

Garmezy, N. (1974). Children at risk: The search for the antecedents of schizophrenia: II. Ongoing research programs, issues, and intervention. *Schizophrenia Bulletin, 1*(9), 55–125.

Garmezy, N. (1991). Resiliency and vulnerability to adverse developmental outcomes associated with poverty. *The American Behavioral Scientist, 34*(4), 416–430.

Garmezy, N. (1993a). Children in poverty: Resilience despite risk. *Psychiatry: Interpersonal and Biological Processes, 56*(1), 127–136.

Garmezy, N. (1993b). Vulnerability and resilience. In D. C. Funder, R. D. Parke, C. Tomlinson-Keasey & K. Widaman (Eds.), *Studying lives through time: Personality and development* (pp. 377–398). Washington, DC: American Psychological Association.

Gerstner, C. R. & Day, D. V. (1997). Meta-analytic review of leader-member exchange theory: Correlates and construct issues. *Journal of Applied Psychology, 82*(6), 827–844.

G-G blasts executives for lack of leadership. (2004, 24 February). *Australian Broadcasting Corporation.* Retrieved from http://www.abc.net.au/news/2004-02-25/g-g-blasts-executives-for-lack-of-leadership/141538

Gilley, A. (2005). *The manager as change leader.* Westport, CT: Praeger.

Gilley, A., Dixon, P. & Gilley, J. W. (2008). Characteristics of leadership effectiveness: implementing change and driving innovation in organisations. *Human Resources Development Quarterly, 19*(2), 153–169.

Glass, D. C. & Singer, J. E. (1972). Experimental studies of uncontrollable and unpredictable noise. *Representative Research in Social Psychology, 4*(1), 165–183.

Glenn, J. & Polygenis, R. (2015). *State update: Western Australia - September 2015.* Retrieved from http://business.nab.com.au/wp-content/uploads/2015/09/WA_-Sep15.pdf

Goffman, E. (1959). *The presentation of self in everyday life.* Garden City, NY: Doubleday-Anchor.

Goleman, D. (1995). *Emotional intelligence.* New York, NY: Bantam Books.

Goleman, D., Boyatzis, R. E. & McKee, A. (2002). *Primal leadership: Realizing the power of emotional intelligence.* Boston, MA: Harvard Business Press.

Gordon, G. G. & DiTomaso, N. (1992). Predicting corporate performance from organisational culture. *Journal of Management Studies, 29*(6), 783–798.

Gore, P. M. & Rotter, J. B. (1963). A personality correlate of social action. *Journal of Personality, 31*(1), 58–64.

Gottfredson, L. S. (1997). Mainstream science on intelligence: An editorial with 52 signatories, history and bibliography. *Intelligence, 24*(1), 13–23.

Graen, G. B., Novak, M. A. & Sommerkamp, P. (1982). The effects of leader-member exchange and job design on productivity and satisfaction: Testing a dual model. *Organisational Behavior and Human Performance, 30*(1), 109–131.

Graen, G. B. & Uhl-Bien, M. (1995). Relationship-based approach to leadership: Development of leader-member exchange theory of leadership over 25 years. *Leadership Quarterly, 6*(2), 219–247.

Graen, G. B., Wakabayashi, M., Graen, M. R. & Graen, M. G. (1990). International generalisability of American hypotheses about Japanese management progress: A strong inference investigation. *Leadership Quarterly, 1*(1), 1–23.

Gravetter, F. & Wallnau, L. (2014) Essentials of statistics for the behavioral sciences (8th ed.). Belmont, CA: Wadsworth.

Green, S. G., Anderson, S. E. & Shivers, S. L. (1996). Demographic and organisational influences on leader-member exchange and related work attitudes. *Organisational Behavior and Human Decision Process, 66*(2), 203–214.

Greenleaf, R. (1977). *Servant leadership.* Mahwah, NJ: Paulist Press.

Greguras, G. J. & Ford, J. M. (2006). An examination of the multidimensionality of supervisor and subordinate perceptions of leader-member exchange. *Journal of Occupational and Organisational Psychology, 79*(3), 433–465.

Griffith, J. & West, C. (2013). Master resilience training and its relationship to individual well-being and stress buffering among Army National Guard soldiers. *The Journal of Behavioral Health Services & Research, 40*(2), 140–155.

Gruber-Baldini, A., Ye, J., Anderson, K. & Shulman, L. M. (2009). Effects of optimism/pessimism and locus of control on disability and quality of life in Parkinson's disease. *Parkinsonism & Related Disorders, 15*(9), 665–669.

Grunberg, L., Moore, S., Greenberg, E. S. & Sikora, P. (2008). The changing workplace and its effects: A longitudinal examination of employee responses to a large company. *Journal of Applied Behavioral Science, 44*(2), 215–236.

Haaga, D. A. F., Dyck, M. J. & Ernst, D. (1991). Empirical status of cognitive theory of depression. *Psychological Bulletin, 110*(2), 215–236.

Hackman, J. R. & Oldham, G. R. (1975). Development of the job diagnostic survey. *Journal of Applied Psychology, 60*(2), 159–170.

Hahn, S. E. (2000). The effects of locus of control on daily exposure, coping and reactivity to work interpersonal stressors: A diary study. *Personality and Individual Differences, 29*(4), 729–748.

Hall, D. T. (2004). Self awareness, identity and leader development. In D. V. Day, S. J. Zaccaro & S. M. Halpin (Eds.), *Leader development for transforming organisations: Growing leaders for tomorrow* (pp. 153–176). Mahwah, NJ: Erlbaum.

Hand, M. P. (2004). *Psychological resilience: The influence of positive and negative life events upon optimism, hope, and perceived locus of control.* Retrieved from ProQuest Digital Dissertations (Order No. AAI3099937).

Hans, T. (2000). A meta-analysis of the effects of adventure programming on locus of control. *Journal of Contemporary Psychotherapy, 30*(1), 33–60.

Handy, C. B. (1995). The empty raincoat: Making sense of the future. London: Hutchinson.

Hardy, S. E., Concato, J. & Gill, T. M. (2004). Resilience of community-dwelling older persons. *Journal of the American Geriatrics Society, 52*(2), 257–262.

Harris, P. R. & Lightsey, O. R. (2005). Constructive thinking as a mediator of the relationship between extraversion, neuroticism, and subjective well-being. *European Journal of Personality, 19*(5), 409–426.

Harrison, R. (1987). Harnessing personal energy: How companies can inspire employees. *Organisational Dynamics, 16*(1), 4–20.

Hart, D., Hofmann, V., Edelstein, W. & Keller, M. (1997). The relation of childhood personality types to adolescent behaviour and development: A longitudinal study of Icelandic children. *Developmental Psychology, 33*(2), 195–205.

Hart, D., Keller, M., Edelstein, W. & Hofmann, V. (1998). Childhood personality influences on social–cognitive development: A longitudinal study. *Journal of Personality and Social Psychology, 74*(5), 1278–1289.

Harter, S. (1998). The development of self-representations. In W. Damon & N. Eisenberg (Ed.), *Handbook of child psychology: Social, emotional, and personality development* (pp. 553–617). Hoboken, NJ: John Wiley & Sons Inc.

Harter, J. K., Schmidt, F. L. & Hayes, T. L. (2002). Business-unit-level relationship between employee satisfaction, employee engagement and business outcomes: A meta-analysis. *Journal of Applied Psychology, 87,* 268–279.

Harvey, M. R. (2007). Towards an ecological understanding of resilience in trauma survivors: Implications for theory, research, and practice. *Journal of Aggression, Maltreatment & Trauma, 14*(1–2), 9–32.

Hätinen, M., Mäkikangas, A., Kinnunen, U. & Pekkonen, M. (2013). Recovery from burnout during a one-year rehabilitation intervention with six-month follow-up: Associations with coping strategies. *International Journal of Stress Management, 20*(4), 364–390.

Hattie, J. A., Marsh, H. W., Neill, J. T. & Richards, G. E. (1997). Adventure education and Outward Bound: Out-of-class experiences that have a lasting effect. *Review of Educational Research, 67*(1), 43–87.

Hautala, T. (2005). The effects of subordinates' personality on appraisals of transformational leadership. *Journal of Leadership & Organisational Studies, 11*(4), 84–92.

Heatherton, T. F., Herman, C. P. & Polivy, J. (1991). Effects of physical threat and ego threat on eating behavior. *Journal of Personality and Social Psychology, 60*(1), 138–143.

Heine, S. J., Lehman, D. R., Markus, H. R. & Kitayama, S. (1999). Is there a universal need for positive self-regard? *Psychological Review, 106*(4), 766–794.

Henning, J. B., Wygant, D. B. & Barnes, P. W. (2014). Mapping the darkness and finding the light: DSM-5 and assessment of the 'corporate psychopath'. *Industrial and Organisational Psychology: Perspectives on Science and Practice, 7*(1), 144–148.

Herd, A. M., Alagaraja, M. & Cumberland, D. M. (2016). Assessing global leadership competencies: The critical role of assessment centre methodology. *Human Resource Development International, 19*(1), 27–43.

Hersey, P. & Blanchard, K. H. (1972). The management of change: III. Planning and implementing change. *Training & Development Journal, 26*(3), 28–33.

Hernández-Torrano, D., Ferrándiz, C., Ferrando, M., Prieto, L. & Fernández, M. C. (2014). The theory of multiple intelligences in the identification of high-ability students. *Anales De Psicología, 30*(1), 193–201.

Herzberg, F. (2003). One more time: How do you motivate employees? *Harvard Business Review, 81*(1), 87–96.

Herzberg, F., Mausner, B. & Snyderman, B. (1959). *The motivation to work.* New York, NY: John Wiley.

Hetland, H., Sandal, G. M. & Johnsen, T. B. (2008). Followers' personality and leadership. *Journal of Leadership and Organisational Studies*, 14(4), 322–331.

Hitt, M. A., Ireland, R. D. & Hoskisson, R. E. (2003). Strategic management: Competitiveness and globalization (5th ed.). Cincinnati, OH: Southwestern College Publishing Company.

Hinduan, Z. R., Wilson-Evered, E., Moss, S. & Scannell, E. (2009). Leadership, work outcomes and openness to change following an Indonesian bank merger. *Asia Pacific Journal of Human Resources*, 47(1), 59–78.

Hinrichs, J. R. & Mischkind, L. A. (1967). Empirical and theoretical limitations of the two-factor hypothesis of job satisfaction. *Journal of Applied Psychology*, 51(2), 191–200.

Hoeve, Y. T., Jansen, G. & Roodbol, P. (2014). The nursing profession: Public image, self-concept and professional identity. A discussion paper. *Journal of Advanced Nursing*, 70, 295–309.

Hoffman. J. N. (2004). Building resilient leaders: Many universities and school districts are creating support mechanisms that increase administrator resiliency and lead to greater retention. *Leadership*, 34(1), 35–38.

Hogan, R. & Blake, R. J. (1996). Vocational interests: Matching of self-concept with the work environment. In K. R. Murphy (Ed.), *Individual differences and behavior in organisations* (pp. 89–144). San Francisco, CA: Jossey-Bass.

Hogan, R., Curphy, G. J. & Hogan, J. (1994). What we know about leadership: Effectiveness and personality. *American Psychologist*, 49(6), 493–504.

Hogan, R. & Ghufran, A. (2011). *Leadership*. Wiley-Blackwell.

Hogan, R. & Hogan, J. (1997). *Hogan Development Survey manual*. Tulsa, OK: Hogan Assessment Systems.

Hogan, R. & Hogan, J. (2001). Assessing leadership: A view from the dark side. *International Journal of Selection and Assessment*, 9(1–2), 40–51.

Hogan, R., Raskin, R. & Fazzini, D. (1990). The dark side of charisma. In K. E. Clark & M. B. Clark (Eds.), *Measures of leadership* (pp. 343–354). West Orange, NJ: Leadership Library of America.

Holden, K. B. & Rotter, J. B. (1962). A nonverbal measure of extinction in skill and change situations. *Journal of Experimental Psychology*, 63, 519–520.

Hollander, E. P. & Julian, J. W. (1969). Contemporary trends in the analysis of leadership processes. *Psychological Bulletin*, 71(5), 387–397.

Holling, C. S. (1973). Resilience and stability of ecological systems. *Annual Review of Ecology and Systematics*, 4(1), 1–23.

Hollnagel, E., Woods, D. D. & Leveson, N. G. (2006). *Resilience engineering: Concepts and precepts*. Aldershot, UK: Ashgate.

Holtz, B. C. & Harold, C. M. (2008). When your boss says no! The effects of leadership style and trust on employee reactions to managerial explanations. *Journal of Occupational Organisational Psychology*, 81(4), 777–802.

House, R. J. (1971). A path-goal theory of leader effectiveness. *Administrative Science Quarterly*, 16(3), 321–339.

House, R. J. & Mitchell, T. R. (1974). Path-goal theory of leadership. *Journal of Contemporary Business, 3*, 81–98.

House, R. J. & Shamir, B. (1993). *Toward the integration of transformational, charismatic, and visionary theories*. San Diego, CA: Academic Press.

Hovland, C. & Janis, I. L. (1959). *Personality and persuasability*. New Haven, CT: Yale University Press.

Howard, A. & Wellins, R. S. (2009). *Overcoming the shortfalls in developing leaders: Global leadership forecast 2008/2009*. Bridgeville, PA: Development Dimensions International Inc.

Howell, J. M. & Avolio, B. J. (1993). Transformational leadership, transactional leadership, locus of control, and support for innovation: Key predictors of consolidated-business-unit performance. *Journal of Applied Psychology*, 78(6), 891–902.

Howell, J. M. & Hall-Merenda, K. E. (1999). The ties that bind: The impact of leader-member exchange, transformational and transactional leadership, and distance on predicting follower performance. *Journal of Applied Psychology*, 84(5), 680–694.

Hoyer, J., Averbeck, M., Heidenreich, T., Stangier, U., Pöhlmann, K. & Rössler, G. (1998). The constructive thinking inventory: Factorial structure in healthy individuals and patients with chronic skin diseases. *European Journal of Psychological Assessment, 14*(3), 226–233.

Huebner, E. S. (2012). Review of applied positive psychology: Improving everyday life, health, schools, work, and society. *The Journal of Social Psychology, 152*(1), 128–130.

Hunt, J. G. (1991). *Leadership: A new synthesis*. Thousand Oaks, CA: SAGE Publications.

Hunt, J. G. & Conger, J. A. (1999). From where we sit: An assessment of transformational and charismatic leadership research. *The Leadership Quarterly, 10*(3), 335–343.

Hunt, J. G. & Larsons, L. L. (1977). *Leadership: The cutting edge*. Carbondale, IL: Southern Illinois University Press.

James, W. (1890). *The principles of psychology.* New York, NY: Holt.

James, W. H. (1957). *Internal versus external control of reinforcement as a basic variable in learning theory* (Unpublished doctoral thesis). Ohio State University. Columbus, OH. Retrieved from PsycINFO (615332801; 1958-05124-001).

Jansen, J. J. P., Vera, D. & Crossan, M. (2009). Strategic leadership for exploration and exploitation: The moderating role of environmental dynamism. *The Leadership Quarterly, 20*(1), 5–18.

Jayawickreme, E., Forgeard, M. J. C. & Seligman, M. E. P. (2012). The engine of well-being. *Review of General Psychology,* 16, 327–342.

Jenkins, L., Demaray, M. & Tennant, J. (2017). Social, emotional, and cognitive factors associated with bullying. *School Psychology Review, 46*(1), 42–64.

Johnson, A., Dey, S., Nguyen, H., Groth, M., Joyce, S., Tan, L., Glozier, N., & Harvey, S. B. (2020). A review and agenda for examining how technology-driven changes at work will impact workplace mental health and employee well-being. *Australian Journal of Management, 45*(3), 402–424.

Johnson, M. C., Birchfield, J. & Wieand, P. (2008). The new leadership challenge: Removing the emotional barriers to sustainable performance in a flat world. *Ivey Business Journal Online, 1.* Retrieved from http://iveybusinessjournal.com/publication/the-new-leadership-challenge-removing-the-emotional-barriers-to-sustainable-performance-in-a-flat-world/

Johnson, R. E., Venus, M., Lanaj, K., Mao, C. & Chang, C. (2012). Leader identity as an antecedent of the frequency and consistency of transformational, consideration, and abusive leadership behaviors. *Journal of Applied Psychology, 97*(6), 1262–1272.

Judd, C. M., Smith, E. R. & Kidder, L. H. (1991). *Research methods in social relation: International edition* (6th ed.). Fort Worth, TX: Rinehart and Winston.

Judge, T. A. (2009). Core self-evaluations and work success. *Current Directions in Psychological Science, 18*(1), 58–62.

Judge, T. A. & Bono, J. E. (2001). Relationship of core self-evaluations traits—self-esteem, generalized self-efficacy, locus of control, and emotional stability—with job satisfaction and job performance: A meta-analysis. *Journal of Applied Psychology, 86*(1), 80–92.

Judge, T. A., Bono, J. E., Erez, A., & Locke, E. A. (2005). Core Self-Evaluations and Job and Life Satisfaction: The Role of Self-Concordance and Goal Attainment. *Journal of Applied Psychology, 90*(2), 257-268.

Judge, T. A., Bono, J. E., Ilies, R. & Gerhardt, M. W. (2002). Personality and leadership: A qualitative and quantitative review. *Journal of Applied Psychology, 87*(4), 765–780.

Judge, T. A., Erez, A., Bono, J. E. & Thoresen, C. J. (2002). Are measures of self-esteem, neuroticism, locus of control, and generalized self-efficacy indicators of a common core construct? *Journal of Personality and Social Psychology, 83*(3), 693–710.

Judge, T. A., Locke, E. A. Durham, C. C. & Kluger, A. N. (1998). Dispositional effects on job and life satisfaction: The role of core evaluations. *Journal of Applied Psychology, 83*(1), 17–34.

Judge, W. Q., Naoumova, I. & Douglas, T. (2009). Organisational capacity for change and firm performance in a transition economy, *The International Journal of Human Resource Management, 20*(8),1737-1752.

Judge, T. A., Thoresen, C. J., Bono, J. E. & Patton, G. K. (2001). The job satisfaction-job performance relationship: A qualitative and quantitative review. *Psychological Bulletin, 127*(3), 376–407.

Judge, T. A., Thoresen, C. J., Pucik, V. & Welbourne, T. M. (1999). Managerial coping with organisational change: A dispositional perspective. *Journal of Applied Psychology, 84*(1), 107–122.

Kahn, R. L., Wolfe, D. M., Quinn, R. P., Snoek, J. D. & Rosenthal, R. A. (1964). *Organisational stress: Studies in role conflict and ambiguity.* Oxford, UK: John Wiley.

Kahneman, D. (2011). *Thinking, fast and slow.* New York: Farrar, Straus and Giroux.

Kantabutra, S., & Avery, G. C. (2010). The power of vision: statements that resonate. Journal of business strategy, 31(1), 37-45.

Kaplan, S. A. & Waller, M. J. (2018). Reliability through resilience in organisational teams. In R. Ramanujam & K. Roberts (Eds.), *Organizing for reliability: A guide for research and practice.* Stanford, CA: Stanford University Press.

Karakas, F. (2009). New paradigms in organisation development: Positivity, spirituality, and complexity. *Organisation Development Journal, 27*(1), 11–26.

Kolzow, D. R. (2014). *Leading from within: Building organisational leadership capacity.* International Economic Development Council.

Katz, D. & Kahn, R. L. (1966). *The social psychology of organisations.* New York, NY: John Wiley.

Kelemen, M. & Rumens, N. (2012). Pragmatism and heterodoxy in organisation research: Going beyond the quantitative/qualitative divide. *International Journal of Organisational Analysis, 20*(1), 5–12.

Kerber, K. W. & Buono, A. F. (2009). Building change capacity: *Client-consultant collaboration and organisational change.* In A. F. Buono & F. Poulfelt (Eds.), Client-consultant collaboration: Coping with complexity and change (pp. 69–87). Charlotte, NC: Information Age Publishing.

Kerlinger. F. N. (1986). *Foundations of behavioral research.* New York, NY: Holt, Rinehart and Winston Inc.

Kernis, M. H. (2000). Substitute needs and the distinction between fragile and secure high self-esteem. *Psychological Inquiry, 11*(4), 298–300.

Kernis, M. H. & Goldman, B. M. (2003). Stability and variability in self-concept and self-esteem. In M. R. Leary & J. P. Tangley (Eds.), *Handbook of self and identity* (pp. 106–127). New York, NY: Guilford Press.

Kernis, M. H., Greenier, K. D., Herlocker, C. E., Whisenhunt, C. R. & Abend, T. A. (1997). Self-perceptions of reactions to doing well or poorly: The roles of stability and level of self-esteem. *Personality and Individual Differences, 22*(6), 845–854.

Kernis, M. H. & Lakey, C. E. (2010). *Fragile versus secure high self-esteem: Implications for defensiveness and insecurity.* New York, NY: Psychology Press.

Keyes, C. L. M. (1998). Social well-being. *Social Psychology Quarterly, 61*(2), 121–140.

Keyes, C. L. M. (2002). The mental health continuum: From languishing to flourishing in life. *Journal of Health and Social Behavior, 43*(2), 207–222.

Keyes, C. L. M. (2004). Risk and resilience in human development: An introduction. *Research in Human Development, 1*(4), 223–227.

Keyes, C. L. M. (2007). Promoting and protecting mental health as flourishing: A complementary strategy for improving national mental health. *American Psychologist, 62*(2), 95–108.

Keyes, C. L. M. & Lopez, S. J. (2009). Toward a science of mental health. In S. J. Lopez & C. R. Snyder (Eds.), *Oxford handbook of positive psychology* (pp. 89–95). New York, NY: Oxford University Press.

Khoo, H. S. & Burch, G. S. J. (2007). The dark side of leadership personality and transformational leadership: An exploratory study. *Personality and Individual Differences, 44*(1), 86–97.

Kimball, L. S. & Nink, C. E. (2006). How to improve employee motivation, commitment, productivity, well-being and safety. *Corrections Today*, 68(3), 66–69.

Kinicki, A. J., McKee-Ryan, F. M., Schriesheim, C. A. & Carson, K. P. (2002). Assessing the construct validity of the Job Descriptive Index: A review and meta-analysis. *Journal of Applied Psychology*, 87(1), 14–32.

Kinman, G. & Grant, L. (2011). Exploring stress resilience in trainee social workers: The role of emotional and social competencies. *British Journal of Social Work*, 41(2), 261–275.

Kinsinger, P., & Walch, K. (2012). Living and leading in a VUCA world. Thunderbird University, 542-555.

Kirmayer, J. L., Sehdev, M., Whitley, R., Dandeneau, F. S. & Isaac, C. (2009). Community resilience: Models, metaphors and measures. *Journal of Aboriginal Health*, 5, 62–117.

Kler, P., Leeves, G. & Shankar, S. (2015). Nothing to fear but fear itself: Perceptions of job security in Australia after the global financial crisis. *Social Indicators Research*, 123(3), 753–769.

Kline, P. (1986). *A handbook in test construction: Introduction to psychometric design*. London, UK: Methuen.

Kline, R. B. (2016). *Principles and practice of structural equation modelling* (4th ed.). New York, NY: Guilford Press.

Kobasa, S. C. (1979). Stressful life events, personality and health: An inquiry into hardiness. *Journal of Personality and Social Psychology*, 37(1) 1–11.

Kobasa, S. C. & Puccetti, M. C. (1983). Personality and social resources in stress resistance. *Journal of Personality and Social Psychology*, 45(4), 839–850.

Koh, W. L., Steers, R. M. & Terborg, J. R. (1995). The effects of transformational leadership on teacher attitudes and student performance in Singapore. *Journal of Organisational Behavior*, 16(4), 319–333.

Korman, A. K. (1970). Towards a hypothesis of work behavior. *Journal of Applied Psychology*, 54, 31–41.

Kotter, J. P. & Heskett, J. L. (1992). *Corporate culture and performance*. New York, NY: The Free Press.

Kramer, R. (2012). Rank on emotional intelligence, unlearning and self-leadership. *The American Journal of Psychoanalysis*, 72(4), 326–351.

Krishnan, V. R. (2005). Leader-member exchange, transformational leadership and value system. *Electronic Journal of Business Ethics and Organisational Studies*, 10(1), 14–21.

Kuoppala, J., Lamminpaa, A., Liira, J. & Vainio, H. (2008). Leadership, job well-being, and health effects: A systematic review and a meta-analysis. *Journal of Occupational and Environmental Medicine, 50*(8), 904–915.

Lachman, M. E. & Firth, K. M. P. (2004). The adaptive value of feeling in control during midlife. In O. G. Brun, C. D. Ryff & R. C. Kessler (Eds.), *How healthy are we? A national study of well-being in midlife* (pp. 320–349). Chicago, IL: University of Chicago Press.

Lachowicz-Tabaczek, K. & Śniecińska, J. (2011). Self-concept and self-esteem: How the content of the self-concept reveals sources and functions of self-esteem. *Polish Psychological Bulletin, 42*(1), 24–35.

Lambert, V. A., Lambert, C. E. & Yamase, H. (2003). Psychological hardiness, workplace stress and related stress reduction strategies. *Nursing & Health Sciences, 5*(2), 181–184.

Lamp, K. E. (2014). *Personal and contextual resilience factors and their relations to psychological adjustment outcomes across the lifespan: A meta-analysis* (Unpublished doctoral thesis). Retrieved from http://ecommons.luc.edu/luc_diss/673/

Landy, J. L. & Conte, J. M. (2016). *Work in the 21st century: An introduction to industrial and organisational psychology* (5th ed.). Oxford, UK: Hoboken Wiley.

Lapierre, M. L. & Hackett, R. D. (2007). Trait conscientiousness, leader-member exchange, job satisfaction and organisational citizenship behavior: A test of an integrative model. *Journal of Occupational and Organisational Psychology, 80*(3), 539–554.

Lawler, E. E. & Worley, C. G. (2012). Designing organisations for sustainable effectiveness. *Organisational Dynamics,* 41(4), 265–270.

Lawrence, S. A. & Callan, V. J. (2011). The role of social support in coping during the anticipatory stage of organisational change: A test of an integrative model. *British Journal of Management, 22*(4), 567–585.

Leary, M. R. & Baumeister, R. F. (2000). The nature and function of self-esteem: Sociometer theory. In M. P. Zanna (Ed.), *Advances in experimental social psychology* (Vol. 32, pp. 1–62). San Diego, CA: Academic Press.

LeBlanc, V., Regehr, C., Blake Jelley, R. & Barath, I. (2008). The relationship between coping styles, performance, and responses to stressful scenarios in police recruits. *International Journal of Stress Management, 15,* 76–93.

Lecky, P. (1945). *Self-consistency: A theory of personality.* Washington, DC: Island Press.

Lee, J. (2005). Effects of leadership and leader-member exchange on commitment. *Leadership and Organisational Development Journal, 26*(8), 655–672.

Lee, J. H., Nam, S. K., Kim, A., Kim, B., Lee, M. Y. & Lee, S. M. (2013). Resilience: A meta-analytic approach. *Journal of Counseling and Development, 91*(3), 269–279.

Lefcourt, H. M. (1976). Locus of control and the response to aversive events. *Canadian Psychological Review, 17*(3), 202–208.

Lefcourt, H. M. (1991). Locus of control. In J. P. Robinson, P. R. Shaver & L. S. Wrightsman (Eds.), *Measures of personality and social psychological attitudes* (pp. 413–499). New York, NY: Academic Press.

Lefcourt, H. M. (1992). Durability and impact of the locus of control construct. *Psychological Bulletin, 112*(3), 411–414.

Lefcourt, H. M. & Davidson-Katz, K. (1991). Locus of control and health. In C. R. Snyder & D. R. Forsyth (Eds.), *Pergamon general psychology series, Vol. 162. Handbook of social and clinical psychology: The health perspective* (pp. 246–266). Elmsford, NY: Pergamon Press.

Lefcourt, H. M. & Wine, J. (1968). Internal versus external control of reinforcement and the deployment of attention in experimental situations. *Canadian Journal of Behavioural Science, 1*(3), 167–181.

Leontopoulou, S. (2006). Resilience of Greek youth at an educational transition point: The role of locus of control and coping strategies as resources. *Social Indicators Research, 76*(1), 95–126.

Levenson, H. (1974). Activism and powerful others: Distinctions within the concept of internal-external control. *Journal of Personality Assessment, 38*(4), 377–383.

Levy, L. H. (1956). The meaning and generality of perceived and actual-ideal discrepancies. *Journal of Consulting Psychology, 20*(5), 396–398.

Lewis, P. S., Goodman, S. H. & Fandt, P. M. (2000). *Management: Challenges in the 21st century* (3rd ed.). Cincinnati, OH: South-Western Publishing.

Liden, R. C., Erdogan, B., Wayne, S. J. & Sparrowe, R. T. (2006). Leader-member exchange, differentiation, and task interdependence: Implications for individual and group performance. Journal of Organisational Behavior, 27(6), 723–746.

Liden, R. C. & Graen, G. (1980). Generalizability of the vertical dyad linkage model of leadership. *Academy of Management Journal, 23*(3), 451–465.

Liden, R. C. & Maslyn, J. M. (1998). Multidimensionality of leader-member exchange: An empirical assessment though scale development. *Journal of Management, 24*(1), 43–72.

Liden, R. C., Wayne, S. J. & Stilwell, D. (1993). A longitudinal study on the early development of leader-member exchanges. *Journal of Applied Psychology*, 78(4), 662–674.

Likert, R. (1967). *The human organisation: Its management and value*. New York, NY: McGraw-Hill.

Lillevoll, K. R., Kroger, J. & Martinussen, M. (2013). Identity status and anxiety: A meta-analysis. *Identity: An International Journal of Theory and Research*, 13(3), 214–227.

Linville, P. W. (1985). Self-complexity and affective extremity: Don't put all of your eggs in one cognitive basket. *Social Cognition*, 3(1), 94–120.

Lipsitt, L. P. & Demick, J. (2011). Resilience science comes of age: Old age, that is. *PsycCRITIQUES*, 36(26). DOI:10.1037/a0023900

Liu, X., Kaplan, H. B. & Risser, W. (1992). Decomposing the reciprocal relationships between academic achievement and general self-esteem. *Youth & Society*, 24(2), 123–148.

Liverant, S. (1960). Intelligence: A concept in need of re-examination. *Journal of Consulting Psychology*, 24(2), 101–110.

Loi, R., Yang, J. & Diefendorff, J. M. (2009). Four-factor justice and daily job satisfaction: A multilevel investigation. *Journal of Applied Psychology*, 94(3), 770–781.

Lord, L., Jefferson, T., Klass, D., Nowak, M. & Thomas, G. (2013). Leadership in context: Insights from a study of nursing in Western Australia. *Leadership*, 9(2), 180–200.

Lorr, M. & Wunderlich, R. A. (1986). Tow objective measures of self-esteem. *Journal of Personality Assessment*, 50(1), 18–23.

Lowe, K. B. & Gardner, W. L. (2000). Ten years of the Leadership Quarterly: Contributions and challenges for the future. *The Leadership Quarterly*, 11(4), 459–514.

Lowe, K. B., Kroeck, K. G. & Sivasubramaniam, N. (1996). Effectiveness correlates of transformational and transactional leadership: A meta-analytic review of the MLQ literature. *Leadership Quarterly*, 7(3), 385–425.

Luft, J.; Ingham, H. (1955). 'The Johari window, a graphic model of interpersonal awareness'. Proceedings of the Western Training Laboratory in Group Development. Los Angeles: *University of California, Los Angeles*.

Luthans, F., Avolio, B. J., Walumbwa, F. O. & Li, W. (2005). The psychological capital of Chinese workers: Exploring the relationship with performance. *Management and Organisation Review*, 1(2), 249–271.

Luthar, S. S., Cicchetti, D. & Becker, B. (2000). The construct of resilience: A critical evaluation and guidelines for future work. *Child Development, 71*(3), 543–562.

Macik-Frey, M., Quick, J. C. & Cooper, C. L. (2008). Authentic leadership as a pathway to positive health. *Journal of Organisational Behaviour, 30*(3), 453–458.

Maddi, S. R. (2011). Personality hardiness as a pathway to resilience under educational stresses. In G. Reevy & E. Frydenberg (Eds.), *Personality, stress, and coping: Implications for education* (pp. 293–313). Charlotte, NC: Information Age Publishing.

Maddi, S. R. (2013). *Hardiness: Turning stressful circumstances into resilient growth.* New York, NY: Springer Science+Business Media.

Maddi, S. R. & Hightower, M. (1999). Hardiness and optimism as expressed in coping patterns. *Consulting Psychology Journal: Practice and Research, 51*(2), 95–105.

Maddi, S. R., Kahn, S. & Maddi, K. L. (1998). The effectiveness of hardiness training. *Consulting Psychology Journal: Practice and Research*, 50(2), 78–86.

Maddi, S. R. & Khoshaba, D. M. (2003). Hardiness training for resiliency and leadership. In D. Paton, J. M. Volanti & L. M. Smith (Eds.), *Promoting capabilities to manage posttraumatic stress: Perspectives on resilience* (pp. 43–58). Springfield, IL: Charles C Thomas Publisher.

Maddi, S. R., Khoshaba, D. M., Harvey, R. H., Fazel, M. & Resurreccion, N. (2011). The personality construct of hardiness, V: Relationships with the construction of existential meaning in life. *Journal of Humanistic Psychology, 51*(3), 369–388.

Madzar, J. (2001). Subordinates' information inquiry: Exploring the effect of perceived leadership style and individual differences. *Journal of Occupational and Organisational Psychology*, 74(2), 221–232.

Maier, S. F. & Seligman, M. E. (1976). Learned helplessness: Theory and evidence. *Journal of Experimental Psychology: General, 105*(1), 3–46.

Mann, R. D. (1959). A review of the relationships between personality and performance in small groups. *Psychological Bulletin, 56*(4), 241–270.

Mann, S. (2006). Review of *Leadership Training. Leadership & Organisation Development Journal*, 27(7).

Mardanov, I. T. & Heischmidt, K. (2008). Leader-member exchange and job satisfaction bond and predicted employee turnover. *Journal of Leadership and Organisational Studies, 15*(2), 159–175.

Markus, H. (1977). Self-schemata and processing information about the self. *Journal of Personality and Social Psychology, 35*(2), 63–78.

Markus, H. & Kunda, Z. (1986). Stability and malleability of the self-concept. *Journal of Personality and Social Psychology, 51*(4), 858–866.

Markus, H. & Wurf, E. (1987). The dynamic self-concept: A social psychological perspective. *Annual Review of Psychology, 38*(1), 299–337.

Marsh, H. W. & Hocevar, D. (1983). Confirmatory factor analysis of multitrait-multimethod matrices. *Journal of Educational Measurement, 20*(3), 231–248.

Marsh, H. W. & Richards, G. E. (1986). The Rotter locus of control scale: The comparison of alternative response formats and implications for reliability, validity and dimensionality. *Journal of Research in Personality, 20*(4), 509–558.

Marsh, H. W. & Richards, G. E. (1987). The multidimensionality of the Rotter IE scale and its higher-order structure: An application of confirmatory factor analysis. *Multivariate Behavioral Research, 22*(1), 39–69.

Marsh, H. W., Smith, I. D. & Barnes, J. (1983). Multitrait-multimethod analyses of the Self-Description Questionnaire: Student-teacher agreement on multidimensional ratings of student self-concept. *American Education Research Journal, 20*(3), 333–357.

Marsh, H. W., Trautwein, U., Lüdtke, O., Köller, O. & Baumert, J. (2005). Academic self-concept, interest, grades, and standardized test scores: Reciprocal effects models of causal ordering. *Child Development, 76*(2), 397–416.

Marsick, V. J. & Watkins, K. (1990). *Informal and incidental learning in the workplace.* New York, NY: Routledge.

Martin, R., Thomas, G., Charles, K. Epitropaki, O. & McNamara, R. (2005). The role of leader-member exchanges in mediating the relationship between locus of control and work reactions. *Journal of Occupational and Organisational Psychology, 78*(1), 141–147.

Maslyn, J. M. & Uhl-Bien, M. (2001). Leader-member exchange and its dimensions: effects of self-effort and others effort on relationship quality. *Journal of Applied Psychology, 86*(4), 697–708.

Maxwell, S. E. (2004). The persistence of underpowered studies in psychological research: Causes, consequences, and remedies. *Psychological Methods, 9*, 147–163.

Maulding, W. S., Peters, G. B., Roberts, J., Leonard, E. & Sparkman, L. (2012). Emotional intelligence and resilience as predictors of leadership in school administrators. *Journal of Leadership Studies, 5*(4), 20–29.

Mayfield, J. & Mayfield, M. (2002). Leader communication strategies critical paths to improving employee commitment. *American Business Review, 20*(2), 89–94.

Maynard, R. A. & Dong, N. (2013). PowerUp!: A tool for calculating minimum detectable Effect sizes and minimum required sample sizes for experimental and quasi-experimental design studies. *Journal of Research on Educational Effectiveness, 6*(1), 24–67. http://dx.doi.org/10.1080/19345747.2012.673143

Mayo, E. (1949). *Hawthorne and the Western Electric Company: The social problems of an industrial civilisation.* London, UK: Lowe & Brydone Printers.

McCall, M. W. (1998). *High flyers: Developing the next generation of leaders.* Boston, MA: Harvard Business Press.

McClane, W. E. (1991). The interaction of leader and member characteristics in the leader-member exchange (LMX) model of leadership. *Small Group Research, 22*(3), 283–300.

McClelland, D. C. (1961). *The achieving society.* Oxford, UK: Van Nostrand.

McClelland, D. C. (1985). *Human motivation.* Glenview, IL: Scott, Foresman.

McDonnell, R. (2008, 27 October). Making sure your business thrives in tough climate: Strong management key to success. *Belfast Telegraph.* Retrieved from https://www.highbeam.com/doc/1P2-19372821.html

McFarlin, D. B., Baumeister, R. F. & Blascovich, J. (1984). On knowing when to quit: Task failure, self-esteem, advice, and nonproductive persistence. *Journal of Personality, 52*(2), 138–155.

Metcalfe, B. A. & Metcalfe, R. J. (2001). The development of a new transformational leadership questionnaire. *Journal of Occupational and Organisational Psychology, 74*(1), 1–27.

Middleton, J., Harvey, S. & Esaki, N. (2015). Transformational leadership and organisational change: How do leaders approach trauma-informed organisational change...twice? *Families in Society, 96*(3), 155–163.

Miller Burke, J. & Attridge, M. (2011). Pathways to career and leadership success: Part 1—A psychosocial profile of $100k professionals. *Journal of Workplace Behavioral Health, 26*(3), 175–206.

Moore-Davis, F. R. (2008). *Impact of spirituality on leader-member exchange and job satisfaction.* Retrieved from ProQuest Digital Dissertations (Order No. AAI3292271).

Morrow, C. C., Jarrett, M. Q. & Rupinski, M. T. (1997). An investigation of the effect and economic utility of corporate-wide training. *Personnel Psychology, 50*(1), 91–119.

Morrow, P. C., Suzuki, Y., Crum, M. R., Ruben, R. & Pautsch, G. (2005). The role of leader-member exchange in high turnover work environments. *Journal of Managerial Psychology*, 20(8), 681–694.

Mumford, M. D., Friedrich, T. L., Vessey, W. B. & Ruark, G. A. (2012). Collective leadership: Thinking about issues vis-à-vis others. *Industrial and Organisational Psychology: Perspectives on Science and Practice*, 5(4), 408–411.

Murphy, K. R. (2006). *A critique of emotional intelligence: What are the problems and how can they be fixed?* Mahwah, NJ: Erlbaum.

Musser, L. M. & Browne, B. A. (1991). Self-monitoring in middle childhood: Personality and social correlates. *Developmental Psychology*, 27(6), 994–999.

Neiger, B. (1991). *Resilient reintegration: Use of structural equations modelling* (Unpublished doctoral thesis). University of Utah, Salt Lake City, UT.

Nelson, D. L. & Quick, J. C. (2009). *Organisational behavior: Science, the real world and you* (6th ed.). Macon, OH: South-Western/Cengage Learning.

Neupert, S. D., Almeida, D. M. & Charles, S. T. (2007). Age differences in reactivity to daily stressors: The role of personal control. *The Journals of Gerontology Series B: Psychological Sciences and Social Sciences*, 62(4), 216–225.

Ng, T. W. H., Sorensen, K. L. & Eby, L. T. (2006). Locus of control at work: A meta-analysis. *Journal of Organisational Behavior*, 27(8), 1057–1087.

Nguyen, J. C. (2002). An investigation of the relationship among the constructs of transformational and transactional leadership and general cognitive ability. *Dissertation Abstracts International Section A: Humanities and Social Sciences*, 63(6-A), 2271.

Niedenthal, P. M., Setterlund, M. B. & Wherry, M. B. (1992). Possible self-complexity and affective reactions to goal-relevant evaluation. *Journal of Personality and Social Psychology*, 63(1), 5–16.

Nissen, M. E. & Bergin, R. D. (2012). Knowledge work through social media applications: Team performance implications of immersive virtual worlds. *Journal of Organisational Computing and Electronic Commerce*, 23(1–2), 84–109.

Noble, K. D. (2001). *Riding the windhorse: Spiritual intelligence and the growth of the self*. New York, NY: Hampton Press.

Norris, F. H., Stevens, S. P., Pfefferbaum, B., Wyche, K. F. & Pfefferbaum, R. L. (2008). Community resilience as a metaphor, theory, set of capacities, and strategy for disaster readiness. *American Journal of Community Psychology*, 41(1–2), 127–150.

Nowak, A. & Vallacher, R. R. (1998). *Dynamical social psychology*. New York: Guilford.

Nufer, S. (2013). The effects of locus of control and leader-member exchange as predictors of stress and burnout in the workplace. *Dissertation Abstracts International, 73*.

Nunnally, J. C. (1967). *Psychometric theory*. New York, NY: McGraw-Hill.

Oades-Sese, G. V., Cohen, D., Allen, J. W. P. & Lewis, M. (2014). Building resilience in young children the sesame street way. In S. Prince-Embury & D. H. Saklofske (Eds.), *Resilience interventions for youth in diverse populations* (pp. 181–201). New York, NY: Springer.

Offutt, M. S. (2011). *An examination of the characteristic, resilience, and leadership practices in public school elementary principals* (Unpublished doctoral thesis). Retrieved from ProQuest Digital Dissertations (Order No. AAI3476498).

Ong, A. D., Bergeman, C. S. & Bisconti, T. L. (2005). Unique effects of daily perceived control on anxiety symptomatology during conjugal bereavement. *Personality and Individual Differences, 38*(5), 1057–1067.

Orth, U., Robins, R. W., Trzesniewski, K. H., Maes, J. & Schmitt, M. (2009). Low self-esteem is a risk factor for depressive symptoms from young adulthood to old age. *Journal of Abnormal Psychology, 118*(3), 472–478.

Orth, U., Robins, R. W. & Widaman, K. F. (2012). Life-span development of self-esteem and its effects on important life outcomes. *Journal of Personality and Social Psychology, 102*(6), 1271–1288.

Overmier, J. B. & Seligman, M. E. (1967). Effects of inescapable shock upon subsequent escape and avoidance responding. *Journal of Comparative and Physiological Psychology, 63*(1), 28.

Palmer, C. (2008). A theory of risk and resilience factors in military families. *Military Psychology, 20*(3), 205–217.

Pangallo, A., Zibarras, L., Lewis, R. & Flaxman, P. (2015). Resilience through the lens of interactionism: A systematic review. *Psychological Assessment, 27*(1), 1–20.

Parkin, A. J. & Java, R. I. (1999). Deterioration of frontal lobe function in normal aging: Influences of fluid intelligence versus perceptual speed. *Neuropsychology, 3*(4), 539–545.

Parry, K. (1998). Grounded theory and social process: A new direction for leadership research. *The Leadership Quarterly, 9*(1), 85–105.

Patterson, M., Warr, P. & West, M. (2004). Organisational climate and company productivity: The role of employee affect and employee level. *Journal of Occupational and Organisational Psychology*, 77(2), 193–216.

Pearson, C., & Porath, C. (2009). *The Costs of Bad Behaviour: How Incivility Is Damaging Your Business and What to Do about It*. New York: Penguin Books Ltd.

Pelham, B. W. & Swann, W. B. (1989). From self-conceptions to self-worth: On the sources and structure of global self-esteem. *Journal of Personality and Social Psychology*, 57(4), 672–680.

Pelletier, K. L. & Bligh, M. C. (2008). The aftermath of organisational corruption: Employee attributions and emotional reactions. *Journal of Business Ethics*, 80(4), 823–844.

Pendse, S. G. (2012). Ethical hazards: A motive, means, and opportunity approach to curbing corporate unethical behavior. *Journal of Business Ethics*, 107(3), 265–279.

Perloff, R. (1997). Daniel Goleman's emotional intelligence: Why it can matter more than IQ. [Review of the book Emotional intelligence. D. Goleman]. *The Psychologist-Manager Journal*, 1(1), 21–22.

Petree, R. D., Broome, K. M. & Bennett, J. B. (2012). Exploring and reducing stress in young restaurant workers: Results of a randomized field trial. *American Journal of Health Promotion*, 26(4), 217–224.

Pfefferbaum, B., Noffsinger, M. A., Wind, L. H. & Allen, J. R. (2014). Children's coping in the context of disasters and terrorism. *Journal of Loss and Trauma*, 19(1), 78–97.

Phares, E. J. (1955). *Changes in expectancy in skill and chance situations* (Unpublished doctoral thesis). Ohio State University, Columbus, OH.

Phares, E. J. (1962). Perceptual threshold decrements as a function of skill and chance expectancies. *The Journal of Psychology*, 53(2), 399–407.

Phares, E. J. (1965). Internal-external control as a determinant of amount of social influence exerted. *Journal of Personality and Social Psychology*, 2(5), 642-647.

Phares, E. J. (1976). *Locus of control in personality*. Morristown, NJ: General Learning Press.

Phillips, A. S. & Bedeian, A. G. (1994). Leader-follower exchange quality: The role of personal and interpersonal attributes. *Academy of Management Journal*, 37(4), 990–1001.

Phillips, R. L., Duran, C. A. & Howell, R. D. (1993). An examination of the multidimensionality hypothesis of leader-member exchange, using both factor analytic and structural modelling techniques. In *Proceedings of the Southern Management Association 1993 Meeting* (pp. X–X). Marietta, GA: Southern Management Association.

Piccolo, R. F., Bono, J. E., Heinitz, K., Rowold, J., Duehr, E. & Judge, T. A. (2012). The relative impact of complementary leader behaviors: Which matter most? *The Leadership Quarterly, 23*(3), 567–581.

Pierce, J. L. & Gardner, D. G. (2004). Self-esteem within the work and organisational context: A review of the organisation-based self-esteem literature. *Journal of Management, 30*(5), 591–622.

Pierce, J. L., Gardner, D. G., Cummings, L. L. & Dunham, R. B. (1989). Organisation-based self-esteem: Construct definition, measurement, and validation. *Academy of Management Journal, 32*(3), 622–648.

Pipe, T. B., Buchda, V. L., Launder, S., Hudak, B., Hulvey, L., Karns, K. E. & Pendergast, D. (2012). Building personal and professional resources of resilience and agility in the healthcare workplace. *Stress and Health, 28*(1), 11–22.

Pisani, N. A. (2009). International management research: Investigating its recent diffusion in top management journals. *Journal of Management, 35*(2), 199–218.

Porter, L. W. & Lawler, E. E. (1968). *Managerial attitudes and performance.* Homewood, IL: Irwin.

Pullen, A. & Rhodes, C. (2008). 'It's all about me!': Gendered narcissism and leaders' identity work. *Leadership, 4*(1), 5–25.

Raskin, R. N. & Terry, H. (1988). A principle components analysis of the narcissistic personality inventory and further evidence of its construct validity. *Journal of Personality and Social Psychology, 54*(5), 890–902.

Rassart, J., Luyckx, K., Berg, C. A., Bijttebier, P., Moons, P. & Weets, I. (2015). Psychosocial functioning and glycemic control in emerging adults with Type 1 diabetes: A 5-year follow-up study. *Health Psychology, 34*(11), 1058–1065.

Raven, B. H. & French, J. R. P. (1958). Group support, legitimate power, and social influence. *Journal of Personality, 26*(3), 400–409.

Ravi, K. R. & Kamalanabhan, T. J. (2005). The role of personality factors in coping with organisational change. *International Journal of Organisational Analysis, 13*(2), 175–192.

Raykov, T. & Marcoulides, G. A. (2006). *A first course in structural equation modeling* (2nd ed.). Mahwah, NJ: Erlbaum.

Razali, N. M. & Wah, Y. B. (2011). Power comparisons of Shapiro-Wilk, Kolmogorov-Smirnov, Lilliefors and Anderson-Darling tests. *Journal of Statistical Modelling and Analytics, 2*(1), 21–33.

Reid, D. W. & Ware, E. E. (1974). Multidimensionality of internal versus external control: Addition of a third dimension and non-distinction of self versus others. *Canadian Journal of Behavioural Science, 6*(2), 131–142.

Reivich, K., Gillham, J. E., Chaplin, T. M. & Seligman, M. E. (2013). From helplessness to optimism: The role of resilience in treating and preventing depression in youth. In S. Goldstein & R. B. Brooks (Eds.), *Handbook of resilience in children* (pp. 201–214). New York, NY: Springer Science+Business.

Reivich, K. J., Seligman, M. E. P. & McBride, S. (2011). Master resilience training in the US Army. *American Psychologist, 66*, 25–34.

Richards, G. E., Ellis, L. A. & Neill, J. T. (2002). The ROPELOC: Review of Personal Effectiveness and Locus of Control: A comprehensive instrument for reviewing life effectiveness. In R. Craven, H. W. Marsh & Katrina B. Simpson (Eds.), *Self-concept research: Driving international research agendas: Collected papers of the Second Biennial Self-concept Enhancement and Learning Facilitation (SELF) Research Centre International Conference, Sydney, Australia, 6–8 August, 2002* (pp. 6–8). Sydney, Australia: University of Western Sydney.

Richardson, G. E. (2002). The metatheory of resilience and resiliency. *Journal of Clinical Psychology, 58*(3), 307–321.

Richardson, G E., Neiger, B., Jensen, S. & Kumpfer, K.. (1990). The resiliency model. *Health Education, 21*, 33–39.

Riggio, R. E. (2008). Leadership development: The current state and future expectations. *Consulting Psychology Journal, 60*(4), 383–392.

Roberts, J. E., Gotlib, I. H. & Kassel, J. D. (1996). Adult attachment security and symptoms of depression: The mediation role of dysfunctional attitudes and low self-esteem. *Journal of Personality and Social Psychology, 70*(2), 310–320.

Robins, R. W., Hendin, H. M. & Trzesniewski, K. H. (2001). Measuring global self-esteem: Construct validation of a single-item measure and the Rosenberg Self-Esteem Scale. *Personality and Social Psychology Bulletin, 27*(2), 151–161.

Robinson, J. P., Shaver, P. R. & Wrightsman, L. S. (1991). *Measures of personality and social psychological attitudes*. San Diego, CA: Academic Press.

Robitschek, C. & Keyes, C. L. M. (2009). Keyes's model of mental health with personal growth initiative as a parsimonious predictor. *Journal of Counseling Psychology, 56*(2), 321–329.

Roethlisberger, F. J. & Dickson, W. J. (1939). *Management and the worker*. Cambridge, MA: Harvard University Press.

Rogelberg, S. G. (2004). *Handbook of research methods in industrial and organisational psychology*. London: Blackwell.

Rogers, C. R. (1959). A theory of therapy, personality, and interpersonal relationships, as developed in the client-centered framework. *Psychology: A Study of a Science, 3*, 184–256.

Rogers, C. R. & Freiberg, H. J. (1969). *Freedom to learn*. Columbus, OH: Merrill.

Rosen, L. H. & Patterson, M. M. (2011). The self and identity. In M. K. Underwood & L. H. Rosen (Eds.), *Social development* (pp. 73–100). New York, NY: Guilford Press.

Rosenberg, M. (1965). *Society and the adolescent self-image*. Princeton, NJ: Princeton University Press.

Rosenberg, M. (1989). *Society and the adolescent self-image* (rev. ed.). Middletown, CT: Wesleyan University Press.

Rosenberg, M. & Pearlin, L. I. (1978). Social class and self-esteem among children and adults. *American Journal of Sociology, 84*(1), 53–77.

Rosenberg, M., Schooler, C. Schoenbach, C. & Rosenberg, F. (1995). Global self-esteem and specific self-esteem: Different concepts, different outcomes. *American Sociological Review, 60*(1), 141–156.

Rosenthal, R. & Rosnow, R. L. (1991). *Essentials of behavioral research: Methods and data analysis* (2nd ed.). New York, NY: McGraw-Hill.

Rotter, J. B. (1954). *Social learning and clinical psychology*. Englewood Cliffs, NJ: Prentice Hall.

Rotter, J. B. (1966). Generalized expectancies for internal versus external control of reinforcement. *Psychological Monographs: General & Applied, 80*(1), 1–28.

Rotter, J. B. (1975). Some problems and misconceptions related to the construct of internal versus external control of reinforcement. *Journal of Consulting and Clinical Psychology, 43*(1), 56–67.

Rotter, J. B. (1990). Internal versus external control of reinforcement: A case history of a variable. *American Psychologist, 45*(4), 489–493.

Rotter, J. B., Liverant, S. & Crowne, D. P. (1961). The growth and extinction of expectancies in chance controlled and skilled tasks. *Journal of Psychology, 52*(1), 161–177.

Rotter, J. B. & Mulry, R. C. (1965). Internal versus external control of reinforcement and decision time. *Journal of Personality and Social Psychology, 2*(4), 598–604.

Rozowski, M. (1989). Examination of the measurement properties of the Job Description Index with experimental items. *Journal of Applied Psychology, 74*(5), 805–814.

Ryff, C. D. (1989). Beyond Ponce de Leon and life satisfaction: New directions in quest of successful aging. *International Journal of Behavioural Development, 12*, 35–55.

Rubin, R. A. (1978). Stability of self-esteem ratings and their relation to academic achievement: A longitudinal study. *Psychology in the Schools, 15*(3), 430–433.

Runyon, K. E. (1973). Some interactions between personality variables and management styles. *Journal of Applied Psychology, 57*(3), 288–294.

Rush, M. C., Schoel, W. A. & Barnard, S. M. (1995). Psychological resiliency in the public sector: 'Hardiness' and pressure for change. *Journal of Vocational Behavior, 46*(1), 17–39.

Russell, C. J. & Kuhnert, K. W. (1992). Integrating skill acquisition and perspective taking capacity in the development of leaders. *Leadership Quarterly, 3*(2), 335–353.

Rutter, M. (1985). Resilience in the face of adversity: Protective factors and resistance to psychiatric disorder. *The British Journal of Psychiatry, 147*(6), 598–611.

Rutter, M. (1999). Resilience concepts and findings: Implications for family therapy. *Journal of Family Therapy, 21*(2), 119–144.

Rutter, M. (2006). Implications of resilience concepts for scientific understanding. *Annals of the New York Academy of Sciences, 1094*(1), 1–12.

Rutter, M. (2012). Resilience as a dynamic concept. *Development and Psychopathology, 24*(2), 335–344.

Salancik, G. R. & Pfeffer, J. (1977). Who gets power and how they hold on to it: A strategic contingency model of power. *Organisational Dynamics, 5*(3), 3–21.

Salovey, P. & Mayer, J. D. (1990). Emotional intelligence. *Imagination, Cognition and Personality, 9*(3), 185–211.

Santos-Ruiz, A. M., Fernández-Serrano, M. J., Robles-Ortega, H., Pérez-García, M., Navarrete-Navarrete, N. & Peralta-Ramírez, M. I. (2012). Can constructive thinking predict decision making? *Journal of Behavioral Decision Making, 25*(5), 469–475.

Sashkin, M. (1988). The visionary leader. In J. A. Conger & P. Kanungo (Eds.), *Charismatic leadership: The elusive factor in organisational effectiveness* (pp. 122–160). San Francisco, CA: Jossey-Bass.

Saunders, I. & Barker, S. (2001). Organisational health: A framework for checking your organisation's fitness for success. *Journal of Change Management, 2*(2), 173–183.

Sawyer, A. C. P., Miller-Lewis, L. R., Searle, A. K., Sawyer, M. G. & Lynch, J. W. (2015). Is greater improvement in early self-regulation associated with fewer behavioral problems later in childhood? *Developmental Psychology, 51*(12), 1740–1755.

Scandura, T. A. & Graen, G. B. (1984). Moderating effects of initial leader-member exchange status on the effects of a leadership intervention. *Journal of Applied Psychology, 69*(3), 428–436.

Schein, E. H. (2009). *The corporate culture survival guide* (rev. ed.). San Francisco, CA: Jossey-Bass.

Schein, E. H. (2010). Organisational culture and leadership. John Wiley & Sons.

Scheuer, E. & Epstein, S. (1997). Constructive thinking, reactions to a laboratory stressor, and symptoms in everyday life. *Anxiety, Stress & Coping: An International Journal, 10*(3), 269–303.

Schiraldi, G., Jackson, T. K., Brown, S. L. & Jordan, J. B. (2010). Resilience training for functioning adults: Program description and preliminary findings from a pilot investigation. *International Journal of Emergency Mental Health, 12*(2), 117–129.

Schlenker, B. R. & Weigold, M. F. (1989). Goals and the self-identification process: Constructing desired identities. In L. A. Pervin (Ed.), *Goal concepts in personality and social psychology* (pp. 243–290). Hillsdale, NJ: Erlbaum.

Schneider, T. R., Lyons, J. B. & Khazon, S. (2013). Emotional intelligence and resilience. *Personality and Individual Differences, 55*(8), 909–914.

Schulte, M., Ostroff, C. & Kinicki, A. J. (2006). Organisational climate systems and psychological climate perceptions: A cross-level study of climate-satisfaction relationships. *Journal of Occupational and Organisational Psychology, 79*(4), 645–671.

Schyns, B. & Von Collani, G. A new occupational self-efficacy scale and its relation to personality constructs and organisational variables. *European Journal of Work and Organisational Psychology, 11*(2), 219–241.

Seeman, M. (1963). An experimental study of alienation and social learning. *American Journal of Sociology, 49*, 270–284.

Segal, Z. V. (1988). Appraisal of the self-schema construct in cognitive models of depression. *Psychological Bulletin, 103*(2), 147–162.

Seligman, M. E. P. (1990). *Learned optimism: How to change your mind and your life*. New York, NY: Pocket Books.

Seligman, M. E. P. (1998). The prediction and prevention of depression. In D. K. Routh & R. J. DeRubeis (Eds.), *The science of clinical psychology: Accomplishments and future directions* (pp. 201–214). Washington, DC: American Psychological Association.

Seligman, M. E. P. (2002). *Handbook of positive psychology*. New York, NY: Oxford University Press.

Seligman, M. E. P. (2011). *Flourish: A visionary new understanding of happiness and well-being*. New York, NY: Free Press.

Seligman, M. E. P., Castellon, C., Cacciola, J., Schulman, P., Luborsky, L., Ollove, M. & Downing, R. (1988). Explanatory style change during cognitive therapy for unipolar depression. *Journal of Abnormal Psychology, 97*(1), 13–18.

Seligman, M. E. P. & Csikszentmihalyi, M. (2000). Positive psychology: An introduction. *American Psychologist, 55*(1), 5–14.

Seligman, M. E. P. & Csikszentmihalyi, M. (2001). Positive psychology: An introduction. Reply to Comments. *American Psychologist, 56*(1), 89–90.

Seligman, M. E., Rashid, T. & Parks, A. C. (2006). Positive psychotherapy. *American Psychologist, 61*(8), 774–788.

Seligman, M. E., Schulman, P. & Tryon, A. M. (2007). Group prevention of depression and anxiety symptoms. *Behavior Research and Therapy, 45*(6), 1111–1126.

Setterlund, M. B. & Niedenthal, P. M. (1993). 'Who am I? Why am I here?': Self-esteem, self-clarity, and prototype matching. *Journal of Personality and Social Psychology, 65*(4), 769–780.

Shapiro, D. H., Schwartz, C. E. & Austin, J. A. (1996). Controlling ourselves, controlling our world. *American Psychologist, 51*(12), 1213–1230.

Shamir, B., House, R. J. & Arthur, M. B. (1993). The motivational effects of charismatic leadership: A self-concept based theory. *Organisation Science, 4*(4), 577–594.

Shamir, B., Zakay, E., Breinin, E. & Popper, M. (1998). Correlates of charismatic leader behaviour in military units: Subordinates' attitudes, unit characteristics, and superiors' appraisals of leader performance. *Academy of Management Journal, 41*(4), 387–409.

Sherer, M. Maddux, J. E., Mercadante, B., Prentice-Dunn, S., Jacobs, B. & Rogers, R. W. (1982). The self-efficacy scale: Construction and validation. *Psychological Reports, 51*(2), 663–671.

Showers, C. J., Abramson, L. Y. & Hogan, M. E. (1998). The dynamic self: How the content and structure of the self-concept change with mood. *Journal of Personality and Social Psychology*, 75(2), 478–493.

Showers, C. J. & KIing, K. C. (1996). Organisation of self-knowledge: Implications for recovery from sad mood. *Journal of Personality and Social Psychology, 70*(3), 578–590.

Shrauger, J. S. & Schohn, M. (1995). Self-confidence in college students: Its conceptualization, measurement and behavioral implications. *Assessment, 2*(3), 255–278.

Shrauger, J. S. & Sorman, P. B. (1977). Self-evaluations, initial success and failure, and improvement as determinants of persistence. *Journal of Consulting and Clinical Psychology, 45*(5), 784–795.

Siber, E. & Tippett, J. (1965). Self-esteem: Clinical assessment and measurement validation. *Psychological Reports, 16*.3c, 1017–1071.

Siu, O., Hui, C. H., Phillips, D. R., Lin, L., Wong, T. & Shi, K. (2009). A study of resiliency among Chinese health care workers: Capacity to cope with workplace stress. *Journal of Research in Personality, 43*(5), 770–776.

Skinner, E. A. (1995). *Perceived control, motivation, & coping.* Thousand Oaks, CA: SAGE Publications.

Smart, J. C. & St. John, E. P. (1996). Organisational culture and effectiveness in higher education: A test of the 'culture type' and 'strong culture' hypotheses. *Educational Evaluation and Policy Analysis*, 18(3), 219–241.

Smith, H. S. & Cohen, L. H. (1993). Self-complexity and reaction to a relationship breakup. *Journal of Social and Clinical Psychology*, 12, 367–384.

Smith, A. F. & Kelly, T. (1997). Human capital in the digital economy. In F. Hesselbein, M. Goldsmith & R. Beckhard (Eds.), *The organisation of the future* (pp. 199–212). San Francisco, CA: Jossey-Bass.

Smith, P. C., Kendall, L. & Hulin, C. L. (1969). *The measurement of satisfaction in work and retirement: A strategy for the study of attitudes.* Chicago, IL: Rand McNally.

Soanes, C. & Hawker, S. (2009). *Oxford dictionary of current English* (4th ed.). London: Oxford University Press.

Solcova, I. & Tomanek, P. (1994). Daily stress coping strategies: An effect of hardiness. *Studia Psychologica*, 36(5), 390–392.

Sonn, C. C. & Fisher, A. T. (1998). Sense of community: Community resilient responses to oppression and change. *Journal of Community Psychology, 26*(5), 457–472.

Sood, A. & Varkey, P. (2011). Resilience training and physician well-being. *Journal of General Internal Medicine,* 26(11), 1243–1243.

Sood, A., Prasad, K., Schroeder, D. & Varkey, P. (2011). Stress management and resilience training among department of medicine faculty: A pilot randomized clinical trial. *Journal of General Internal Medicine, 26*, 858–861.

Sowislo, J. F. & Orth, U. (2013). Does low self-esteem predict depression and anxiety? A meta-analysis of longitudinal studies. *Psychological Bulletin, 139*(1), 213–240.

Spangler, N. W. (2012) *Employer perspectives on stress intervention and resilience building: A qualitative study.* Retrieved from ProQuest Digital Dissertations (Order No. AAI3434780).

Sparrowe, R. T. & Liden, R. C. (1997). Processes and structure in leader-member exchange. *Academy of Management Review,* 22(2), 522–552.

Spector, P. E. (1982). Behavior in organisations as a function of employee's locus of control. *Psychological Bulletin, 91*(3), 482–497.

Spector, P. E. (1997). *Job satisfaction: Applications, assessment, causes and consequences.* Thousand Oaks, CA: SAGE Publications.

Stauser, D. R., Ketz, K. & Keim, J. (2002). The relationship between self-efficacy, locus of control and work personality. *Journal of Applied Psychology, 68*(1), 20–44.

Steele, C. (1988). The psychology of self-affirmation: Sustaining the integrity of the self. *Advances in Experimental Social Psychology,* 21(2), 261–302.

Stewart, D. E. & Yuen, T. (2011). A systematic review of resilience in the physically ill. *Psychosomatics, 52*(3), 199–209.

Stewart, I. & Joines, V. S. (2011). TA tomorrow. *Transactional Analysis Journal, 41*(3), 221–229.

Stipancic, M., Renner, W., Schütz, P. & Dond, R. (2010). Effects of neuro-linguistic psychotherapy on psychological difficulties and perceived quality of life. *Counselling and Psychotherapy Research,* 10(1), 39–49.

Stogdill, R. M. (1948). Personal factors associated with leadership: Survey of literature. *The Journal of Psychology,* 25(1), 35–71.

Stogdill, R. M. (1974). *Handbook of leadership: A survey of theory and research.* New York, NY: The Free Press.

Story, J. S. P. & Barbuto, J. E., Jr. (2011). Global mindset: A construct clarification and framework. *Journal of Leadership & Organisational Studies, 18*(3), 377–384.

Stutchbury, M. (2010). Paradox in economic policies. The Australian. http://www.theaustralian.com.au/national-affairs/commentary/paradox-in-economic-policies/

Sui, Y., Wang, H., Yue, Y. N. & Luthans, F. (2012). The effect of transformational leadership on follower performance and satisfaction: The mediating role of psychological capital and the moderating role of procedural justice. *Acta Psychologica Sinica, 44*(9), 1217–1230.

Svindseth, M. F., Sorebo, O., Nottestad, J. A., Roaldset, J. O., Wallin, J. & Dahl, A. A. (2009). Psychometric examination and normative data for the Narcissistic Personality Inventory 29 item version. *Scandinavian Journal of Psychology, 50*(2), 151–159.

Swann, W. B., Jr. (1990). To be adored or to be known? The interplay of self-enhancement and self-verification. In E. T. Higgins & R. M. Sorrentino (Eds.), *Handbook of motivation and cognition: Foundations of social behavior* (Vol. 2, pp. 408–448). New York, NY: Guilford Press.

Sy, T., Tram, S. & O'Hara, L. A. (2006). Relation of employee and manager emotional intelligence to job satisfaction and Performance. *Journal of Vocational Behavior, 68*(3), 461–473.

Sylvester, M. H. (2009). *Transformational leadership behavior of frontline sales professionals: An investigation of the impact of resilience and key demographics* (Unpublished doctoral thesis). Retrieved from ProQuest Digital Dissertations (Order No. AAI3387358).

Syndell, M. A. (2008). *The role of emotional intelligence in transformational leadership style* (Unpublished doctoral thesis). Capella University, Minneapolis, MN. Retrieved from ProQuest Digital Dissertations (Order No. 3320725).

Taffinder, P. (1995). *The new leaders. Achieving corporate transformation through dynamic leadership.* London, UK: Kogan Page.

Tajfel, H. (1981). *Human groups and social categories.* Cambridge, UK: Cambridge University Press.

Tannenbaum, R. & Schmidt, W. H. (1958). How to choose a leadership pattern. *Harvard Business Review, 36*, 95–101.

Taylor, J. A. (1953). A personality scale of manifest anxiety. *The Journal of Abnormal and Social Psychology, 48*(2), 285–290.

Taylor, M. C., Cornelius, C., & Colvin, K. (2014). Visionary leadership and its relationship to organisational effectiveness. Leadership & Organisation Development Journal, 35(6), 566-583.

Taylor, S. E., Kemeny, M. E., Bower, J. E., Gruenewald, T. L. & Reed, G. M. (2000). Psychological resources, positive illusions, and health. *American Psychologist*, 55, 99–109.

Tedeschi, R. G. & Calhoun, L. G. (1995). Trauma & transformation: *Growing in the aftermath of suffering*. Thousand Oaks, CA: SAGE Publications.

Tejeda, M. J., Scandura, T. A. & Pillai, R. (2001). The MLQ revisited: Psychometric properties and recommendations. *The Leadership Quarterly*, 12(1), 31–52.

Terman, L. M. & Oden, M. H. (1947). *The gifted child grows up: Twenty-five years' follow-up of a superior group*. Palo Alto, CA: Stanford University Press.

Tesser, A. (1986). Some effects of self-evaluation maintenance on cognition and action. In R. M. Sorrentino & E. T. Biggins (Eds.), *Handbook of motivation and cognition: Foundations of social behavior* (pp. 435–464). New York, NY: Guilford Press.

Tharenou, P. (1979). Employee self-esteem: A review of the literature. *Journal of Vocational Behavior*, 15(3), 316–346.

Thierry, C. (2005). Integral leadership: A research proposal. *Journal of Organisational Change Management*, 18(3), 211–229.

Tichy, N. & Devanna, M. (1986). *The transformational leader*. New York, NY: Wiley.

Tierney, P., Farmer, F. M. & Graen, G. B. (1999). An examination of leadership and employee creativity: The relevance of traits and relationships. *Personnel Psychology*, 52(3), 591–620.

Trickett, E. J. (1996). A future for community psychology: The contexts of diversity and the diversity of contexts. *American Journal of Community Psychology*, 24(2), 209–234.

Trzesniewski, K. H., Donnellan, M. B. & Robins, R. W. (2003). Stability of self-esteem across the life span. *Journal of Personality and Social Psychology*, 84(1), 205–220.

Tsai, K. & Yang, S. (2013). Firm innovativeness and business performance: The joint moderating effects of market turbulence and competition. *Industrial Marketing Management*, 42(8), 1279–1294.

Tsui, A. S. & O'Reilly, C. A. (1989). Beyond simple demographic effects: The importance of relational demography in superior subordinate dyads. *Academy of Management Journal*, 32(2), 402–423.

Tubbs, S. L. & Schulz, E. (2006). Exploring a taxonomy of global leadership competencies and meta-competencies. *Journal of American Academy of Business, Cambridge, 8*(2), 29–34.

Tvedt, S. D. & Saksvik, P. Ø. (2012). Perspectives on the intervention process as a special case of organisational change. In C. Biron, M. Karanika-Murray & C. Cooper (Eds.), *Improving organisational interventions for stress and well-being: Addressing process and context* (pp. 102–119). London: Routledge.

Twenge, J. M. & Campbell, W. K. (2009). *The narcissism epidemic: Living in the age of entitlement.* New York, NY: Free Press.

Ulrich, D. (1998). *Champions of change: How CEOs and their companies are mastering the skills of radical change.* San Francisco, CA: Jossey-Bass.

Vallacher, R. R. & Nowak, A. (1997). The emergence of dynamical social psychology. *Psychological Inquiry, 8*(2), 73–99.

Van den Heuvel, M., Demerouti, E., Schreurs, B. H. J., Bakker, A. B. & Schaufeli, W. B. (2009). Does meaning-making help during organisational change? Development and validation of a new scale. *Career Development International, 14*(6), 508–533.

Van Knippenberg, D. & Sitkin, S. B. (2013). A critical assessment of charismatic and transformational leadership research: Back to the drawing board? *The Academy of Management Annals, 7*(1), 1–60.

Van Velsor, E. & McCauley, C. D. (2004). Our view of leadership development. In C. D. McCauley & E. Van Velsor (Eds.), *The Centre for Creative Leadership handbook of leadership development* (2nd ed., pp. 1–22). San Francisco, CA: Jossey-Bass.

VandeWalle, D. (1997). Development and validation of a work domain goal orientation instrument. *Educational and Psychological Measurement, 57*(6), 995–1015.

Varker, T. & Devilly, G. (2012). An analogue trial of inoculation/resilience training for emergency services personnel: Proof of concept. *Journal of Anxiety Disorders, 26*(6), 696–701.

Vecchio, R. P., Justin, J. E. & Pearce (2008). The utility of transactional and transformational leadership for predicting performance and satisfaction within a path-goal theory framework. *Journal of Occupational and Organisational Psychology, 81*(1), 71–82.

Villanueva, D. & Djurkovic, N. (2009). Occupational stress and intention to leave among employees in small and medium enterprises. *International Journal of Stress Management, 16*(2), 124–137.

Vroom, V. H. & Yetton, P. N. (1973). *Leadership and decision-making.* Pittsburgh, PA: University of Pittsburgh Press.

Vroom, V. H. & Jago, A. G. (1988). *The new leadership: Managing participation in organisations.* Englewood Cliffs, NJ: Prentice Hall.

Wagnild, G. (2009). A review of the resilience scale. *Journal of Nursing Measurement, 17*(2), 105–113.

Wagnild, G. M. & Collins, J. A. (2009). Assessing resilience. *Journal of Psychosocial Nursing and Mental Health Services,* 47(12), 28–33.

Wagnild, G. M. & Young, H. M. (1993). Development and psychometric evaluation of the resilience scale. *Journal of Nursing Measurement, 1(2),* 165–178.

Waldman, D. A., Ramirez, G. G., House, R. J. & Puraman, P. (2001). Does leadership matter? CEO leader attributes and profitability under conditions of perceived environmental uncertainty. *Academy of Management Journal, 44*(1), pp. 134–143.

Walker, S. N., Sechrist, K. R. & Pender, N. J. (1987). The health-promoting lifestyle profile: Development and psychometric characteristics. *Nursing Research, 36*(2), 76–81.

Walker, A. G., Smither, J. W. & Waldman, D. A. (2008). A longitudinal examination of concomitant changes in team leadership and customer satisfaction. *Personnel Psychology, 61*(3), 547–577.

Wallston, B. S., Wallston, K. A., Kaplan, G. D. & Maides, S. A. (1976). Development and validation of the health locus of control (HLC) scale. *Journal of Consulting and Clinical Psychology, 44*(4), 580–585.

Walumbwa, F. O., Wang, P., Lawler, J. J. & Shi, K. (2010). The role of collective efficacy in the relations between transformational leadership and work outcomes. *Journal of Occupational and Organisational Psychology, 77*(4), 515–530.

Wanberg, C. R. & Banas, J. T. (2000). Predictors and outcomes of openness to changes in a reorganizing workplace. *Journal of Applied Psychology,* 85(1), 132–142.

Warr, P. (1990). The measurement of well-being and other aspects of mental health. *Journal of Occupational Psychology, 63*(3), 193–210.

Wasden, S. T. (2014). *A correlational study on transformational leadership in higher education leadership* (Unpublished doctoral thesis). University of Idaho, ID.

Wasylyshyn, K. M. (2008). Behind the door: Keeping business leaders focus on how they lead. *Consulting Psychology Journal*, 60(4), 314–330.

Wayne, S. J. & Green, S. A. (1993). The effects of leader-member exchange on employee citizenship and impression management behavior. *Human Relations*, 46(2), 1431–1440.

Wayne, S. J., Shore, L. M. & Liden, R. C. (1997). Perceived organisational support and leader-member exchange: A social exchange perspective. *Academy of Management Journal*, 40(1), 82–111.

Weiner, I. B., Schmitt, N. W. & Highhouse, S. (2012). *Handbook of psychology, volume 12. Industrial and organisational psychology* (2nd ed.). Hoboken, NJ: John Wiley and Sons.

Weiss, D. J., Dawis, R. V., England, G. W. & Lofquist, L. H. (1967). *Manual for the Minnesota Satisfaction Questionnaire 22*. Minneapolis, MN: Industrial Relations Centre, University of Minnesota.

Weiss, H. M. & Adler, S. (1984). Personality and organisational behavior. *Research in Organisational Behavior*, 6, 1–50.

Wells, L. E. & Marwell, G. (1976). *Self-esteem: Its conceptualization and measurement*. Beverly Hills, CA: SAGE Publications.

Werner, E. E. (1982). *Vulnerable but invincible: A longitudinal study of resilient children and youth*. New York, NY: McGraw-Hill.

Werner, E. E. (1995). Resilience in development. *Current Directions in Psychological Science*, 4(3), 81–85.

Werner, E. E. & Smith, R. S. (1992). Overcoming the odds: *High risk children from birth to adulthood*. Ithaca, NY: Cornell University Press.

Wershow, H. J. & Reinhart, G. (1974). Life change and hospitalization: A heretical view. *Journal of Psychosomatic Research*, 8(6), 393–401.

Wheeler, J. V. (2008). The impact of social environments on emotional, social and cognitive competency development. *Journal of Management Development*, 27(1), 129–145.

Wiese, S. L. (2011). *The downside of self-esteem stability: Does stability impede flexibility?* Retrieved from ProQuest Digital Dissertations (Order No. AAI3420061).

Weissman, N. L. (2009). *The relationship between leadership styles of directors of accredited higher education respiratory care programs and faculty satisfaction, willingness to exert extra effort, perceived director effectiveness, and program outcomes*. Retrieved from ProQuest Digital Dissertations (Order No. AAI3319732).

Wilson, W. R. (1967). Correlates of avowed happiness. *Psychological Bulletin,* *67*(4), 294–306.

Wissing, M. & Van Eeden, C. (2002). Empirical clarification of the nature of psychological well-being. *South African Journal of Psychology, 32*(1), 32–44.

Wolf, E. J., Harrington, K. M., Clark, S. L. & Miller, M. W. (2013). Sample size requirements for structural equation models: An evaluation of power, bias, and solution propriety. *Educational and Psychological Measurement, 76*(6), 913–934. DOI:10.1177/0013164413495237.

Wolin, S. & Wolin, S. J. (1996). The challenge model: Working with strengths in children of substance-abusing parents. *Child and Adolescent Psychiatric Clinics of North America,* 5(1), 243–256.

Wolkind, S. & Rutter, M. (1985). Separation, loss, and family relationships. In M. Rutter and L. Hersov (Eds.), *Child and adolescent psychiatry: Modern approaches* (2nd ed., pp. X–X). Oxford: Blackwell.

Wylie, R. C. (1979). *The self-concept: Theory and research on selected topics.* Lincoln, NE: University of Nebraska Press.

Xenikou, A. & Simosi, M. (2006). Organisational culture and transformational leadership as predictors of business unit performance. *Journal of Managerial Psychology, 21*(6), 566–579.

Yeung, A., Warner, M. & Rowley, C. (2008). Guest editors' introduction: Growth and globalization: Evolution of human resource management practices in Asia. *Human Resource Management, 47*(1), 1–13.

Youssef, C. M. & Luthans, F. (2007). Positive organisational behavior in the workplace: The impact of hope, optimism, and resilience. *Journal of Management, 33*(5), 774–800.

Yukl, G. (1998). *Leadership in organisations* (4th ed.). Englewood Cliffs, NJ: Prentice Hall.

Yukl, G., Kim, H. & Falbe, C. M. (1996). Antecedents of influence outcomes. *Journal of Applied Psychology,* 81(3), 309–317.

Yukl, G. & Mashud, R. (2010). Why flexible adaptive leadership is essential. *Consulting Psychology Journal,* 62(2), 81–93.

Zeigler-Hill, V. (2010). The interpersonal nature of self-esteem: Do different measures of self-esteem possess similar interpersonal content? *Journal of Research in Personality, 44*(1), 22–30.

Zeigler-Hill, V., Clark, C. B. & Beckman, T. E. (2011). Fragile self-esteem and the interpersonal circumplex: Are feelings of self-worth associated with interpersonal style? *Self and Identity, 10*(4), 509–536.

Zenger, T. R. (1992). Why do employers only reward extreme performance? Examining the relationships among performance, pay, and turnover. *Administrative Science Quarterly, 37*, 198–219.

Ziller, R., Hagey, J. Smith, M. D. & Long, B. (1969). Self-esteem: A self-social construct. *Journal of Consulting and Clinical Psychology, 33*(1), 84–95.

Zolli, A. & Healy, A. M. (2012). *Resilience: Why things bounce back*. New York, NY: Free Press.

www.ingramcontent.com/pod-product-compliance
Lightning Source LLC
Chambersburg PA
CBHW022054210326
41519CB00054B/359